Herding Cats
and other Greek Tales

Dave Burnham

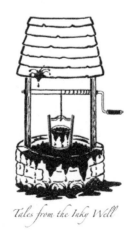

Tales from the Inky Well

A few names in this publication have been changed to protect the identity of the individual.

Visit the author at: http://www.adastralpodcast.com

At the author's request all profits from this book will be donated to the Animal Charities detailed at the end of the book entitled "Charities"

Cover designed by Dave Burnham
Inky Well logo designed by Rene Burnham
Photographs by Dave and Sue, Trisha, Karen and Andy, Lynda, Gaynor, Nick, Hanna, Linda, Martin and Ilias
Editing by Sue Burnham

Published by Kindle Direct Publishing
In association with The Inky Well

ISBN 9798411090192

Also by DJ Burnham

SCIENCE FICTION
Flux
Novel
Test Drive
Volume 1 of the collected short stories of DJ Burnham

ANTHOLOGIES
Anthropomorphs
A short story which appears in a speculative fiction anthology entitled "Silverthought: Ignition" (2005)
Published by Silverthought Press

Thriskia's Life Bank
A short story which appears in Issue 1, Volume 1 of "The Literary Bone" (2007)

Mortal Coil
A short story which appears in a speculative fiction anthology "Thank You Death Robot" (2008)
Published by Silverthought Press

Tales from The Inky Well

(Inky Well logo designed by Rene Burnham)

CONTENTS

For Wendy

About the Author

Born in the 1960s, Dave's family regularly upped sticks and moved as his father progressed in his career with Freightliners container company and later with Railfreight: from London to Hampshire, Yorkshire, Berkshire and Suffolk. As a consequence, he learned to make friends quickly and the constantly changing array of school teachers (along with a with a necessity for frantic note-taking as a student) combined to give him one of the worst examples of hand-writing on the planet – well, that's his excuse.

He developed a passion for music and for Science Fiction from an early age, expanding his musical and literary horizons as a student while starting to write poetry and create artwork (inheriting his mother, Irene's, artistic side.)

Dave formed the short-lived concert project, *The Natural Transport Company*, in the 1990s working with Roy and Nick Harper, as well as one-off concerts for a variety of other favourites. In 1998 Dave organised a short tour for The Dayglo Pirates (the UK's premiere Jethro Tull tribute band).

In 1996 Dave and his wife visited the Greek island of Skiathos for a holiday, which immediately felt like a second home to them. Over the subsequent years they have had many enjoyable holidays on various Greek islands and have developed a deep love for the country and her people (and cats!). Those holidays gave a much-needed break from work, the opportunity to explore, discover the unique gifts of each island and the chance for Dave to sit and write his short stories.

Some of these stories written under the name of DJ Burnham have subsequently been published by online webzines such as Silverthought,

Bewildering Stories and Aphelion. In 2005 his story *Anthropomorphs* appeared in print as part of a speculative fiction anthology: Silverthought Ignition. More appeared in other anthologies over the coming years. In June 2006 his story *The Spoils of War* appeared on the Variant Frequencies podcast narrated by Rick Stringer. The idea of podcasting his stories sowed a seed in Dave's mind and in 2009 he released the first episode of his own podcast *"Ad Astral"*, going on to release 36 episodes to date. They all have immersive sound effects and many have voice actors playing a variety of roles in a radio theatre style. *Test Drive* Volume 1 of DJ Burnham's Collected Short Stories was published in 2007 and a novel *Flux* was published in 2010. Since then his short stories have been released as podcasts on Ad Astral.

Dave is also a keen gardener and in October 2006 he appeared on BBC2's Gardener's World as part of their Chilli Trial and he has had an allotment plot in Brighton since 2014.

You can find out more at: www.adastralpodcast.com

Introduction

I've been writing for over 20 years to date, but until now it's been mainly Sci-Fi, poetry and the occasional album/concert review. However, my wife (Sue) and I bit off more than we could chew in 2020, when we decided to adopt a Greek cat and as the complicated process went along she said:

'You couldn't make this up! You really should write a book about it!'

I think she may have been joking at the time, but it struck me that it might be a great idea to write something non-fiction for a change. It might also serve to assist anyone else who might decide to adopt a rescue animal from Greece, which we believed would be a relatively easy process. How wrong we were!

The story became more than just a tale of bureaucratic David and Goliath. It tells the tale of a lucky little Greek cat named Teddy; the epic struggle and rollercoaster ride of emotions we felt in overcoming the obstacles in adopting him; the stories of other Greek cats, the people who rescue and neuter them and more besides.

The process of writing the story also gave me the opportunity to reminisce about some of the wonderful Greek holidays we have had over the years. I've also tried not to get too bogged down in what became a legislative quagmire and have tried not to "knowledge the fun out of" the story. So I have included an Appendix which may be of some help if you're trying to/or thinking of adopting a cat or a dog from Greece. We were all learning on the job and it seemed to be a case of constantly-shifting goalposts, but I hope this book might give some helpful advice and act as a guide to the situation as I understood it at the time of writing.

Any proceeds from the sale of this book they will be split between some of the Greek Animal Charities (who kindly helped us as we tried to make sense of the labyrinth of bureaucracy unleashed by the UK's exit from the EU on 31st January 2021) and also Brighton's City Cat Shelter. I'll tell you more about them at the end of the book, but those who helped us were:

The Greek Cat Welfare Society (UK) – GCWS
Greek Animal Rescue – GAR
Caring for the Animals Trust – CARAT
Nine Lives Greece
Brighton City Cat Shelter

In the end, over 40 different people were involved in Teddy's adoption and we're very grateful to each and every one of them. Some played greater roles than others, but they all kindly helped us and are included in the 'Thanks' section at the end.

The story has been built from a combination of emails, Facebook posts, texts, WhatsApp and Messenger messages, telephone calls and my own recollections of the – relatively – recent events. I drew the line at smoke signals and semaphore, but had they been available they would, no doubt, have played a part. It was also fascinating to go-back through photographs of previous holidays and re-live some very pleasant recollections of times spent in that wonderful part of the world.

Some names relating to Teddy's tale have been changed for privacy, but the events and storyline are all pretty much exactly as they unfolded over 10 months between October 2020 and July 2021. To help with the timeline I've included the dates as we go along.

The photographs in the printed and Kindle book versions are in Black and White, but you can see all of them in colour (and I may post updates here, too) at:

www.adastralpodcast.com/herdingcats.html

You can also join the book's Facebook group to comment, share your own animal adoption stories and see updates at:

facebook.com/groups/1471681759877496

Lastly, thanks for reading this book, I do hope you enjoy it.

Part One

Herding Cats

Purrlogue

I believe cats to be spirits come to earth. A cat, I am sure, could walk on a cloud without coming through: Jules Verne

Since October 1987, we've had ginger cats in our lives. So far, they had sort of found us.

Tigger, and Anand's cartoon of the day we moved house

Tigger came to us just before the great storm of October 1987. One day Sue was chatting to a neighbour over the fence in the back garden, when a little ginger and white cat walked up one arm, over her shoulders, back down the other arm and then trotted up the back steps and into the house. She settled down to sleep on the sofa and never left. Various enquiries were made to try and find her owners, but to no avail. After about 6 months we discovered that her original owner had had a baby and acquired a puppy, so Tigger had decided to move house. Her original owner didn't mind, so stay she did. She was a very loving little soul, albeit slightly eccentric with an oddly poor sense of balance. She only managed to catch one thing in her life: a long-dead yellow canary, which was stiff as a board and probably expired when its aviary blew down in the hurricane, but she was so proud when she bought it home. It was – as it always is – terribly sad when she passed away in January 2003, aged about 18, but she had enjoyed a lovely life with us.

In late December 2020 Sue's daughter moved into temporary accommodation at a nearby pub. Her recent ex-boyfriend had bought her a tiny kitten as a present a few weeks beforehand who she'd named Simba, but the pub wasn't a good environment for him (resident dog, next to a busy road and no outside space). So she asked us if we would look after him until she found somewhere more permanent to live. Naturally we agreed, and I woke up around 2am that first night to find a little furry bundle curled up on my chest, nose poking out from under the duvet: that was the start of things. A couple of weeks later Sue popped her head round my home office – Simba was curled up on my lap as I worked on the computer. Her daughter wanted to know if we'd consider keeping Simba on a permanent basis? I was utterly delighted and so happy to have the little cat in our lives permanently: when I looked down I swear he was nodding vigorously ... probably just purring...

In February 2020 our dear old Simba passed away aged nearly 17.

Simba

The Amazing Mr. Bimble

Our first meeting
Curled in a palm
Under the duvet
Sheltered from harm

Saturday morning string mouse
Magnetic cat fishing
Cartoon running through the house
On laminate flooring

Duvet tunnel daytime shift
Hoover monster short shrift
Curled summer flower pot
Winter claim on warm spot

Distributed collars
As others would favours
Chased his own tail
Cat behaviour

The ginger ninja
Mark of Simba
White sock paw
From under the door

Voiced his joy in mother tongue
Zoom groom tune
Grew into his purr
Friday treat all laid on
Your usual table, Sir

Out through the flap
In through the window
Tickly tummy
Legs akimbo

Evening greeting
Meeow…eh oh

You could set your watch
So set in his ways
Mouse post notch
Lord of all he surveyed

Access all areas VIP
Abu Simba Bimble Marmaduke Pftang Pftang Olé Biscuit Barrel
Dear old friend
RIP

(Dave Burnham 2020)

Chapter 1

Down to the bone

October 2020

The smallest feline is a masterpiece: Leonardo da Vinci

Trisha's heavily-pregnant cat, Hera, had disappeared – Schrödinger-ed! She was days away from giving birth and there was no sign of her, hidden away somewhere having found the best spot for her "nest".

A couple of days later Trisha's friend, Rebecca, was riding her bike up the mountain behind Trisha's house when she spotted Hera and another three ginger kittens. They went back and managed to capture her and two of the kittens, but there was no sign of the third.

Some time passed and it seems that Rebecca was cycling past the same spot up the mountain when she saw a raggedy little ginger bundle. She shot back down the hill and returned on scooters with Trisha, parking at the bottom of the steep track. Rebecca tried to crawl under the barbed-wire fence into the field catch the little kitty. She raised her head and saw Trisha who had entered into the field by the gate, which was lucky because it was usually locked. The little kitten was lying on his side half-heartedly trying to gnaw on a dry old bone, clearly starving and close to death. He was so thin and weak that he could hardly manage to stand. Trisha picked him up and put him into the cat carrier. Rebecca carried him all the way down the mountain on her bike, feeling as if her arms would break whilst holding on to the cage. There was no way she was going to let go (and she felt thankful for her time spent in the gym!). Finally they reached Trisha's house and gave the little kitten – whom they christened "Teddy" – some proper food and they recovered with a well-deserved glass of wine each!

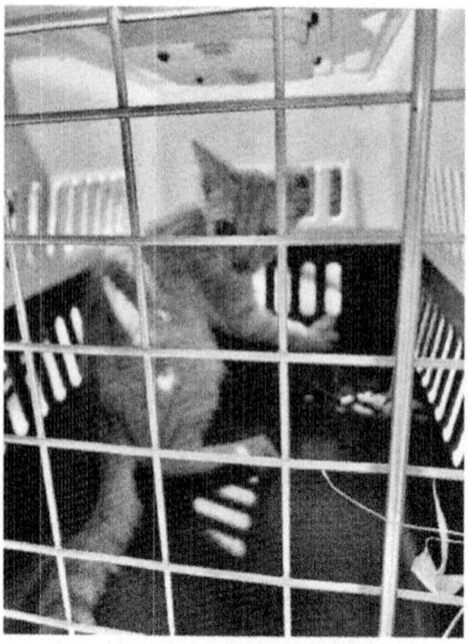

Rebecca says of that day: ‘Just a brilliant day that I will never forget, ever!’

22.10.20

Teddy had a check-up with the vet, Nikos, plus his first set of vaccinations and a microchip inserted.

24.10.20

Meanwhile, in the UK, Sue and I were sitting in our living room in Brighton. There was a post on Facebook from The Greek Cat Welfare Society (UK) with a picture of an absolutely gorgeous little kitten. Trisha’s contact details were given for anyone interested in adoption.

'Dear friends, sweet Teddy is looking for a home, if you would like to offer him a home he would be the happiest in the world. Thank you.'

'Hello, Teddy here. I am being treated royally at the moment as I need to build up my strength. I am still very thin as three months on bin scraps is not good for a growing kitten. I have a little area of my own with a Teddy bear. Rebecca checks on me all the time with nourishing food. I would really love a forever home. I am placid and affectionate.

Purrrrr please. Love Teddy.'

'What do you think?' Sue asked me.

'Oh, yes!' I replied.

25.10.20

The next day we sent an email to Trisha:

'Hello Trisha,

We've seen the Facebook post regarding Teddy, and would like to ask you how we might go about arranging to adopt him in the UK (we live in Brighton). We'd love to be able to offer Teddy a loving, forever home. What sort of information do you require from us? And what do we need to know/do in order to go about adopting him? We have had 2 cats over the past 30 years; our last one sadly passed away aged 17 in February this year. We now feel able to offer a good home to another cat/kitten and having visited Greece over many years, would be pleased to adopt a Greek cat in need. We look forward to hearing from you. Best wishes, Dave and Sue Burnham.'

Trisha sent us some more photos of Teddy and explained the next steps.

Trisha: 'My friend Rebecca is looking after him. He stays in a kitty park in the guest room. He has a toy dog with a beating heart so that he doesn't feel alone. Gourmet kitten food. Dry and wet ... he's been wormed and flea ampule applied.'

Dave: 'Fabulous, it's so good to know he's in such kind and expert hands. We like to give a mix of wet and dry food, too. We used Advocate for flea/tic/worms. The vet practice near us is excellent.'

Trisha: 'That's good to know you have a good vet. We feed so many here. We went to the Vrisoola forest today and fed all the cats there. It is a dumping ground for unwanted cats and kittens. We have made a hideaway for them with individual bed boxes inside.'

Dave: 'We're always humbled by people like you on the many islands we've visited over the years. We have friends who often travel to Athens and work with Nine Lives there and we had a friend who used to be involved with PAWS (Paros Animal Welfare).'

Trisha: 'I know Cordelia of Nine Lives, we worked together with our vet sterilizing in Piraeus. A lady in Hove adopted a blind cat from me and a black kitten.'

28.10.20

The following day Trisha sent us a video of little Teddy having a wash, it was the first time he'd had the energy to clean himself.

Dave: 'Aw, that's such a good sign - both the energy and the motivation. 😸 I'm on the allotment awaiting a horse manure delivery: it's the allotment holder's version of Christmas. One of the allotment cats came to see me, meowing his head off, partly wondering what I'm doing here in the wind and rain, and partly to complain about the weather, I think. 😂 The tail end of hurricane Epsilon doesn't have the warmth of the meltemi! 😂 The grey cat is Dorian, one of the allotment cats who lives nearby and often comes to visit.

This is Neo. He lives on the allotments all year. Thanks to Facebook I now know his original owner and I keep her updated on how he's doing (we've tried taking him home to her, but he keeps coming back). I've got to know the owners of the cats who visit us and keep an eye on them. Really white: a challenge in the allotment environment. 😸'

Dorian and Neo on the allotment in Brighton

Trisha: 'I have two white cats one is blind, both rescued. Fhivosis is blind and the owner wanted me to put him to sleep as a small kitten. He is about 5 now.'

Asprooli

'This is Asprooli his brother. Asprooli was losing his fur and very thin as his 93-year-old owner had died. I helped his owner by giving him some cake and company.'

29.10.20

Trisha: 'I am taking Teddy to the vet this weekend for a check-up.' 🐱

Dave: 'Hopefully his check-up will be all good. Need to be sure that he's in robust health. We're keeping a close eye on things this end. The pandemic (Covid) infection rate is climbing again so when we reach a stage at which Teddy is safe to travel we need to make sure there won't be transfer problems this end. If we get a National lockdown we might need to hang on? I really hope Brexit doesn't have a negative impact on pet passport compliance and transportation logistics for Greek cat welfare in the longer term.

30.10.20

Trisha: 'Teddy is now upstairs in my conservatory room along with Tommy another rescue.' 😸

Dave: 'He looks much perkier! Nice that he's sociable with Tommy, too. We also need to think about helping with funding. We'd like to make sure that your costs are covered (vet, food, transport etc etc).'

Trisha: 'Thank you very much. I will sort out ASAP. Going to vet tomorrow morning.' 😸😸😸

Dave: 'Before the pandemic the nursing home looking after my mother had regular visits from the pet therapy folks. This time last year they brought kittens in!'

Dave at the nursing home on pet therapy kitten day

Trisha: 'What a gorgeous grey. Just when people need animal therapy it stops!' 🐱🙀

Dave: 'I know, it's a real shame ... the staff wondered if they should frisk me before I left in case I tried to smuggle him out.' 😸

Chapter 2

Oh for a TARDIS

November 2020

Cats may walk by themselves, but there are times when they need our support:
Nicholas Dodman

2.11.20

Dave: 'How did Teddy's vet check-up with Nikos go? As anticipated, the UK is back in lockdown from Thursday until sometime in December. The government are publishing further specific guidance before Thursday. Not sure how all this will affect animal transport logistics.'

Trisha: 'Kalimera, Dave. He was only on the island on Sunday morning and was so busy taking teeth out of a rescued kitty he ran out of time. I have booked Teddy in for Thursday for his vaccinations. He had flea and worm treatment as soon as we found him. I have asked Nikos to write out a list of the costs which could be paid directly to the him. I will be applying for a grant from Greek Cats soon to do a TNR programme; unfortunately on the island there are very few volunteers.'

With the UK back in lockdown it meant I wouldn't be able to see my mother in her nursing home for a little while, but I knew she was in good hands, just like Teddy was. Greece was also in lockdown, so Trisha had to text for permission before going outside and had to obtain special authorisation to feed the street cats: the police were stopping people and asking to see their phones and their permission texts. She likened it to Alcatraz, but it seemed the Greek government were taking things very seriously.

16

Teddy was getting stronger every day and Asprooli would wash him from time to time, getting used to Teddy and Tommy curling up next to him; Trisha sent us a photo of the three of them together.

Asprooli, Tommy and Teddy

Dave: 'Okay, now that's the calendar photo! Tommy and Teddy look like they've just watched an episode of Dr Who and are hiding behind Asprooli instead of the sofa.'

Trisha: 'Ha-ha Asprooli is incredibly warm, plump and cosy.

Tommy was one of five kittens and found refuge with an experienced bin cat called Hopi. I went to feed them every night, but the bigger cats out-competed Tommy and he got steadily thinner. He got cat flu and couldn't smell the food, so I got him in my bag and he wriggled all the way home. I took him to Nikos for a check-up and he was diagnosed with a breathing problem. Luckily Michael was here and took over looking after him, but Tommy is living with me now because Michael is stuck in the UK due to Covid. Tommy was so skinny. We hope that that he will eventually go to live with him, but his breathing problems could be exacerbated by the journey.'

Tommy

Dave: 'Wow, well done. It's really hard to believe he's the same cat in those photos!'

22.11.12

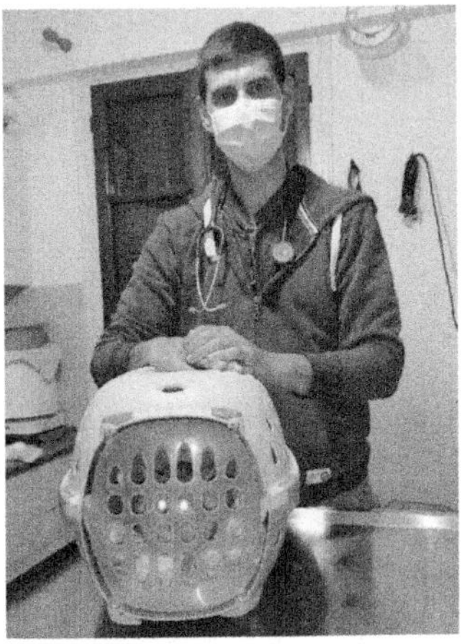

Nikos with Teddy

Trisha: 'Teddy had his second Tricat vaccinations and his first Rabies shot today.'

Dave: 'Great, sounds like good progress. The UK comes out of lockdown next week, but we're still in 'Tier 2'. Not sure about logistics, but I guess it's down to Nikos giving the go ahead on Teddy's overall strength and having a safe transfer corridor if/when the Greek lockdown is lifted/reduced.'

Trisha: 'It sounds like we may have a problem with Traces – whatever they are – when it comes to transport. I hope there will be a solution soon: I have 6 cats waiting to go. Teddy will be ready to go maybe after a month, along with Vincent, Ari, Simbi and Danae, but for now my house is full! 🙀 I am waiting to hear from Thompson Pet Travel.'

Dave: 'So, it's sounding like January. Would love to climb in a Tardis and pop over to visit kitty central 😻.'

Trisha: 'Your Tardis would be very welcome here...👾 You could throw in a few days holiday🏖️⛱️. Teddy agrees.'

Meanwhile, I joined the Thompson Pet Travel Facebook page and began to learn about some of the problems effecting the future of animal transfers from the EU. Eurotunnel had changed its rules so that a maximum of 5 animals would be allowed through at any one time, but then they back-tracked so DEFRA-registered transporters were still permitted to take 20 animals. There were more rules to contend with though and Eurotunnel were unable to cope with the overwhelming number of queries and requests for the new "business account". It seemed as if Eurotunnel were creating their own set of rules above and beyond DEFRA regulations. In combination with increasing difficulty in obtaining the necessary paperwork (Traces) at the Greek end, all this was making the job of pet transport from the EU to the UK practically impossible.

Things were starting to look a lot less certain for Teddy travelling to join us in the UK and there was still the spectre of Brexit looming on the horizon.

TRACES, by the way, (The Trade Control and Expert System) was an online system for health certification and tracking consignments of animals or animal products coming into or out of the UK; but it was going to be superseded after Brexit in January 2021.

Chapter 3

The Feline Dynasty

December 2020

No matter how much the cats fight, there always seem to be plenty of kittens:
Abraham Lincoln

Trisha started to tell me tales of some of the desperate cats that had passed through her care and how rewarding it was to help them pull through and find loving homes. Cats like Winnie who was found outside a holiday resort by Martin. She had one eye full of maggots, half a jaw and was rake thin. She'd lived with Trisha for two years when a lady who had heard about her work through Greek Cats Welfare visited her on the island. She picked Winnie up for a cuddle and asked if she could have her: Winnie now lives a happy life in Greenwich.

Although we really wanted Teddy to travel to the UK with Thompson Pet Travel, we were also keeping our options open in case things became even more complicated after the UK officially left the EU in January 2021. Various customs checks were on the increase and there were already substantial delays at Calais for both the tunnel and the ferry port as miles of lorry queues built up. Andy from Spartan Cats was looking into other possibilities, but with a limit on the number of animals that could travel per person and the ongoing changes, it sounded like other options were going to be increasingly more expensive. Even if we were able to find an animal courier still undertaking transport into the UK, Teddy's comfort and safety was always of paramount importance, so we would just have to wait and see how things developed.

I did a bit of internet research and found an article on Eurotunnel's new rules. They claimed that the "sheer volume" of dogs being brought through had become untenable and there were concerns about their welfare. Various animal charities had flagged the tremendous hike in prices being charged for puppies during lockdown and how that could be fuelling smuggling. (In my view it would have been more sensible to place an age limit on animal transport to try and prevent that issue.) The UK Lockdowns had most likely played their part in people becoming desperate for the company of a dog or puppy and the annual pre-Christmas surge in demand wasn't helping. After a huge petition managed to clarify matters, Eurotunnel announced they were going to exempt registered charities and businesses from the 5 animal limit, but license application was never going to be easy. Community interest companies didn't qualify and even those that did were struggling with the all the red tape involved. Meanwhile, the rescue shelters were filling up and with winter kicking in, the weaker animals left on the street were likely to succumb to the cold.

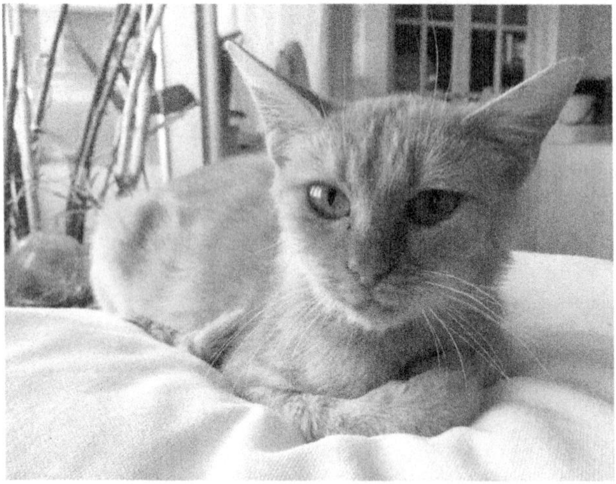

5.12.20

Trisha sent me a photo of Teddy relaxing on a cushion after his breakfast. I sent her a picture of me in PPE with my Mum, having finally been allowed back to see her in a separate, dedicated visiting building at her nursing home. I showed Teddy to her and, despite her dementia, she tickled his face on my phone screen with her finger and said, 'Hello, pretty'. I decided to send some funds to Trisha to help cover Teddy's food costs: meanwhile, we dreamt of waking up to Teddy's little face next to ours!

Lily and Fluffy

Trisha told me another story: 'Some years ago Andy and I found two newborns in the forest with their umbilical cords still attached. We fed them every four hours with kitten milk and they grew up to be beautiful cats – Lily and Fluffy. Michael and I flew with Aegean Airlines to Paris with three cats: two in the cabin, one in the hold. An animal courier taxi picked us up in Paris, we travelled to the UK and Lily and Fluffy went to Oxfordshire and Ella to Scotland. A lady in the UK had a car boot sale to raise the money to pay for their transport.'

We chatted some more about famous cat lovers, such as Freddie Mercury, Joni Mitchell, Debbie Harry and Mark Twain.

Twain had some fabulous cat quotations, here are a couple:

If man could be crossed with a cat, it would improve man, but deteriorate the cat.

When a man loves cats, I am his friend and comrade, without further introduction.

We talked about the recent Queen biopic, Bohemian Rhapsody and how it had been on at her local Greek cinema (a treat for those with balconies overlooking the outdoor screen).

One of Trisha's friends had been due to fly out from Israel, but had to cancel due to Covid. I sympathised and hoped that she could come in Spring when the orchids were in the fields. We chatted a bit about gardening. I'd recently built a rose arch and prepared a border at my mother's nursing home ready for planting up in April. I told her the bamboo canes on my allotment had rather novel eye-protectors on them – many an *Ouzo 12* cork waves in the breeze on the plot to keep us from eye injury. Teddy apparently had developed a taste for *Felix* and *Royal Canin* and Trisha joked that he had gone from street cat to royalty in one step, with a very healthy appetite.

Sometimes Robert would come over from the mainland and bring a *Dreamies* party mix.

Trisha: 'So funny that humans who love their animals just love buying treats and toys and beds. I have just ordered another recycled plastic cat house. I already have a block of three, two below and one penthouse above. My husband wished I would buy him houses and treats. It does get cold here on the mountain side. The stairs have cat beds all the way up.'

Dave: 'Wow, it's a city for the feline dynasty.'

Trisha: 'With 25 rescued cats and kittens it's not possible to have visitors. My house is on the mountain with the mountain inside. Teddy isn't sure if he's inside or outside, except it's warmer than outside. The *Cave room* is cut out of the rock. Usually it's only my husband and I and the cats here in the winter.'

Dave: 'An old friend of ours on Paros has a giant rock at the front of his house which they built onto: there was no way they were going to shift it. Originally it was a farmer's cottage. Great view of the islands from a picture window in his back garden.'

Christmas Day 2020

Trisha: 'Happy Christmas from Teddy and all of us. He had his second rabies vaccination three days ago. Teddy and Asprooli are sitting in front of the wood burner.'

Danae and Vincent

Trisha: 'Danae is singing Christmas songs and Vincent is enacting "God Rest Ye Merry Gentlemen".

Dave: 'Happy Christmas to you, too. Give Teddy an extra festive tickle from us.'

Trisha: 'Will do. He really is a lovely little lad ... purrs all the time.'

Boxing Day 2020

Teddy

Trisha: 'Teddy says "Happy Boxing Day".'

Dave: 'Aw, Happy Boxing Day back to Teddy from Sue and me.'

Trisha: 'That's me and Moustaki – that's Greek for moustache; he has a ginger one. Moustaki was dumped by the owners outside the vet. He heard me walk by and meowed. I recognised his voice (to a non-cat person they don't believe he has a different meow) he had stomatitis and had to have teeth out. We raised money for his operation. His original owners had got a kitten so they didn't want him anymore! Now I, or Demos, feed the little boy who has grown into a big ginger cat.'

Dave: 'Ha, yeah, they all have widely different meows. Things have improved a lot since we first started going to Greece in the 90s, we used to hear stories of people returning to Athens after the tourist season and abandoning animals ... hopefully they will come to understand in time.'

Primrose

Trisha: 'We did a sterilizing programme today, then the heavens opened and it rained thunder and lightning and one of my cats, Primrose, hasn't turned up for dinner. She's scared of the other cats and they chase her. She was chased last year and she ran into a bike and broke her leg so badly she was in the clinic for 12 weeks. She was nearly wild when I took her home, but I managed to calm her down and even found a home for her, but she is so scared of other cats the adoptee could not adopt her. I am going to give the kittens their night snack now and then go and look for Primrose again.'

Dave: 'Oh dear, it's always a worry when they go walkabouts. The two who regularly come to visit me on the allotment are really friendly. Dorian is the grey and lives about quarter of a mile away and regularly walks up to the allotment on his own. The white cat is Neo and he lives about one and a half miles away and despite taking him back to his owner he keeps coming back to the plot. He has a lovely home, but just seems to want his independence in the "wild". Our last cat, Simba, wouldn't have anything to do with other cats. It's a shame, but they're all different, generally avoiding one another's territories (many of Brighton's cats seem to operate in the gardens on a time share basis).'

Trisha: 'This is feeding the forest cats and kittens and catching some for neutering. There have been more kittens dumped in the forest, poor things. I would take them home, but there's no room at the Inn. They look like little Bengals.'

Dave: 'Thank goodness you're there for them. Neutering is so important. Sue once had a bit of a debate about neutering male cats with a taverna owner: anyone would've thought she was suggesting he cut his own off!'

Trisha: 'I know they get quite upset at the thought. That happened today. The pizza lady contacted me for three of hers. When I got there she said they are her boys, as if they were her own sons, and was having second thoughts. I told her they can go on the rampage for miles. I trapped them in the dropper cages then transferred to the green cages. She was distraught but I told her it was in their best interests.'

Dave: 'Hmmm ... joined up thinking required. I totally understand that it's a deep cultural thing; it will get better as the next generation of Greeks grow up. Maybe it also relates to Greek Orthodox dictates being extrapolated into nature?'

Trisha: 'Yes, true. I tell them humans have upset the balance of nature and some understand, usually the younger generation. Mind you there's an old lady from a nearby, remote village who's gung-ho to do the lot!'

Dave: 'Bless her ... I assume you're not referring to male taverna owners as well?"

Kristi: 'They are very hard to convince.' 😂

Dave: '... and probably even harder to catch.' 😂

We talked about the Brexit deal and wondered if it might help to clarify things for the future of animal transport. We had flights to Athens booked for June and had been planning to travel to Sifnos, but a trip to Poros instead might be possible and then we could fly Teddy back with one of us. There were still many unknowns though, such as whether we would have had our coronavirus vaccinations by then, what the restrictions might be, how Brexit might affect travel, and so on.

Trisha: 'I cannot find Primrose! Really worried now as she always comes back for food.' 🙀

Dave: 'Oh no, it's so distressing. If she has problems with other cats did you have another place for her to stay?'

Trisha: 'Sometimes she stays in the room downstairs as it's an empty bedroom, but she is too scared to come inside upstairs now as we have so many rescued cats and kittens. When she had her accident I found her after 10 days.'

Dave: 'If you know the direction from which she comes back to the house, you could try taking a little *cat house* a few hundred yards away from your place, pop some food in it and hope for the best, but I guess there aren't many spare cat houses just now. How about some kind of box with a cat-sized entrance?'

Trisha: 'I have 6 cat houses outside, but she won't use them. I walked up to the nightclub earlier because I found her there last time, but no luck. She could be anywhere because we are on an open mountainside.'

Dave: 'Ooof! You can only do so much. You need some sleep and to keep it all together for the rest of the feline dynasty (let alone you and yours). Just have to hope she'll find her way back. Much less likely to get shut in anywhere this time of year.' 🤞 🤗

29.12.20

I came across some information that directed me to a UK government page about bringing your pet dog, cat or ferret into the country (Ferret? Really?). The overview seemed okay, referring to the need for the animal to have been microchipped, vaccinated against rabies and have either a pet passport or a health certificate. This was the first I'd heard about a "Health Certificate" (little did I realise at this stage that the Health Certificate was to be the cornerstone and lynchpin of the whole pack of cards: so important, it warranted a mixed metaphor – or possibly Minotaur.)

Anyway, scrolling down I came across this:

"You must follow extra rules if the animals will be sold or rehomed in Great Britain. See the section on 'Goods Subject to Sanitary and Phytosanitary Controls'."

Alarm bells began to ring and the link took me to a Policy paper on "The Border Operating Model". This was a 159-page PDF document. As we were planning to give Teddy a new home in the UK, it looked like this might apply to us. Oh dear, that would be some heavy bedtime reading. There was also talk of a 'declaration of ownership' to confirm that you were not planning to sell or transfer ownership.

(*Written declaration for the non-commercial movement of animals referred to in Article 25(3) of Regulation (EU) No 576/2013*)

As I carried on with my research, it looked like the Animal and Plant Agency, DEFRA (Department for Environment, Food and Rural Affairs) and the Animal Health and Veterinary Laboratories Agency were all going to need to be involved. The more I read, the more difficult and complicated the whole thing started to look.

I contacted Trisha and asked if she had found Primrose yet.

Trisha: 'I have called and called, asked my neighbours, but she has just disappeared. The 2 times she disappeared before was when she broke her leg and when she wasn't well. I found her both times because she comes when I call. But now, nothing. There was a big storm yesterday. Leon did that, too, vanished then knocked on the door three days later. What do they do? Where do they go? Primrose does not like socialising with the other cats and won't come in the house anymore unless it's just me there.

It was a long day. Robert, our volunteer, and I took the sterilised cats back to their habitat. Then we fed the street cats and went to the forest to clean the bowls and feed the cats and kittens. We reorganised the cat shelter in the forest and put a large duvet inside it.'

Dave: 'I've been doing some further research into the post-Brexit regulations for animal transport now that the UK will no longer be part of the EU. It looks a bit boggling, but I'll try to pick through it. Also, it looks like the vets here in the UK are only offering in-surgery urgent vaccines and urgent neutering and have gone over to video/phone consultation only, because the number of new Covid cases has gone through the roof. Bearing that in mind, if Greece still comes out of lockdown on 7th Jan, it looks best if Teddy has any booster vaccines and neutering carried out at your end. Obviously, I'm happy to pay Teddy's vet bill. It could also further affect all travel arrangements if the Covid situation continues as it is here. These are such difficult times.'

Trisha: 'They are indeed. I will look after Teddy until he goes to you. He doesn't go out and has a huge room that looks like its outside anyway 😺. I have 5 waiting to go. Our vet has already sterilized Vincent, who is waiting to go. I think it's much easier to do it here.'

Trisha: 'These two have been in their new home for a few years now: Wispa and Roly. I found them running randomly in the middle of the road as tiny kittens. The adoptee loves them.'

'This is Freddie. When we found him he was sick with cat flu. Named after Freddie Mercury.

Here's Freddie in his new home with the other adopted cat, Thomas. Thomas was adopted from me as well. His new dad, Peter, asked me for another kitty to keep Thomas company. It's so uplifting when new parents send updates of their adopted kitties.'

Dave: 'We can guarantee to send you regular pictures and updates on Teddy.'

Trisha: 'I look forward to them.'

Chapter 4

Primrose Path

January 2021

I would like to see anyone, Prophet, King or God, convince a thousand cats to do the same thing at the same time: Neil Gaiman.

Trisha asked me how things were with us in the UK being back in lockdown, so I let her know that I'd managed to see my mother through a glass door at her nursing home. She couldn't hear me, but I managed to make her laugh by pulling funny faces. I asked if there was any sign of Primrose.

Trisha: 'So good to be able to see your mum and make her laugh, what a lovely son. On Friday I went looking for Primrose up the mountain above our house. It was getting dark so I asked my husband to come with me. We walked the stretch at the top then I told my husband to go down the steps as the hill is so steep and it was nearly dark. It's all woodland at the top of the mountainside (it is a mountain, but low) I rushed to my bike and twisted my ankle on a loose stone. However, I picked up hubby, drove home, fed cats, cooked and looked for Primrose. Then agony set in on my ankle so ice, then a hot cloth and my husband's old crutches. Next day I stayed in for a while then just before dark I went next door again to the derelict night club – several of my cats followed. The club was locked but music was playing inside 👻👻👻👻. This is where I found her before, so I called and called for ages and had almost given up when I heard a cacophony of meows followed by a niaw, coming from inside the club! She came bouncing over, jumping up and down on the other side of the glass doors. I woke the owner up from his siesta – he came out donning his dressing gown – and opened the club. Primrose had got in through the window at the start of the storm and the owner had come in and shut it to keep the wind and rain out, not realising she was in there. Five days locked inside no food or water, she was so hungry!' 😹

Primrose returned

Relieved at finding Primrose, Trisha went shopping for collars and found Teddy a nice green one. Asprooli ended up with a diamante pink bling number. I'd just started writing a new story for my Ad Astral podcast so we exchanged messages about that and then talked about the situation with Covid. Greece still had a curfew and the UK was back in lockdown. Trisha was missing the company of her girlfriends. She had her husband for company, but it wasn't the same as girly chats. Rebecca, who has a house next door to Trisha and found Teddy, normally came out to the island in April for the summer, but 2021 was looking uncertain.

We talked some more about cat food and animal transport options. At that stage Thompson Pet Travel were deep in the process of trying to understand and negotiate all the new regulations and figure out whether it would be viable or even possible for them to continue bringing dogs and cats from Greece to the UK. Their current mission was to try to get a licence from Greece, as the UK were now saying they had to have an EU licence as well as their UK DEFRA licence. Their van already fitted, and exceeded, the criteria required, but who knew what other rules and regulations would be added on? There were some other options to explore, but Trisha had used Thompson before and they had such a good reputation. Time would tell.

Animal Couriers looked like another possible option and Trisha's friend was in touch with several other animal welfare organisations, but the situation was both complex and confused. It was starting to look less likely that the animal couriers would be travelling to Greece as there was now talk about "Travel Corridors" and possible isolation rules that could further complicate matters.

Trisha: 'Here's Teddy sitting by the fire with Barry on the left and Asprooli on the right. Teddy is so sweet and charming; purrs all the time. What a different cat from the starving kitten Rebecca found. It's still tear-jerking remembering that picture of a terrified kitty trying to eat a dry old bone.' 🙀

Dave: 'It's incredible how your care has not only saved Teddy's life, but also how well he's doing. I updated our Wills over the weekend and wrote a new clause as our cat-loving Grecophile friends (Karen and Andy) have agreed to look after Teddy should anything happen to us: belt and braces cat care.' 😉

Trisha: 'Yes, I've done something similar for all the cats here.'

A couple of days later some more news was released. I contacted Trisha:

Dave: 'New quarantine rules and proof of negative tests are coming in, plus closure of some travel corridors. Hopefully they will find a way round that for lorry drivers. It must be a nightmare for animal couriers ... they could get as far as France only to be turned away.'

Trisha: '🙀😳Well I hope it's sorted out. 🙏 Teddy is already selecting his suitcase and a new collar 🎒.'

Chapter 5

The Enigma Code

February 2021

One reason that cats are happier than people is that they have no newspapers:
Gwendolyn Brooks

6.2.2021

For the rest of January 2021 we traded occasional messages and Trisha sent me several pictures of Teddy, including one of him sitting on the cat activity tower wearing a new collar, sent by Rebecca. Such a gorgeous little boy. We were trying to keep our hopes up that there would still be a way to get him to us, despite the ever-increasing obstacles.

Lynda Thompson and her team at Thompson Pet Travel, and all the other animal transport companies, had been spending endless hours trying to unearth information from deep within the DEFRA and UK government websites aiming to understand what the rules would be for the transportation of pets with the new, post-Brexit regulations. As I read their updates and continued with my own research, it all sounded horribly draconian, with any lack of compliance risking anything from travel delays to seizure of the animals with even the possibility of them being destroyed! The European Commission released information on Border Control Posts at specific French sea ports, namely St. Malo, Caen and Calais (with no mention of the Eurotunnel). It was "Tales of the Expected" regarding the lack of forward planning and organisation for Border Control Posts on the UK side. It seemed as if there hadn't been anything done about it at all, and the Posts hadn't even been scheduled to begin activity until sometime in the Summer of 2021.

I also gathered that applications for the additional European transport licences were taking forever to be processed – Greece has always been rather notorious for its 'sluggish' bureaucracy (but possibly not helped in this instance by the applications being for 'pet transportation'). It sounded like another problem was the use of a "one size fits all" form, so that applications were based on transporting agricultural livestock, rather than being specifically for cats and dogs (not known for requiring emergency treatment for broken horns, hoof rot or hoisting gear to upright them in transport stalls).

Further details then began to emerge about the paperwork and compliance that would be required. Now that the UK had become a non-member state, a Health Certificate would be required for Teddy to travel to the UK. A pet passport would also be required although, rather strangely, that only appeared to apply to the UK in its new non-member status. Teddy's vet would issue a pet passport as routine, but it highlighted the potential raft of other – possibly more complex – peculiarities in relation to the UK.

We would have to find out how to make a Customs Declaration for Teddy and he would now be subject to VAT! Yep, VAT on a cat...

In addition to that, we would have to make an 'IPAFFS' declaration for an animal import.

Lynda from Thompson PT posted an update on their Facebook page:

'Stella Blue has undergone a makeover, she is pristine inside! We had everything ready last year, but no time to actually strip her out and do the work. So she's newly painted inside, new insulation including lifting the floor to insulate underneath. A new, smart-looking roof, new walls all painted or varnished. Electrics all redone with new lighting, a new heater that can run independently through the night and many other extras too. None of this work would have been possible without the brilliant help of Frank and

Rachel....Frank is a genius, I don't think there's anything this man can't do!!! Thanks so much!!! Stella is way above fully compliant as she already was to receive our existing licence, (which we still need to enter the UK) so there is no reason for her not to pass! But, Greece has only ever issued ONE licence so far in the whole country, so we shall see ...'

Stella Blue's makeover

25.2.21

News emerged that the Deputy Minister of Interior, Stelios Petsas, had announced that Greece was introducing new regulations for pet owners and sellers, as well as stricter penalties for animal abuse. This was a pre-election commitment by Kyriakos Mitsotakis, the Greek Prime Minister.

He said: 'The framework for pets shows our humanity.'

The draft bill now explicitly included the five internationally-recognized animal freedoms. These are: freedom from hunger and thirst, freedom from unnecessary suffering and strain, freedom from pain, injury and illness, freedom from fear and anxiety, and the freedom to express normal behaviours in appropriate living conditions.

There would also be a new digital health book accessible by vets and owners alike, as well as fines for infringements and an education programme to increase awareness of pet welfare.

The bill also set out to establish a comprehensive programme for the management of stray animals by the local Municipalities and participation of Animal Welfare Organisations in a supervisory framework.

A 'National Register' of pets, strays, adoptees, welfare organisations, shelters, breeders and vets was proposed to bring everything together. It also outlined proposals to limit the number of births per animal to regulate reproduction and incentives for owners to take better care of their pets.

All of these measures and the establishment of a National Complaints Line.

It looked as if things were starting to change in favour of the animals, reducing exploitation, suffering and harm. Of course, these proposals were met with a certain amount of mistrust and suspicion, but there was no doubt it represented a step in the right direction.

26.2.21

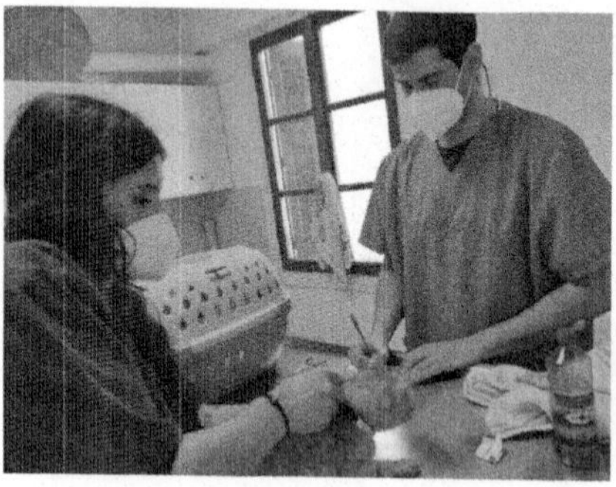

Nikos and Litsa with Teddy

Teddy recovering

Teddy was successfully neutered. Trisha said he was sleepy for a while, but managed a snack in the evening (very Teddy!). She sent me a copy of the vet bill so I could look into paying it as it was the least I could do, and his little operation and micro-chipping ticked two more of the boxes towards compliance with the growing mountain of paperwork.

Chapter 6

The Mystery Vets

March 2021

The human race can be divided into two categories: ailurophiles and ailurophobes – cat lovers and the underprivileged:
David Taylor

1.3.21

I made a note of Teddy's microchip number and registered him in the UK with Petlog: it was all beginning to feel real! Then I emailed Thompson Pet Travel, having seen their Facebook post about a visual guide to IPAFFS. I explained that we'd adopted Teddy and would like to enquire if they could bring him to the UK on a future trip. I also thanked them for their extraordinary commitment in tackling the very difficult and frustrating situation: the triple whammy of Covid, Brexit and the illegal animal trade conspiring to increase its complexity. I then got in touch with Trisha, sending her all I knew so far by email and we had a chat on WhatsApp:

Dave: 'Hiya, I've emailed Thompson for their guide on the new regulations. Looks like every animal will need a Health Certificate. I haven't got to the bottom of the VAT situation, but it looks like there's a nominal value placed on a cat at £60 so I guess it's 20% of that. I think they might be encountering expensive Covid testing, too (the lovely transport folks, not the cats and dogs ... I assume.)

Trisha: 🙀🙀 'They are making it so difficult for all of us trying to rehome animals that would just be abused on the street. I have to sneak around one bin in the dark, or when the old witch who lives there has the curtains drawn, to feed a limping kitty. Otherwise she comes out of her house yelling at me.'

Dave: 'I wish they'd inject everyone with a shot of empathy as well as the vaccine! Covid will eventually come under a degree of control, but Brexit was always going to be an administrative nightmare. I'll send you what I know so far about the new paperwork and regulations.'

Trisha: 'Oh, Lord, this IS a nightmare!'

Dave: 'I hope it can be overcome, but maybe we need to coordinate with Greek Cat Welfare Society HQ and any other charities we're friends with so we can gather all the information and experience on the new situation and create a comprehensive guide for all of you?'

Trisha: 'I just sent the information to Cordelia at Nine Lives Athens and Andy at Spartan Cats. I have Tommy that can only go by plane with Michael as he is a very nervous cat and has a breathing problem. My friend Rachael wants to take 5 of my rescued cats.'

Dave: 'If you're in touch with Cordelia let her know about me and Teddy and tell her that Sue and I are Karen and Andy's fellow Grecophile friends in Brighton.' 😉 (We've known Karen and Andy for some years and had a lovely long weekend with them in Athens in 2015. They often spend time in the city and have got to know Cordelia, helping her out on her rounds feeding the stray cats in Athens. Karen has written a little piece about that for the end of the chapter on Athens).

Trisha: 'Andy has another lead with a Greek transport company called Pet Transport from a lady called Victoria in Athens. I'll look into it.'

Dave: 'Interesting, I guess we need to know how they are getting on with the new regulations, the Greek Ministry Vet, awareness of UK VAT advance payment and chip registration/documentation and the testing regulations, as Calais Border Control seem to be insisting on full Covid tests (animal transport might have fallen outside the "transport driver exemption" rulings, but I'm not sure). It makes you wonder if the Greek authorities might be slightly more kindly disposed towards a Greek animal transport company 🤔. Traces have been superseded by the Health Certificate (that also enables more than 5 animals per vehicle through Border Control). It certainly could smooth the acquiring of paperwork at the Greek end. Border Control may be picky at the Calais end (plus VAT and chip registration at UK arrival). Sounding hopeful though. Be good to know if they've had a successful trip in the last 3-4 weeks. I even have a tiny suspicion that French Border Control may look less favourably on UK drivers, but that might be short-lived and relate to threatened blockades.'

Trisha: 'I've heard of another company that transport livestock and take a few pets as well. Sounds like they just scoot through without all the extra paperwork.'

Dave: 'Hmmm, sounds a bit dodgy. Worth knowing more, though.'

3.3.2021

Trisha: 'Teddy and the rescues. Asprooli is the big white, Tommy black and white and Nefeli small black and white.'

Dave: 😻😻😻 'Teddy and the Rescues would make a great band name.'

Trisha: 'Thank goodness Rebecca spotted Teddy up in the mountain. Whatever star he was born under it was a lucky one when you two came along! I am thinking there must be others all the time, so Rebecca and I are going to try and sterilize a few up there.'

Dave: 'The transport companies have to be registered with IPAFFS (Import of products, animals, food and feed system) and I think I will have to do something with that, too.

Meanwhile, I guess you've seen the new Health Certificate, but I've attached a copy of what I think it looks like coming from the EU end, in case you need some information.'

6.3.21

Trisha: 'We did a sterilizing programme today as Nikos had a donation from a lady who adopted a kitten we rescued called Artemis.'

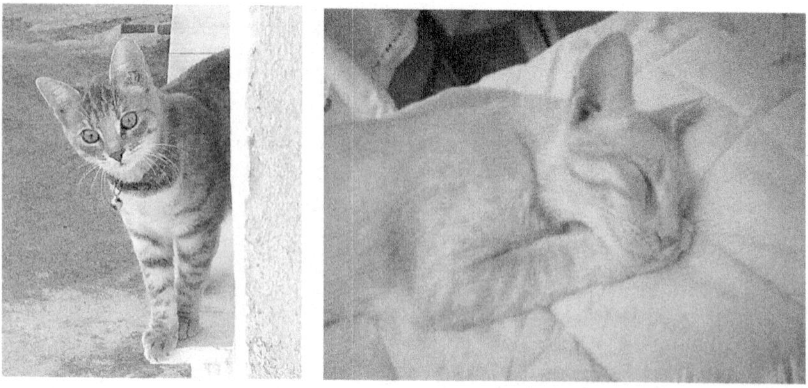

Artemis and Simbi

Here's their story:

"Hi everyone I am Simbi. I was born on a yacht. Sounds posh doesn't it? But here is what really happened. My mum, who lived in the port of Piraeus in Athens, was looking for somewhere to give birth to her kittens, one of them being me. She saw the ideal place under the tarpaulin of a lifeboat on a yacht – no one seemed to be on board. Mum gave birth to me and my sisters Artemis and Ariadne whilst she went off for food. Meanwhile, the yacht crew came back and sailed away to the island of Poros! What does a three-week-old kitty do? Meowwww! Luckily one of the crew heard me and contacted Trisha who took us in. Michael then fostered us for a while and fed us with kitty milk from a bottle. Needless to say we thrived and eventually Artemis was adopted by a kind lady called Marina in the UK. I am still looking for a forever home."

We sterilized 3 boys and one girl today. They are all in an apartment for aftercare. When we have funds from Greek Cats we will do a big programme.

My friend just wrote to me she is stuck in Greece worrying she may never get back to the UK. She said we have had pandemics before and they died out, but this one is mutating and mutating. So, is something else going on?'

Dave: 'The variants are occurring in countries that aren't managing the situation well (frankly that includes the UK) which is giving the virus a chance to thrive and evolve. To put things in perspective 'Flu changes every year.

As long as the genetics of the spike protein don't change too much then the current vaccines will be able to confer some protection and there are loads of different vaccines that have been or are being developed around the world.

It thrives on our being social animals.

SARS and MERS were overcome, but those countries have more "compliant" populations.

In many respects your friend is probably better off in Greece.'

Trisha: 'She is in Ermioni on the Peloponnese and very lonely as it's just her and her doggy. We still have 9.00pm curfew in the week and 7.00pm curfew at weekends. The police go round and round looking for culprits to fine. We cannot go further than 2 miles from our home without permission. We have to state why we are going out on our mobile phones by a number: 6 is for exercise, 2 is to go to the bank and so on. I will send her your message to reassure her that there isn't a conspiracy going on.'

Dave: 'It's very hard being on your own, I sympathise. The curfews are heavy, but my goodness, compare Greece's figures with the UK's and you can see it's worth it.

'Flu pandemics have been the main ones (other than plagues) but the worst in recent times is AIDS.

Anyway, there's no conspiracy, but mankind needs to drastically alter meat consumption and animal husbandry, let alone looking at the global human population increase.'

9.3.21

Rachel at Thompson Pet Travel replied to my email and explained the process.

It seemed we needed to contact the Ministry Vet responsible for Poros Island to see if they would issue a Health Certificate. It sounded like there was some resistance at this point in time, possibly due to a lack of information on what the Ministry Vets were required to do, having been used to the old Traces system. Rachel attached a blank example of the new Health Certificate so that I could see what it looked like and what it involved. Some Ministry Vets were signing, stamping and issuing reference numbers for the pre-filled certificates, whilst other Ministry Vets were following the new protocols and completing them online, so it seemed there was already a lack of uniformity in procedure.

Teddy would need to travel with a record of his vaccinations and as long as it was all certified by his local vet it didn't necessarily have to be in the form of a pet passport (but as we already had one for Teddy I decided to stick with that as our evidence base).

He would need to be declared via IPAFFS and I would also need to engage an agent to deal with both the import declaration in the UK and the associated customs declaration. But there was no point in starting on all that lot until we knew if we could get a Ministry Vet to actually issue or verify his Health Certificate. The same would apply to booking a place on the transport bus.

Rachel also sent me a helpful guide on how to make the IPAFFS declaration and said she would pass my kind words and support on to Lynda and Julia.

I thanked her for her help and for the information, and asked a few more questions...

We'd been in touch with Nikos (Teddy's local vet) and it looked as if Poros came under the area of the Local Competent Authority based somewhere in Piraeus (in other words, the Greek Ministry Vet responsible for Poros Island was located in Piraeus). Nikos was willing to complete Teddy's Health Certificate for us, but it seemed that it could only be "officially" issued by a State Vet. It was beginning to sound like the Health Certificates could be issued by the animal's own local vet in many, (if not all) other EU countries, but that this was not the case with Greece. If so, that would add an extra layer of complexity, as we would have to find out where the "Mystery Ministry Vet" was, get their agreement to authorise Teddy's Health Certificate and try to make an appointment for that (at a time when someone else could attend on Trisha's behalf).

I had heard that a dog was unable to travel because a Ministry Vet had not completed the Health Certificate correctly in several places and thus rendered the paperwork (and therefore everything else) invalid. By the time they discovered the error it was too late to get it corrected as the Ministry Vet had left the office. It seemed that these new forms were going to be a big problem.

However, I tried to remain positive and contacted Trisha.

Dave: 'Hi Trisha. Just sent you an email from Rachel at Thompson Pet Travel, looks like they're up for it! Woohoo!'

Trisha: That's good news indeed 😻. I'm waiting to hear back from Victoria in Athens to see what her company can do to help with the paperwork. It also sounds like the livestock transport company are up and running, too. Ministry Vet involvement has been a problem in the past with Traces, but I will ask our local vet about it. I am not sure what the Health Certificate involves. Is it for the vaccinations plus rabies, flea treatment and worming?'

Dave: 'I'll look into it tomorrow. Thing is, Health Certificates for all animals travelling also means Thompson can cross the English Channel with more than 5 animals, making it viable for them.'

Trisha: 'I prefer Lynda because I know her and the animals are well taken care of.'

Dave: 'Everything I've seen and read about them makes me feel that they are definitely the ones to go with if we can.'

Ares

Trisha: 'Special food tonight for my aging kitty and for Princess who has had 4 teeth out. 🙀 We also released the kitty, Lucy, who was sterilised on Saturday, she went off like a rocket. Pat is a saint and helps me with catching cats, recovery, meds, feeding etc. The cat in the photo is Ares (Mars), he is supposed to be in the UK with Rachael. He wouldn't stay indoors without me with him so he hangs around with Poppy and Co.'

10.3.21

Dave: 'Hi, Trisha. I've done some more research and have sent a further itemised enquiry to Rachel at Thompson and have copied you in. If we can work through the detail we may be able to establish protocols for transport of the other cats, too. I think it's worth pursuing.'

Trisha: 'That would be great. We have a very sad, dying kitty and no vet here. It's very strange as he was eating with gusto last night and we thought he would last out until Nikos got here tomorrow but he is slipping away. Very sad.'

Dave: 'Oh no, that's very upsetting for you all.'

Trisha: 'Thank you so much for being so helpful with the pet travel people. I am so busy with cats and my husband who has health problems. I am going to do another application to Greek Cat Welfare today for funds for a sterilizing programme. They are very good. We haven't done a big TNR (Trap Neuter Release) for a year. There are so many not sterilized. It looks like I will start back at work next month so I want to do it soon. I am very sad about the poor kitty.'

Dave: 'I'm still learning about the Health Certificate. I think we might need your vet's help with it.'

Trisha: 'I will ask Nikos. It would be much better to use Lynda because we know the company and have used them many times. I would like to send Vincent with Teddy. I was disappointed as one lady has decided not to take Danae. Such a shame. We have been in contact and I sent loads of photos and she was so looking forward to adopting her. My friend Rachael may adopt her or otherwise she just stays with me.'

11.3.21

Trisha: 'A local dog rescuer has used the other livestock transport company, she says it isn't complicated. They say nothing has changed regarding the government vet certificate and UK regulation, animals can still travel with ordinary pet passports.'

Dave: 'That doesn't sound right to me, unless they only take a few animals at a time. Plus, it may not be a very comfortable experience, especially for the cats, in a big, boomy livestock transporter.'

Trisha: 'I know what you mean. Anyway, I'm going out to feed the street cats. Teddy is relaxing with his roommates. Well, Andy (Spartan Cats) put it in perspective. He said if we can fly to the moon surely we can send some kitties to the UK?' 😸🚀🌕

Dave: 'Ha, yeah, although NASA didn't have the incompetent UK Brexit Deal fools to deal with.' 😂

12.3.21

And so the rollercoaster continued, as a friend had sent me an article from the Guardian suggesting an about-face by the UK government on import checks. British Customs were due to begin the control of animal products, live animals and plants and associated products from 1st April 2021 (including the much-discussed, so-called 'high-risk' foods such as sausages). These sanitary and phytosanitary (SPS) controls, would require consignments to have the correct documentation, including import and health certificates signed by vets on arrival in Britain. However, the network of Border Control Posts were still being built and wouldn't be ready in time for the 1st April date, so the UK government was forced to delay the introduction of import checks by six months. The anticipated scenario of "piss-ups and breweries" was now coming to pass, but it only related to border checks so we still needed all the paperwork for Teddy.

Dave: 'Hi, Trisha. I got a bit excited with yesterday's news update, but it doesn't apply to transport companies bringing more than 5 animals. Anyway, Rachel is being really helpful with guidance and information. I heard back from another UK-based animal courier and they sound very good, but they sort of leave it up to me to sort out the paperwork, plus Thompson are a known and very reliable company to you. Could I have photos of Teddy's Pet Passport so I can have all the vaccination information etc.'

Trisha: 'Okay, I'll ask our vet. I'm struggling with a TNR application spread sheet at the moment.'

As requested, Teddy's pet passport photos came through and I asked for a few more details such as batch numbers for the vaccinations. Victoria (from the Transport company based in Athens who Trisha was in touch with) also needed a Health Certificate, so I wondered if she might actually be able to visit the Ministry Vet and help with that aspect as it would make life much easier with regards to the special codes and details from both the vet and the transport company themselves.

Dave: 'Nikos, your vet is such a helpful and lovely guy. I don't suppose he has a list of State/Ministry Vets by any chance? I'm having trouble finding out who these "Mystery Vets" are and where they are.'

Trisha: 'He thinks it would be easier by car or plane. Cordelia at 9 lives uses the plane. I have a kitty, Tommy, who is so nervous I simply cannot send him in the bus overland. Michael is going to fly out when he can to take Tommy and hopefully two of Cordelia's as it makes the price of the pickup taxi cheaper if there are more cats. Maybe we could add Teddy and Vincent, but I don't know ... and then there is Ari, another forest cat.'

Dave: 'Wow, the Poros kitty family tree must be amazing.'

Trisha: 'The yacht kittens were found under a tarpaulin on a yacht after three days at sea. The people on the yacht had left Piraeus without knowing the kittens were on board, so Mum was left behind. Somehow they got hold of my number and rang me and asked if I was the "Poros Cat Hotel?" 😹😂 So, I collected them with Michael and then when Michael I left I took over. The yacht people paid for some food, vaccinations and sterilizing. Very kind. Oh, I want to go to bed now, but Rosie is asleep on my pillow!'

14.3.21

Trisha: 'We managed to catch Athena yesterday and get her sterilised. She's been avoiding us for weeks. We took her to recover in the apartment after her operation. She was half coming round when she tried to get out of the cage. I tried to push her back in and her tooth caught my hand with a light bite. Thankfully the chemist stayed open for me to have a tetanus jab. Now Pat our volunteer after carer has just sent me a text and said Athena got out again and is in the apartment so I have to go and try and get her back in the cage. Marina wants to adopt her but I think she may be a bit too wild to go to a UK home.'

Athena

Dave: 'Tricky one ... would probably mellow with time, but could cause issues. Hope the bite wasn't too bad, good idea to get the tetanus jab.'

Trisha: 'Thank you. The bite wasn't too bad, but I did it to be on the safe side. If she won't go back in the cage I will leave her free in the apartment. Hopefully she won't destroy the furniture. We take all the recoveries there but they are usually in cages.' 😬

Dave: 'Butterfly net?' 🦋😹

Trisha: 'I think that maybe our only option.' 😂

Later that day

Dave: 'Hope things went okay with Athena. Let's see what Victoria comes back with, but the possible option of Teddy travelling with Michael by aircraft sounds very tempting. Obviously we'd be happy to help with transport/travel costs.'

Trisha: 'Athena is okay, we left her in the apartment and didn't try to put her back in the cage as she is still recovering from her op'. I fed the street cats earlier and now mine are staring at me! Cordelia is texting me because our homeless lady at the port in Piraeus is in hospital again and there is no one to feed the street cats at the port: very worrying. I spoke to Michael and he has already been ill with Covid, but he has the long term symptoms and is not too good. He is up for taking the cats when he is ok to fly out, so, it may be a while. Tommy can only go with Michael. The local dog rescuer came up to my house this afternoon and said that the livestock company truck had just done a trip and there were cats in the trucks as well and they were all delivered safely. I don't know why but I'm not convinced. We will see how we go with Victoria, but really I want to use Lynda.' 🙆

Dave: 'These are strange times. I'm sorry to hear that Michael has had long Covid. I hope Cordelia can find someone to help feed the cats. My 2nd vaccine is scheduled for 3rd June so I might be able to get a vaccine passport a few weeks after that (just thinking about options).'

Trisha: 'You are good. I try to have as many "Plan Bs" as possible. My nephew has put up his hand to do a pick-up in Paris if necessary. He has already done a UK pick-up for Marina and adopted an abandoned puppy found by an oil press.'

The weather had turned colder in Greece and Trisha had to go and do her rounds feeding the street cats that sat expectantly on the walls around the island and by the bins. There were about six separate feeding sites to visit in all. Victoria was going to look into the Health Certificate situation and report back to Trisha. Although Thompson were emerging as the favourites, a Greek-owned company might make things easier if they could assist with the paperwork directly with the Ministry Vets, which would make life less stressful for the charities, but time would tell.

19.3.21

Trisha: 'I had a cat emergency. It was Rubin. He had collapsed and couldn't stand up. Nikos was in Piraeus so we had to take him to Ligourio, 40 minutes away. He had a urinary blockage, poor boy. He will be okay. I am taking Athena back to her stamping ground today and will try and catch another two this weekend for sterilizing.'

Rubin

Dave: 'Hope Rubin will be okay. I'm a bit fuzzy after my first AstraZeneca Covid jab. How about a Zoom chat sometime, I've got an account for Family and Friends?'

Trisha: 'I don't have Zoom. My family have asked me to have Zoom chats, but I'm embarrassed to say that the house is all over the place and a mess at the moment, plus I'm surrounded by cats leaping around the place and interrupting any attempts at Zoom, plus my husband will keep popping in and I'd be in my pyjamas. Can we go for a chat on the landline after I've done the next sterilisation? I was also going to ask you that once all this Covid is over and I can get to the UK would it be ok to visit you both?'

Dave: Ha-ha, believe me, we don't mind cats, randomly-appearing husbands or pyjamas ... plus my office is all over the place as well: Sue just lets me get on with it. We can have a chat on the landline or the mobile, whatever. Yes, of course! If you're in the UK and Covid is behind us you'd be most welcome to visit. Might try and meet up with Karen and Andy, too (our Grecophile chums and Cordelia's friends).'

Athena hiding on the kitchen cupboards

Trisha: 'I can't catch Athena, she's still hiding above the kitchen cupboards.'

Dave: 'Try waving an olive branch at her, that should do the trick if she lives up to her namesake.'

Trisha: 'Ha, yeah, I'll try that. Nope, Athena still won't come down from above the kitchen cupboards.😳 Rainbow Rose is still in a bad mood 🙀and 😢Matilda is recovering, but gave us the evil eye when we tried to put water in the cage. The apartment smells of sardines that we are using to try and entice Athena down. I am going back home. They are comfortable for the night.' 🌙

Dave: 'Cats are all captains of their own boats. You are such a patient soul.'

Kristi: 'Ha-ha, I have a Greek husband!'

Dave: 'Ti na kanoume;' (*What can we do?*)

Trisha: 'That's about right. 😂 It's his favourite expression.'

Dave: '... and mine.'

Trisha: 'We could learn a lot from cats. The look of disdain if I give them *Whiskers* instead of *Felix* or *Gourmet* ...'

Dave: 'Ha-ha-ha, yeah. We know that look ... as if to say: "Hmmmm ... and this is?"'

Trisha: 'I asked my husband if I could employ a butler... Err, humm, I mean for the cats.'

Dave: 'Never a truer word than, "Dogs have owners ... cats have staff".'

Trisha: 😂😂 'They do indeed, so funny. Especially mine. I am going to the mainland with special permission next week. Pat is going to feed them and when I gave her instructions I realised how spoilt they are. Oh, I said, Willow eats *Gourmet Gold*, Percy hates *Whiskers*, Molly will only eat there, Tommy likes a second helping on the kitchen worktop, Haliberi eats outside with Teddy bear, Primrose dines late in the granny studio, Monty likes dry food, Hector will only eat *Felix*, Princess has had 4 teeth out so only wet food and has to be *Gourmet* pate. Rosie is 19 and eats Sheba. Vincent Corleone eats anywhere and everything all day, Nefeli steals food from all the plates and Teddy loves *Felix* and is always hungry. Next the litter trays🙈, water bowls and then the outside cats. Poor Pat has asked for a dress rehearsal.' 🤔🙀

Dave: 'Wow, that's quite some list of requirements ... good for Pat! ... actually, it's more like stage notes for the National Opera.' 🎭

Pat with Rainbow Rose and Matilda

25.3.21

Trisha and I had a long chat on the phone today: 25th March, Greek Independence Day. It was fascinating to hear about her life on the island and also her life in Greece for three decades. We discussed all the possible routes to get Teddy and Vincent over to the UK and touched on what we knew so far about the new regulations. Unfortunately, Pat was unwell so Trisha couldn't go to the mainland. Hopefully Pat didn't have Covid, but she was waiting for a test.

By the end of March it was looking likely that Covid tests might be carried out on lorry/transport drivers arriving in the UK, due to the rising cases in France and the increase in variants. If so that may delay the transport company's onward journey to a UK pick-up point. I wondered if it would be a lateral flow test or the longer-winded PCR? More unknowns.

Chapter 7

Mission Impossible

April 2021

As anyone who has ever been around a cat for any length of time well knows cats have enormous patience with the limitations of the human kind:
Cleveland Amory

5.4.21

We continued to explore transport options and Trisha sent me further updates on her cat feeding rounds. GCWS sent the vet a donation for neutering so things were extremely hectic on the island of Poros. Trisha had been in touch with a friend on the mainland in Piraeus who said she might be willing to visit the Ministry Vet there for us to submit the paperwork for Teddy. Greece was increasing its bureaucratic processes in response to Brexit and even those Brits who'd lived there for years were having to obtain new ID cards and driving licences. Whereas in the past things had been a bit more lackadaisical with reliance on a wing and a prayer, this now seemed to be changing.

Dave: 'If your friend was able to help us with the Health Certificate and the Ministry Vet visit I'm sure we could compensate her for her expenses and her time. We'd have to have a booked transport date beforehand, because – as I understand it – the Health Certificate is only valid for 10 days from date of issue, so the timing is crucial. If she is willing to help we'll need a really good plan of action.'

Trisha: 'It's a lot of work for people to rescue the animals, foster them, sort out passports/vaccinations etc, etc. I am not quite sure what Andrea would need for the Ministry Vet. Is it pet passports plus your identity card or passport?'

Dave: 'I've made a note to do some more research tomorrow. I think it's the original Pet Passport (not copies). On my list is trying to find out from Thompson if others have managed to get Health Certificates and how they've gone about it. Maybe they could put me in touch with a successful applicant who would be willing to talk to me and give advice.'

Trisha: 'That would be so helpful 🙂. I am getting very stressed about all this as I don't want our adoptees to pull out because it is taking so long – two have already! It's stopping me from taking any more rescues. I wanted to foster another kitten but I don't have any more room. My husband is so understanding, I don't think many husbands would like 5 cats in the tv room, 4 in the bedroom, 4 in the rock room, 8 on the veranda, 2 in the bathroom window area, cat houses and beds everywhere, cat toys he keeps falling over and 5 litter trays 🙀😬. I said we should move out and leave the house to the cats, but he likes the views 😀.'

Dave: 'I completely understand, he's a very tolerant chap, but there is a limit. I wonder if you have to get Health Certificates for air travel? Maybe not if you're sending less than 5 at a time. I think I read somewhere that Aegean suggested they were required, but I'll have to double check. The problem also seems to be the lack of distinction between charity and commercial, let alone adoption versus ownership.'

Trisha: 'I've heard that they can go as the traveller's own cats and Michael could take up to 5. When we did the Paris run with Michael we had 2 of my kitten rescues and Ella. Michael was asked to take Ella out of the cage and we'd only just picked her up so we had no idea what she was like. Michael gave me this "Oh, Lord look" and went into a private room with Ella. Luckily Ella was amenable 😺and all ok, but 5 of them 😬? Ella now lives in Scotland.'

Dave: 'Yikes, you never know how a cat might react under unfamiliar circumstances at the best of times. Aha! Actual ownership - interesting. I guess that would have to be reflected in the Pet Passport and possibly the microchip registration as proof of destination.'

We had some information/feedback about the livestock transport company. It sounded like one of the cats or dogs had escaped en-route and they'd apparently done nothing about trying to recover it. Another story was circulating about a similar situation of transport without official documentation a while ago, with several dogs impounded somewhere on the Adriatic coast of Italy as a result. Their owner had to fight for two years and spent thousands of pounds trying to get them back: there were some other animals on that trip, but they were never seen again.

Dave: 'Looks like our concerns have been more than validated.'

Trisha: 'Indeed! I asked a while back if someone else could do Traces for me, but the Ministry said it had to be me, Lynda has let me know that it is possible now to have a representative. I'm waiting to hear back from Andrea or maybe someone I know in Athens. At least we know there's a way round it and if Lynda can do the trip I would be so happy, because I'll know the kids will be safe with her. Just the thought of Teddy or any of my wards escaping fills me with horror 🙀.'

Dave: 'Likewise! Let me know as soon as you hear if Andrea is willing to help with the Ministry Vet visit. Once we know that piece of the puzzle we need to establish a travel date with Thompson so we know when to make the appointment and be inside the 10 day validity window (did I mention that it's only five days for dogs? Something to do with worming treatment just before they leave.) Looks like it's all in the timing. I'm still trying to find out if there's a list of Ministry Vets anywhere.'

7.4.21

Trisha: 'Here's Teddy with Asprooli and Nefeli.'

Dave: 'He looks very content – hope he won't get lonely on his own. Sue likes his green collar.'

Trisha: 'He will be fine. Nefeli will eventually go to Rachael in Herefordshire. Yes, she's right, green goes with ginger. I will send it with him. He still has his bling collar but I was saving it for best.' 😸

Lynda posted a Facebook update on the latest Thompson Pet Travel journey as they made their way through Italy. It was lovely to see the dogs and cats on their way to the UK and it filled me with hope and confidence. I posted a comment:

Dave: 'You are really remarkable, your determination and care is humbling! I'm in touch with Rachel ironing out some details and then hope to be able to arrange the Health Certificate for Teddy to make the journey with you in due course. It's been a rollercoaster of emotions these recent months, but it feels like – with your amazing help – we could actually do it. Xxx'

Lynda: 'I do hope so Dave, we'd love to have Teddy aboard the Freedom Bus! X'

Dave: 'Thank you so much, Lynda, the hope of actually getting him here with us in Brighton means a great deal. Would anyone who has been successful with a cat be able to let me know their experience with obtaining the Health Certificate, too, I wonder?'

Shortly after that there was another comment on the post.

Helen Evans: 'Hi, Dave, if Teddy is coming over on the next vehicle please let us know at Skypets International as we arrange all the customs formalities for entering the UK for the team at Thompson x'.

Dave: 'Thanks so much, Helen - I'll be in touch shortly' 👍😻😘

8.4.21

I received a reply from Rachel at Thompson about my concerns and queries. In my 30 years as a healthcare professional, dealing with both specific and general bureaucracy, I'd never had such a helpful and comprehensive reply to a complex topic like this: it was nothing short of spectacular. She went through the Health Certificate, step-by-step, guiding me through all the stuff I'd never encountered before. There was apparently no list of Ministry Vets, so they remained "Mystery Vets" at this stage, but I was determined to track down the Vet responsible for the Poros region. She also sent me a "nomou 105" form, which was an official Greek authorisation form for appointing someone to represent you.

I had thought that the customs agent would handle the UK IPAFFS notification, but it seemed they didn't. However, Rachel sent me further guidance on how to do that as well. She flagged that I might need an EORI (an *Economic Operators Registration and Identification number*), but the customs agent would advise me.

She also asked if I had "Adoption Papers" for Teddy? That was the first I'd heard of those, so further research would be required.

We had set a date for Teddy to board the Freedom Bus. It would be 11th May.

So, now I had all the information on what was required and a date to aim for. It seemed extraordinary that all of this would be necessary to bring one little ginger pussycat to our home in the UK, but at least I had more to work with, thanks to Rachel.

Within the hour I had contacted Helen at Skypets International with Teddy's departure date and had an email from the UK government gateway/DEFRA confirming that they had registered me, so I could proceed with the import notification.

I contacted Trisha.

Dave: 'Hi Trisha, things are coming together! I've heard back from Rachel and she's been a star. Once I've ironed out the paperwork I'll let you know the window of opportunity for the Ministry Vet visit.

Can you get the address of the Ministry Vet from Nikos? There's no online list of MVs.'

Trisha: 'I was so stressed. Last night I woke at 4.00am feeling sick and worried. I dreamt I could not find Vincent and I wanted to buy my friend's new skirt. How bonkers is that?'

Dave: 'I totally understand. I'm 99% confident we can sort out the cat transport and I will produce a comprehensive step-by-step guide along with contact details. I'm just about to have a crack at doing the IPAFFS bit, writing guidance as I go along.'

(The IPAFFS – *Import of products, animals, food and feed system* – details are in the appendix so I'll spare you that here, but once I'd got all the information it really wasn't too difficult.)

9.4.21

Lynda made it back to the UK with her "Freedom Bus" full of dogs and a couple of cats. Delays at Calais meant she had to get another Covid test or risk it being out of date on arrival, plus missing their slot on the train, so had to go by Ferry to Dover, but they did it! Really encouraging news.

10.4.21
Trisha: 'Hello, Dave, it was full on again today. Nikos does not know the address of the government vet, sorry 🤔. I got home really late as we were taking the recovered cats back and catching more. I was told off by one man as he did not want me to sterilize the female, but he has about 12 cats and none of them look great. I took one of the last batch of kittens home. Can't believe some of these people. 🤷'

Dave: 'Okay, looks like I'll have to contact the Greek government. I'm waiting for confirmation of the travel date for Teddy of 11th May. I've just found out that we'll need some Adoption Papers for Teddy and they might come from the local Municipality. On the plus side, Rachel also sent me a special Declaration of Responsibility form for Andrea to represent us; I translated it so I could figure out how to fill it in. Once/if Andrea confirms I'll fill in her name. I've done the IPAFFS and have a *UNN* notification number which the Ministry Vet has to have for the Health Certificate. I'm making loads of notes as a guide to the process. Hey! I'm an official UK importer now. Anyone want a dog, cat or ferret?'

Trisha: 'Last time I tried to get Adoption Papers the guy at the town hall had no idea what I was talking about. Are you sure we need them?'

Dave: 'Yep, looks like it. It's one of the pieces of the puzzle that I'm waiting to hear back about from Rachel. I'm guessing that there was a different system/Ministry Vet for Traces ... plus the new regulations show that it has to be the Ministry Vet responsible for the specific Municipality in which the animal resides.'

Trisha: 'I have just been trying to find Ministry Vets on the Greek government websites, but no luck so far. No wonder this country is in such a muddle, everything is so complicated. They have now declared that in order for expats to stay here we need to give our thumb print in an office outside Athens, not everyone can do that!'🙄🥴

Dave: 'An elderly friend of mine in Paros (married to a renowned Greek surgeon) is having a struggle with her ID card: long story, but it's affecting her being able to get her Covid jab.

Hmm, so, there's no online list of Ministry Vets in Greece ... that's a pain.'

Trisha: 'One of my rescue friends is so stressed about it, I think it's making her ill. To top it she and her husband have been asked to leave their apartment of 17 years due to her work with cats. They made her give away her old cat that she had had for over 10 years. So mean. Robert is looking after the cat.'

Dave: 'It seems such a bizarre volte face from previous Greek attitudes to people. I feel so sorry for her.'

Trisha: A lot of this new attitude is due to Airbnb. They think they can make a summer killing and charge 100 euros per night in August instead of 400 per month, so people are being turfed out of their homes.'

Dave: 'Hey ho. I'll try and deal with as much of the paperwork as I can from this end and just get you to do a few key things that I can't do from here. The next thing is to confirm that Andrea will help, otherwise it might mean a trip to Piraeus and I know that is super-difficult for you. I could try my friend in Athens, but I'm not sure how comfortable she'd feel about travelling to Piraeus as she's very careful about Covid and public transport, plus issues trying to get the vaccination.'

Trisha: 'Thank you so much, all paperwork stuff does my head in. It's like an exam paper. Oh Lord, I know the answer to the first question on the exam paper 🤔 ... name ... 🤪.'

Dave: 'Ha, most people feel the same about paperwork. My aim is to produce sufficient guidance that it will enable you and adoptees to deal with the process smoothly and have a list of everything you need to take to the Ministry Vet and to give to Thompson. Anyway, go get some sleep my friend ... sounds like it's been a long day.'

Trisha: 'I have more cat-catching tomorrow. Night-night 🌙.'

11.4.21

I had a brainwave in trying to track down the "Mystery Vets" and to try to find out some more about what was required with the "Adoption Papers". Sue and I are friends with a wonderful lady called Kate Daisy Grant who is a fabulous singer-songwriter and is married to an old friend of ours called Nick Pynn, who is an extraordinarily-talented multi-instrumentalist. I had a sudden bout of joined-up-thinking in that they adopted a lovely Greek rescue dog called Lemon in 2020, so I wondered how they went about it. Turns out a chap called Andrew found Lemon in a dog shelter in Amfissa, Central Greece, and he is involved in fundraising for Greek Animal Rescue. Kate very kindly set up a Messenger group and copied me in, so I sent a message out.

Dave: 'Thanks, Kate xx. Hi Andrew, just wondered if you might have some info? No problem if not. I'm trying to adopt a rescue cat and things have become very complicated, as I've no doubt you're aware.'

In next to no time Andrew had hooked me up with Diane and Nena from GAR. I explained that (at that stage) I was trying to compile guidance for others who were all at sea with the new regulations and that I had managed to get quite a bit done for my own adopted cat.

Dave: 'The two stumbling blocks at the moment are:

1/ Actually finding out who the Ministry Vet is for the Municipality of Poros (men/women of "Mystery" rather than Ministry): even the Vet for Poros doesn't know who the MV for Poros is. I'm on the verge of phoning the head of all Greeks vets in Athens: yep, I've actually got her phone number and email.

2/ Getting hold of a template/PDF of these "Adoption Papers" so we're in with a fighting chance of getting them signed/stamped by the Municipality of Poros (last time the rescue lady asked them about a year ago they said they didn't know what she was talking about). Any help you might be able to offer with those two things would be fabulous. Thanks again for taking the time to get back to me, Best wishes Dave Burnham.'

Diane kindly offered to help me with the IPAFFS and Nena looked into the other issues. It sounded like they had myriad Messenger groups on the go, trying to help people with the nightmare of the new paperwork. I was bowled over by their phenomenal kindness and willingness to help me, especially as they must have been overwhelmed.

Nena sent me details and advice on completion of the Health Certificate – actually written by a Ministry Vet – as well the whereabouts of the Ministry Vet who covered Poros. She then sent me a redacted copy of how the key pages of the Health Certificate should look once the Ministry Vet had stamped and signed them and had entered the all-important reference number.

Running my eyes over the paperwork I spotted a familiar vehicle registration number from my own IPAFFS in the transport section – it was Thompson Pet Travel. The very people we were hoping would take Teddy to the UK and who I had earlier referred to in our conversation as the "really good pet transport company that the rescuer (Trisha) has used in the past" ... small world! 😂

I let Trisha know that I had some lovely people from Greek Animal Rescue helping me and that it looked like they also worked with Thompson Pet Travel.

Dave: 'Take a look at this. My Greek isn't quite up to the task but I think Nena's sent me a screenshot of the Ministry Vet's details in Piraeus?'

Trisha: 'Yes, I think I know more or less where it is.'

Dave: 'Okidoki, if we have a name, a location and a telephone number to make an appointment then we're winning. I'll keep you up to speed 😉. I'll check the translation with a couple of friends and then run some internet searches.'

Trisha: ' You must be going nuts trying to sort this out, but what foxes me and Andy (of Spartan cats) is that people are managing to get these certificate things. I think my brain is frying, I'm a bit tired tonight ..."

Dave: 'Trust me, the mists are clearing and I'm getting a much better idea of how to deal with it. Take it easy, chill and have a good night's sleep. As yet no one has completed a Health Certificate 100% correctly, my aim is for us to be the first 😉.'

Trisha sent me some more photos and updates of her activities before she went to bed.

Trisha: 'This is Fouli. She is 82 and her husband is 90. She has to use a stick because she has had an operation on her knee. She feeds the street cats every day. She came with me and Robert today to collect cats for sterilising. We collected 5 and she is going to take them home for recovery.

At home she has over 50 cats. Her husband Panayiotis drives her round to feed the cats and has made a little hut for injured or sick kitties. She is looking after a blind kitty as well as her siblings.'

Trisha: 'I have been trying to catch Matilda for over a year now and finally managed it with an ordinary snap trap and sardines. I already have one of her kittens at home.'

Trisha: 'This is a new boy on the block. He lives on a wall.'

Trisha: 'This is Robert transferring from a dropper cage to green carry off, also assisted by Fouli.'

(A drop trap is an essential tool for the TNR trapper. Compared to a normal box trap, cats are not as wary of going in and so don't need to be as hungry. It can be used for selectively trapping a particular cat.)

News came in that Kyriakos Mitsotakis had become the first Greek Prime Minister to publicly visit a shelter for homeless and abandoned animals. It was World Stray Animals Day so he went to Iliopouli (a suburban municipality in South East Athens) to show his support.

He said: 'Given the World Stray Day, I wanted to be with you, to thank you for the great work you are doing and to discuss, of course, the new bill for pets, which we will put to public consultation within the next ten days. We will wait with a great interest for your comments, and I believe that it can be voted by the end of May.'

It was interesting that he chose a shelter run by volunteers who were given the chance to air their grievances and concerns, rather than the easier route of a well-funded, government-approved animal hospital. The photograph of him with a stray dog called Peanut was widely distributed and it sounded like he planned to adopt him. Clearly it was underlining the new bill, but it also sent the right message and looked to be yet another positive step in raising awareness about animal welfare.

12.4.21

I sent a message to another friend, Mark, (who I knew through mutual admiration of the legendary singer-songwriter, Roy Harper), attaching the screenshot of the Ministry Vet's whereabouts. Mark's wife, Kat, is Greek so I thought she might be able to help with translation.

Mark: 'Kat will be home in a bit. What do you think it says, by the way?'

Dave: 'Something about the Islands and possibly agriculture, hopefully along with the address of the elusive Ministry Vet's office.'

A short while later Mark let me know it was indeed the address I was hoping for, so another piece of the puzzle fell into place.

Teddy's place on the Freedom Bus was confirmed for 11th May so I paid the deposit. Rachel came back to me about some of the other on-going queries. It seemed that an agreement of some sort needed to be drawn up in the form of Adoption Papers. Rachel knew both Diane and Nena so hoped that they might be able to help me with that. The Health Certificate was asking for "Approval Numbers" for the person sending Teddy and for the person receiving him. Rachel thought it might only apply to animal products, but would try to look into it.

I had been working my way through the Health Certificate form, filling in bits that I already knew the answers to and compiling a list of the sections that still needed some information gathering. I was also working on a range of dates to check to see if Trisha's friend would be free, so I could get Trisha to contact the Ministry Vet and book an appointment. I figured the sooner we tried then the better the chance of getting a day/time that worked to keep within the Health Certificate's 10 day validity for arrival in the UK.

We would need to ask Nikos to sign and stamp the actual Health Certificate (as it would relate the content of the Pet Passport to the Health Certificate). My plan was to pre-fill it so the Ministry Vet would only need to sign and stamp it, complete the bottom section and issue the reference number that would finalise the IPAFFS notification. If I made it sound easy to myself then I might start believing it …

I updated Trisha on a busy day's progress via email and contacted her by WhatsApp in the evening.

Dave: 'Hi there. It snowed this morning!!! ❄'

Trisha: 'Hello, Dave, I have just got home. I read your message twice. I don't understand where the health certificate is found to be filled in. 🤔 I have to sleep now. My husband has his 2nd Covid vaccination at 8.00 tomorrow morning and wants me to go with him … in case he grows a second head after🙀🤕. I will contact Andrea tomorrow. Night 🌙'

Dave: 'Don't worry. I'll explain everything as we go along. I've already got the Health Certificate and am well on the way to filling it in. Once I've done that I'll send it to you so you can print it out for Nikos to stamp and sign. Then it can go to Andrea who will take it to the Ministry Vet. They will stamp and sign it and issue a reference number, then it will come back to you and go with all the other documents when Teddy sets off. Really, don't worry, I'm taking care of all the details and will advise as we go along 😉. Good luck to your husband tomorrow, send him my best wishes ... he will be fine.'

Trisha: 'Thank you, Dave.'😺

13.4.21

Dave: 'Hi, Trisha. As far as I can work out it looks like we might need to register Teddy's transponder microchip to me as his 'owner' on the Greek system. Hopefully it's something Nikos can help us with. Once that's done it might then be possible to get the Adoption Papers from the Municipality. Hope today went okay with your husband's 2nd jab.'

Trisha: 'Yes, he was ok, a bit sleepy. Are the Adoption papers a necessity? Because last time no one had any idea what I meant. 🙈'

Dave: 'Glad he's ok. Yeah, looks like the Adoption Papers are needed. I'm waiting for further clarification from Rachel at Thompson and/or help from Nena at GAR.

I spoke with their Customs Agent today and got that bit set up – they didn't know about the Adoption Papers (or something called "Approval Numbers" on the Health Certificate) and suggested I phoned the government DEFRA helpline, which I did. I eventually got through to a charming lady, who was very happy to talk to someone who wasn't biting her head off about new regulations that aren't her fault, for a change ... but she didn't have an answer to Adoption Papers or approval numbers either.

I tried GCWS but they say they're not involved in the actual adoption process so suggested I try Greek Animal Rescue ... who I'm already in touch with and I have just sent another message to them.

I will eventually get to the bottom of it, but the clock is now ticking towards the 11th May departure date and I've paid a deposit to reserve Teddy's place on the bus.'

Trisha: 'I have contacted Andrea. Without you doing all the leg work it would be impossible. In fact I was going to say fly out, have a break, stay in our holiday apt. Take Teddy and a couple of others back with you on the plane. ✈️ Anyway if all goes well I will know for Vincent who will go next along with Aries and Nefeli.😺🌼

Ha, now you can see why Greece is such a nightmare to do anything official; my husband said he has to confirm he has had his 2nd vaccination. So, I said ok, where? Well, they said the guys in the office know. What office, what guys? So I ring the doc in charge. Oh yes, she says, do it on the internet. What address I say? It's there on the internet, she says. Apparently I have to find out now from the Naval school where my husband was an officer years ago 🤔 ... wish me luck.'

Dave: 'Ha, yeah, I always knew from other people's stories it was a pain. The Egyptians invented bureaucracy, but the Greeks turned it into something second only to Greek Orthodoxy ... mind you, you would've loved the paperwork associated with dentistry. I received 3 documents when I bought my practice in 1987 ... I had to provide 400 when I sold it in 2017!'

'Meanwhile, Neo the white cat, is giving me headbutts on the allotment.'😻

14.4.21
Trisha: 'Andrea is up for the government vet stuff, but I'm not sure about Adoption Papers.'

Dave: 'That's great news about Andrea. I think there's a way of sorting out our own Adoption Papers. I've been chatting to Rachel and Diane on Messenger while standing in the queue for my barber in Brighton: they're actually in the same room together in Athens and just realised they were talking about the same cat, Teddy! Can you believe the coincidence? I'll let you know the outcome a bit later.'

Diane explained to me the ins and outs of the adoption paperwork. If we could figure out how to affect a private adoption, so Teddy was transferred to me on an acceptable piece of paperwork, we'd have it well on the way to being tied up. However, it was beginning to sound like different Ministry Vets from different regions had different approaches to the logistics. In my research I'd come across something in Greek law (LAW NUMBER. 4039/2012 Article 5 Part 1...oh yeah, I was now getting full-on nerdy with this nonsense) which suggested that, technically, a kitten should be registered to its owner within a couple of months of birth. Rather like the plans for the Hyperspace Bypass through Earth in Douglas Adams' *Hitchhiker's Guide to the Galaxy*, it sounded like this wasn't common knowledge in Greece to anyone except the lawmakers. We also touched on having to get a 'Declaration of Responsibility' for Trisha's representative at the Ministry Vet appointment – as she couldn't leave Poros herself.

A couple of hours later I'd had my locks lopped and messaged Trisha.

Dave: 'Okay, my head feels a bit lighter now. You could barely see the floor there were so many post-lockdown haircuts going on!'

Trihsa: 'Ha-ha, sounds like your barber had his work cut out!'

Dave: 'He shears sheep in his spare time 😂. Anyway, I need to look into registering Teddy's chip and so on with the Greek database and then I've got a template for Adoption Papers from Diane that I can use as the basis for officially adopting Teddy from you. I'm going to ask Rachel (at Thompson) what's the latest we could cancel the booking for Teddy's trip without losing the deposit for a potential future booking. This is in case we can't get the Adoption Papers in time. (The Customs Agent and new VAT rules means I will have to pay them, too, so I've got to watch the budget).'

Later that evening I sent a message to my Greek allotment friend, Eva.

Dave: 'Yassou, Eva. Random question, but do you know how someone would register their cat in Greece? Wondering if there was somewhere on line (in Greece) that you could register the kitten in your name. Hope all's ok with you, Dave x.'

Eva: 'I will forward your question to a friend who lives in Greece because I have been away for the last 12 years and I am not sure what the answer is lol.'

Dave: 'Ha, thafmasia, Efcharisto Poli. 😺😘'

Eva: 'Are you adopting a Greek cat, then?'

(I sent her a photo.)

Eva: 'Aw, he's a lucky beauty.'

Dave: 'Isn't he just. I am learning a great deal about Greek bureaucracy...and UK! Ti na kanoume; 😁. Ya.' (*What can we do?* 😁 *Bye.*)

15.4.21

Just as I was chatting to Nena on Messenger, Nikos let me know that Teddy could be registered by his assistant, Litsa, in my name. I asked Trisha for Litsa's email address and started to put together a large list of all the information she was likely to require to undertake Teddy's registration (the Greek authorities like to have your father and mother's names, your place of birth, passport number, inside leg measurement ...). The next stage would be to contact the Ministry Vet and find out what they needed.

Trisha: 'Photos of Teddy. He really is Mr Super-Purrer. He won't keep still this morning.'

Dave: 'He's such a fabulous colour, too. Ants in his pants in prospect of a journey on the bus. 😉'

Trisha: 'Ha-ha. I am proud of the gingers in my care. They look super and I am especially proud of Teddy because he was in such a state.'

Dave: 'He, and they, are a testament to your skills xx.'

Trisha: 'Awww, thank you, and you have been amazing helping me through all this. I struggle with paperwork and documents and legal stuff.'

Dave: 'We'll get there ... and hopefully for the other adoption kitties. There will be bursts of information coming your way, but I'll try to keep each stage concise and clear. It very much sounds like there is no such thing as official Adoption Papers from the Municipality🙃🤪, hence them being confused when you asked them way back when. We'll write our own.

I'll send you the phone number and email address for the Ministry Vet, plus a list of what we need to know, including what their fee is?'

Trisha: 'I've just heard from Andrea. She's free on 6th May and would like the first appointment in the morning. She can collect the documents I send her from the ferry before then and hopefully get them back to us on the Flying Dolphin after the appointment.'

Dave: 'Fabulous! Please pass my thanks on to Andrea and we need to pay her for her time and trouble.'

16.4.21 (Friday)

Trisha: 'Kalimera.. No one is picking up at the government vet office.🙄 I will try later. As soon as I have all the info I will send it to Andrea so she has it ready.'

Dave: 'Let me know if you still can't reach them by this afternoon. There could be a reason, such as there being another number or limited opening hours due to Covid (although you'd think it would divert) or maybe they're round the corner drinking coffee.'

By the afternoon there was still no reply. I'd managed to obtain the phone number for the head of all vets in Greece so I suggested Trisha tried phoning her to see what the problem was in reaching our Ministry Vet.

Trisha: 'Okay, I'll give that a go. I need to feed my cats now, 😺Rubin's on urinary dry food, Rosie has old lady *Gourmet*, Monty gets sardines with an antibiotic hidden inside and Halliberi eats *Felix* with a hidden antibiotic.'

Dave: 'Have you heard the saying: *People that hate cats will come back as mice in their next life*?'

Trisha: 'That could apply to a few people on this island. My cats will enjoy chasing them.'

Dave: 'Ha, cosmic feline schadenfreude.'

17.4.21

I had completed the Health Certificate by now, so I emailed it to Trisha so she could print it and have it ready for Nikos to sign once we had a date for the Ministry Vet. I asked her if Nikos liked ouzo or something else we could give him to say thank you. Meanwhile, Dorian visited me on the allotment again so I sent her a photo of him on the greenhouse roof.

Trisha: 'What a lovely photo of Dorian, looks like a painting. I know Nikos likes wine.'

Dave: 'Sounds like a plan.'

18.4.21

The Greek Prime Minister Kyriakos Mitsotakis announced on his Instagram account that he had adopted a stray dog called Peanut and commented, "Open your arms and save a stray. The truth is that I did not choose him, he chose us." He was already settling in to the Maximos Palace (Mitsotakis' official residence). He followed in the footsteps of the President of Greece, Katerina Sakellaropoulou, adopting a rescued kitten named Calypso from the non-profit organization Animal Welfare Karpathos in November 2020. There was an element of suspicion from some that it was a publicity stunt coinciding with the new bill on animal welfare, but with the significant increase in strays following the Greek financial crisis anything that could highlight the issue had to be a good thing.

19.4.21 (MONDAY)

Trisha: 'Still no answer from the Ministry Vet or the head of the vets. People have told me it can be difficult to get hold of them, but others must be managing. Shall I ask Andrea if she might pop in to see them?'

Dave: 'Yikes! Yeah, if Andrea's willing to swing by that could certainly be an option. I think I've worked out where the offices actually are now, so I'll send an address and a map. We need to get an appointment so I can confirm Teddy's place on the bus with Rachel and Friday looks like the deadline for that. I think the others who are sending animals with Thompson use different Ministry Vets, because there are quite a few of them covering different regions in Greece. Umm ... it's not Pascha – *Easter* – coming up is it?'

Trisha: 'No, Easter is 2nd May. Andrea suspects they may be closed because of Covid.'

Dave: 'Ah, now it makes sense. Ha, by the way, I sent all that information to Litsa for Teddy's registration, but I forgot my own date of birth! Anyway, she has that now.'

Later that day Trisha managed to speak to the head of vets who was able to confirm that the Piraeus office was currently closed on Mondays and Fridays due to Covid restrictions. At least we knew there was a fighting chance of getting hold of the Ministry Vet tomorrow ...

Chapter 8

Saint Gertrude the ~~Apostle~~ Apostille (Patron Saint of Cats)

April 2021

It is a truth universally acknowledged that a man in possession of a warm house and a well-stocked fridge must be in want of a cat:
Heather Hacking

20.4.21

Today was a good day.

I received an email from Litsa attaching Teddy's official Greek database microchip registration certificate with a note of congratulations from her.

Dave: 'Efcharisto para poli, Litsa. You have made a little ginger cat and his new owner very happy.'

Litsa: 'Greece is making our life difficult with the papers, but I think that everything will be alright and soon Teddy will be yours! He is already yours!'

Dave: 'Hi Trisha, Litsa has just sent me Teddy's Greek registration certificate, bless her.'

Trisha: 'Kalimera. Great! I managed to get through to the Ministry Vet. She is trying to find out what information I need to send to the office.'

Dave: 'Ooh, well done for getting hold of her! Did you manage to get an appointment?'

Trisha: ‘She told me I could not send Teddy on his own to the UK ... pause for thought on that one⁉. Here you are Teddy here is your suitcase and *Felix* sandwiches, off you go.🎒🧢✈️😻’

Dave: ‘Oh dear. The Health Certificate has the transporter’s details on it and they will have a full bus so it should be obvious. Maybe it’s just a tick-box standard statement?’

Trisha: ‘Maybe. I spoke to her again and she is sending me an email with all the information they require. I’ll send it to you later. She said maybe it can all be done by email.’

Dave: ‘What? Really? Flippin’ ‘eck, that would make our lives easier! I’m off to the allotment for an hour or two to de-stress.’

Trisha: ‘Don’t blame you. I Nearly fell off my chair.’😝

Dave: ‘If they can do that we’ve got to make sure the Health Certificate gets dated 6th May so it doesn’t become invalid on entry into the UK – also got to watch out for Easter.’

Trisha: ‘🐣🐥We are still in lockdown over Easter. Thank goodness, can’t stand all the noise. Of course, no one will work. Oh, she said something about needing an *Apostillee*.’

Dave: ‘A whatee?’

Trisha: ‘I don’t know. I think she said something about a certificate from the Hague.’

Dave: ‘No idea! Hopefully it will become clear in her email.’

I now had some example Adoption Papers to work with from GAR so I wrote some private Adoption Papers for Teddy. They also asked if the Health Certificate had to be filled in electronically as, presumably, that could make it possible to do by email. Mind you, it could also make it more complicated. Time would tell.

Later that day

Trisha: ‘Litsa helped me with catching cats today. We rescued Flora (who is so thin and can’t eat because she doesn’t have any teeth) and Poppy, the village resort cat who is old now. We’ve got them all in the apartment and Pat is checking them over. It’s been a busy day so I will read the Ministry Vet’s email and send it later or in the morning.’

Dave: ‘Thank you and well done. It’s lovely to put a face to the amazingly helpful Litsa. Just the sort of person you need on your team. Is Litsa Nikos’ nurse, assistant, veterinarian co-pilot?’

Litsa

Trisha: 'Litsa is full of energy and is super helpful. I think Litsa is all of those. Nikos has been training her in vet work. She has reorganised his clinic – repainted it – sorts out his timetable and assists him with operations and does the bookings.😁'

Dave: 'Wow, a Renaissance Woman!'

21.4.21

I woke up about 6am wondering what would be in the replies from the Ministry Vet, so I got up and turned on the computer. I ran the email through Google Translate and her advice matched everything I'd done to date, so things looked good. There was no mention of the hitherto unheard of certificate from the Hague.

Dave: 'She hasn't said anything about the Apostille and everything in the email is addressed by our documents so, I'm composing a reply ... it could take a while.'

Trisha: 'Greek offices are notorious for paperwork and I think they employ clones 😳, maybe you should have a cup of tea or coffee first.'

Dave: 'I might try and get some sleep later, but the clock is ticking for Teddy's place on the bus. Um, did you say there were two emails from the Ministry Vet? I've just got one.'

Trisha: 'Yes, you should have a rest later. I am just going to get up to face the feeding of the 5000.😹 Er, oh, yes. I'll send you the other one now.'

When I translated the second email from the Ministry Vet things started to get more complicated. She wanted a certificate of approval of transport, but as far as I knew that had been entered on the Health Certificate as part of the IPAFFS submission. Then there was something about an approval code for the transport and a list of the towns they would pass through on the journey plus the hours. Again, IPAFFS just requested the countries and it was all listed as part of that. Maybe this was more to do with commercial transport of livestock?

Then came the killer:

Ministry Vet: 'This is to be signed by the owner of the animal and signed and validated with the stamp of the Hague (Definitely) it is like original signatures enclosed.'

There was this Apostille thing again ... and what is to be signed? The Health Certificate? The transport approval? The journey plan? I had a sinking feeling that a whole new can of worms had just been opened.

There followed a succession of messages between Trisha and I for further information and clarification.

I responded to the Ministry Vet's requests to the best of my ability. Following some frantic online research I suggested that as the Health Certificate and IPAFFS were not published as public documents, then an Apostille might not be required. I sent all the documents I had prepared, requested an appointment for 6th May and asked what the fee was. She said she would show my email to the head of department, but by then it was getting close to 2pm in Greece and their office would be closing for the day.

Meanwhile, Lynda posted an update on their current trip. They were in warm and sunny Italy having had a thorough examination of all the paperwork at Brindisi. The Italian police and customs officers sounded like a nice bunch, laughing, joking and when the animal inspection took place, others left what they were doing to come and see them, with lots of oohs and ahhs. They wanted to see the Health Certificates, but their expressions suggested they didn't really know what they were looking at.

22.4.21

The Ministry Vet emailed me again requesting the Owners Page of the Pet Passport and various proofs of identity. The Apostille was needed on the Adoption Papers, "... according to Greek National Law as confirmed by the Directorate". There was no way I could to get an Apostille from the UK government and send a copy to Greece in time for the appointment on 6th May to get the Health Certificate stamped and signed.

Nena suggested I should call the Greek Embassy and ask them to certify my signature from a copy of my passport and get them to send that direct to the Ministry Vet, along with verification of the declaration of the authority for the person representing me. They should, theoretically, accept a document from any official body that could certify or validate my signature and it might not need to be an Apostille. If I lived in Greece a local police station could do this. Nena also offered to write the wording for the nomou 105 Declaration of Authority in Greek for me – so incredibly kind. I relayed that information to the Ministry Vet and sent the other documents she had requested.

Ministry Vet: 'A strike has been scheduled for 6th May so it would be more appropriate to make an appointment for the 5th or 7th.'

'You're joking?', I thought to myself, before checking it out online. Sure enough there was a transport workers strike announced for the 6th May. It looked like the ADEDY – the Civil Servants Confederation – had also declared a 24-hour strike to mark Labour Day.

I had understood that their offices were closed on Mondays and Fridays but the Ministry Vet assured me that they would be there and someone had been assigned to issue the Health Certificate.

I phoned the Greek Embassy in London, which had just opened for that day's business. They gave me an email address to send my request to, asking that I included the contact details of the Ministry Vet as the verification's destination in case it could be emailed directly.

Back came a reply:

Greek Embassy: 'Dear Sir, Following the communication with the competent Veterinarian Authority in Piraeus Greece, it turns out that you were never requested to seek the verification of your ID by our Embassy, which is not done by mail either way. You were only asked to **affix the Apostille stamp, issued by the British Authorities, on the agreement of adoption of your cat**. This is a standard procedure for the verification and legalization of all original documents issued by the Authorities of the UK, as a member state of the Hague Convention.
Hence, this Embassy may not accommodate your request.'

There seemed little point in arguing that the *original documents* were written by me and I was not an *Authority of the UK*. Nena emailed the Greek Embassy on my behalf, as well, but to no avail.

Teddy was happily curled up asleep on Trisha's office computer chair, blissfully unaware of the administrative chaos flying back and forth between Greece and the UK.

Dave: 'Hi Trisha. The Ministry Vet that we have to use is insisting on an Apostille for the actual Adoption Papers I'm losing the plot. I am really tired, have a headache and don't feel too good.'

Trisha: 'I'm not surprised 😟what a performance. Have a lie down and a break.'

Dave: 'Once we have Andrea's details I will send them to Nena so she can write another document in Greek to accompany the Declaration of Responsibility. If we can't get this finally in place then, sadly, it looks like we won't be able to get Teddy.'

Trisha: 'Do you mean never get Teddy or just delayed? It is nuts all this work for one little kitten to go to the UK.'

Dave: 'I've just arrived at the allotment to reset my head a bit. If the Ministry Vet won't play ball with Nena's help then there will be little that we can do at this point.'

Later that day.

Trisha: 'I really don't understand. Why they are making it so difficult?'

Dave: 'It's a direct consequence of Brexit and they're now following the resulting rules that apply to Greece. I get the feeling that a lot of it is the luck of the draw on which Ministry Vet your area comes under and what the local Municipality are like from the point of how they apply the rules and associated bureaucracy. Sue's worried about the effect of the stress on my health, but I really want to see it through.'

Trisha: 'I don't blame her, you are doing all the work and I am so worried, too. I am sorting out sterilizing this weekend and can't think straight. I will ring the Ministry Vet's office again tomorrow. It's crazy … I wonder if that is the office we absolutely have to use?'

Dave: 'Don't worry to phone the Ministry Vet. Leave it to Nena now, she understands these difficult situations far better than we do. I have provided everything, but this Apostille thing is a pain and it's not entirely clear which document(s) it really applies to, because it might also be the 'Declaration of Responsibity' as well. Poros comes under that office so there's nothing we can do. Let me know if Andrea can do either of those other dates. It feels like Greek bureaucracy has tied itself up in knots and strangled the life out of reason.'

23.4.21

I approached a Public Notary in Brighton to see if they could help with an Apostille, but it might still take a while and may not be back in time for the Ministry Vet appointment we had booked, plus I wouldn't get much change from £200. So, I did some more research that suggested this was something I could do myself for about £40, but there were likely to be some delays due to Covid-related staffing issues.

Dave: 'Andrea has been in touch with her ID so I've passed that info on to Nena. People are really fighting our corner.'

Trisha: 'Andrea is very reliable. I busied myself cleaning till 4.00 am this morning, but I suddenly felt more positive. Bit tired now though.'

Dave: 'Sue calls the last couple of months "a rollercoaster of emotions".'

Trisha: 'Indeed. I certainly wouldn't be able to do all you have done. I may eventually move back to the UK, but how I will bring my cats I have no idea. Apparently in Aegina the animal welfare have a van and volunteers drive to the UK and back with 5 cats. The animal couriers should lobby the government for their stupid rules. Point out the millions of cats that are poisoned or killed.'

Dave: 'It's highly complicated, but it could be that we don't need the Adoption Papers after all … I don't know yet … the complexities of Greek law. I am now entered in the Pet Passport as Teddy's owner, plus being his registered owner on the Greek database. I have paid his vet bills and towards his food. He is my cat to all intents and purposes. If we can say that he has been gifted to me as one of your cat's kittens then surely we don't need the Adoption Papers?

Anyway, if you could get your local print shop to print the Health Certificates so Nikos could sign and stamp them that would be great.'

Trisha: 'Rebecca (Becks) who first found Teddy on the mountain side sent me a text. I'll send it to you. She calls me Lara – as in Lara Croft' 😂

Rebecca: 'JUST UNBELIEVABLE LARA CROFT ... you are amazing 🤩 ... Teddy just looks out of this world. I will be so sad 😭 not to see him, it was the best adventure ever, finding Teddy💕. Nearly going to cry 😢 now. Oh dear, Becky, sort yourself out. Absolutely great Dave has been able to fight for Teddy to get there, very kind. The Video of Teddy is beautiful, I just love his purring💕. I will watch all the videos of Teddy forever. I hope Dave will send some videos and photos to you. You have done fantastic work with all this Brexit and documentation stuff, well done! Just cooking Greek stifado. Good luck xxxxxxxx.💕💕🤩🤩🤩🤩😍'

Trisha: 'I told her you were amazing and struggling with all the Greek bureaucracy.'

Dave: 'Aw, that's so lovely. If we're successful we could form a Teddy Group on WhatsApp and I'll post photos etc xx.'

Frida

Trisha: 'Simba, who has injured his leg, got out and he has an appointment with Nikos tomorrow. My neighbour has just informed me that they are having the insect spray guys round on Monday to spray the entire house, trees and garden, that means all the cats' bedding and cat houses will have to come indoors and they don't all get on. 😾😾😾 I hate the sprays, so toxic. My neighbours are going off for the day. Frida has her head permanently on one side due to cockroach spray. Do you know when it will be safe to put the cat houses back and let the cats out? I can't keep all 25 in the house 🙈.'

Dave: 'If the spray gets into grass etc it'll probably a couple of days, maybe a few hours if it's just sprayed around generally.

I heard from Rachel (at Thompson) about 40 minutes ago. It comes down to whether we can get anywhere with the embassy via Nena, lap of the gods stuff.'

24.4.21

Dave to Nena: 'Could you talk to the Ministry Vet for me? We need to tell her that Teddy is my cat and the Adoption Papers are not necessary. We need to know if the authorisation can be validated by the Greek Embassy and if that is okay for her, or if the MV still has to have an Apostille – in which case I will have to book Teddy's journey/transfer with Thompson for later in the year to give me time to get the Apostille. We need to know that the Ministry Vet agrees with one of these options. Thank you so much, efcharisto poli.'

25.4.21

Trisha: 'Kalimera. I'm with Nikos and Litsa. I brought Simba in yesterday as he had been limping for a week. I thought his leg may be fractured, but luckily it's not broken. Nikos is signing Teddy's Health Certificate in a moment.'

Dave: 'Hiya. Beautiful photos of you both with Simba and send Nikos my thanks. 😸 I've been thinking it over having got some sleep and stepped back for 24 hours. Let's get the Adoption Papers signed and then email me a copy.

I am phoning the UK government legalisation office tomorrow morning to see if they could do a rapid Apostille. It is difficult for Andrea on 5th/7th, but she still insists that I go ahead and make an appointment as early in the day as possible. She also doesn't trust the Civil Servants to be in work the day after the strike so, I'm going to try for the 5th.'

26.4.21

Dave: 'I really have to confirm the trip with Thompson today, so if there's still a problem with the Ministry Vet I'll lose the full cost of the transport, not just the deposit. It feels like too big a gamble in the current situation, plus it's a Monday so it's likely that the Ministry Vet won't be in the office if Nena tries to reach her.'

Trisha: 'Okay, let me know what happens. I have 25 hissing cats in the house due to the cockroach stuff.'

Dave: 'Oh dear, did they spray yesterday or today?'

Trisha: 'This morning and some of the cats got out.'

Later that morning Nena let me know that she couldn't get hold of the Ministry Vet.

Dave to Nena: 'Okay, Nena, thank so much for your help as always, we will try next week to contact them. I think I will make a new document including a Nomou 105, owner papers etc. I will make sure the Ministry Vet is satisfied with the contents and then get the UK government to issue an Apostille if the Ministry Vet is still demanding it. I am going to postpone Teddy's trip until June. Please let me know if I could make a donation to you. Have a Καλό Πάσχα! Big Love Dave xxx'

Dave to Trisha: 'Just had a message. Tales of the expected. Nena can't reach the Ministry Vet and as it's Holy week she reckons they've all gone off to start slaughtering lambs ready for the traditional Easter Sunday roast. I thanked her for everything she has done and wished her Καλό Πάσχα! (Good Easter) She's an angel ... I need to find a way of repaying her kindness and Diane's. Meanwhile, having spoken to them I was advised that the UK government Legislation process for an Apostille takes 10 working days plus postal time.

So, we're cancelling the trip on 11th May to give us time to get the paperwork together without the extra pressure and loss of the full transportation fee.

I've let Rachel know and asked her to give Nena a hug for me when she can. She was very understanding and sorry that Teddy wouldn't make the trip this time, but very supportive and encouraging that we'll get there in the end. I've also let Andrea know.'

Trisha: 'Okay, it would be good to know if the Apostille is really necessary. Maybe I will try and get Vincent on the next run as well.'

Dave: 'We could try ... wouldn't like to guarantee it at this stage. I'll only book a trip with Thompson when everything is in order and the same would have to be true for Vincent. Too much to think about today. I'm sending an email to the Ministry Vet, I'll copy you in.'

To the Ministry Vet from Dave (also translated into Greek in the email):

'I understand that the new regulations following Brexit have given you a great deal of extra work and I sympathise.
Teddy was given to me.
I have paid Teddy's veterinarian bill.
I have been paying for Teddy's food.
I am Teddy's owner in the Pet Passport.
I am Teddy's owner on the ΠΙΣΤΟΠΟΙΗΤΙΚΟ ΗΛΕΚΤΡΟΝΙΚΗΣ ΤΑΥΤΟΠΟΙΗΣΗΣ (Certificate of Electronic Identification).
Teddy is my cat.

All I want to do is bring him home.

I checked with the UK Government Legalisation Office and they would not be able to issue an Apostille in time for the 5th May appointment at your office.
I have to pay the full transport fee today and the risk of losing it is too great. So, I have cancelled the booking with Thompson Pet Travel and my representative will not come to your office until the papers are correct.

I wrote the Adoption Papers because I thought it was necessary in Greek Law, even though Teddy is my cat. He is living with his temporary guardian until he can travel to the UK. Please can you advise me in the circumstances exactly what is really required? I will then continue to do my best to satisfy the requirements. Once that is done I will have to re-apply for the IPAFFS notification, produce a new Health Certificate, book a new transport date and make a new declaration for the customs and VAT.

Thank you for your kind help, your patience and your understanding.

Ευχαριστώ πολύ

Very best wishes,

David Burnham'

Reply from the Ministry Vet:

'We will be glad to fill in the health certificate once all documents are as demanded. The certificate will be completed when your representative visits. The passport has a specific field that should be filled by the veterinarian in Poros 48-72 hours prior to the departure.

Best regards'

Chapter 9

Double Trouble

May 2021

One cat just leads to another: Ernest Hemingway

Having now cancelled Teddy's place on the Freedom Bus, Sue said to me: 'You've spent hours on this, jumped through every hoop and bent over backwards and still the Ministry Vet comes up with more things to be done; perhaps it's time to give up?'

There had been moments when things felt like they were spiralling out of control and it had certainly crossed my mind, but every time I saw a photo of Teddy I knew I couldn't let go of him. Sometimes you come so far with something in life you just have to see it through. The other factor goading me on was that it presented a way of making a stand against the apparent helplessness of a situation both beyond my control and not of my doing: I was fighting for Teddy's future.

Troy by the harbour in Poros

Trisha sent me a picture of a cat called Troy enjoying the sunshine by the harbour. I had a vision of Teddy similarly enjoying the sun in our back garden curled up in a flower pot like his predecessor.

I decided I had to keep going!

There seemed to be a difference of opinion between the Ministry Vet's office demand and the prior experience of the Greek Animal Rescue team with regards to the Apostille. The Ministry Vet wanted an Apostille for the Adoption Papers. All the other advice was telling me it should be for the Declaration of Authorisation (nomou 105) for my representative to visit their offices. I pondered for some time. If I did one and not the other then it would almost certainly be rejected and I'd be back to square one. I wasn't going to put myself under any pressure by creating a deadline for the transport date until all the paperwork was in place, but on the other hand I didn't want to waste time and money in the interim.

Then I had an idea.

Nena had very kindly produced a document with the correct wording for the Declaration form in both English and Greek. I knitted together a PDF document with a covering introductory page, then the adoption agreement, then the nomou 105, then Nena's document – all numbered so they could be stapled together. By applying for an Apostille for the entire document that would cover everything, so there could be no argument and no further demands on that front.

I printed it out, filled in the Legalisation Department of the Foreign and Commonwealth Office's online application and got it in the post. An email popped in a couple of hours later:

'Please ensure your documents have been certified by the relevant authority with an original wet ink signature, stamp, or seal of a practising solicitor or public notary in the UK.'

Oh dear. That little nugget of information hadn't appeared anywhere in the online application and the form had already left the Post Office. Great! So they had told me (too late) that even though they were a government Legalisation Office someone else had to also certify the document first. I'd just have to wait and see what happened.

6.5.21

Meanwhile, having managed to work out what I thought was the entire raft of paperwork required to get Teddy to the UK, it then seemed logical to see if I could also get Trisha's other kitten, Vincent, to his new owner in

Birmingham. So, I contacted Martin by email and set out a plan. I explained where we'd got to and that people were still feeling their way through the quagmire of bureaucracy resulting from Brexit (including the Greek officials), but I was willing to help him if needed. Might as well go for "Double Trouble".

Martin: 'This sounds like an absolute nightmare. Do you have any idea at all when Vincent might be making the trip? Thanks.'

Dave: 'Hi Martin. Not sure at present, I'm still battling with the UK Legalisation Office for Teddy's Apostille. My guess would be late June.'

7.5.21

Tales of the expected.

Dave: 'Kalimera, Trisha. The Legalisation Office sent the paperwork back as apparently it has to be witnessed and stamped by a solicitor before they will authorise it (seems they're as bad as Greek bureaucrats 😂🙃). Luckily the solicitor who acts for my Mum has a colleague in the office who is qualified to do it, so I'll drive over to Worthing in the next few days and get them to witness and certify another copy of the Adoption Papers while I hang around.

So many people have been so kind to help us get there.' ❣️

Trisha: 'That is wonderful.' 😻

11.5.21

Thompson set off on their next journey from Greece to the UK. Teddy should have been on board, were it not for all the nonsense over the Apostille. One of the animal passengers had the incorrect microchip number on their paperwork and there was no way it could be changed within hours, so sadly that one didn't make the trip either.

18.5.21

Dave: 'Fingers crossed for the Apostille. I think it might be around 22nd June for the next attempt at getting Teddy on the Freedom Bus.'

Trisha: 'Teddy is one lucky kitty. I am hoping this week will be back to fairly normal. Started my new project back at work. Will send pics.' 🌼🍇🍷

Dave: 'Did you want to try to get Vincent on the 22nd June trip, too, or shall I let Martin know that we're still trying to clarify the Ministry Vet's requirements for him?'

Trisha: 'I was wondering what to write to Martin, he's been through a lot recently. I'm not really sure what's best, but it would be good to send Vincent with Teddy. I think Vincent will help Martin because as with most gingers he is cheeky like Teddy. Teddy is better behaved than Vincent. Teddy is such a lovely boy, he's always purring.'😺

Dave: 'Okay, let's give it a go.'

Trisha: 'I have repetitive strain in my left thumb radiating up my arm because I carry the rubbish down with one hand whilst driving my motor bike ... you know that song ... *Once upon a time I was falling in love, now I am just falling apart*? I'm getting an electric car.'

Dave: 'Sounds like a good idea, for the planet and for your thumb.'

19.5.21

Trisha took delivery of her little electric car to get her round the island with the cat food. It was a one person vehicle with a fairly short range, but would be perfect for the island and feline "meals on wheels". Like all electric cars it was very quiet and even more so being small. We joked about it needing an external speaker playing a recording of Teddy purring or several cats meowing loudly, so people would know she was coming.

Trisha: 'It's quite a phenomenon here, there's nothing else like it on the island.'🚐

Dave: 'Fabulous, it's just the thing for island life. I've heard that the Greek government want to move away from lignite mining to fuel their power stations. Lignite is pretty unpleasant stuff with less actual energy value than hard coal, so it produces more air pollution in comparison. Greece is blessed with sunshine and wind, so even based on pure economics investing in renewables would make better financial sense for your country, let alone the environmental benefits.

Sifnos is an interesting case in point. The Sifnos Island Cooperative wants to move towards a plan of total energy autonomy. It's a really neat idea. They want to build a huge water reservoir high up on the hillside and fill it with sea water by using wind turbines. The electricity generated by the wind turbines would supply the grid, as well as filling the reservoir. A hydroelectric station would also generate power and if the wind dropped there would still be enough sea water to cover the energy requirements for the island. It's such an elegant solution, I love it. There's a website you can look at: www.sifnosislandcoop.gr.'

Trisha: 'That sounds fabulous. Such a good idea.'

Later that day.

Dave: 'I've just got back home. The Apostille arrived in today's post, I've actually got it! I dashed over to RePrint near Dyke Road and got Richard there to scan it so I can send it to the Ministry Vet in the morning.'

Trisha: 'That's great news! Let me know what she says.'

20.5.21

Dave: 'How long does it take for a letter to reach you from the UK and do they arrive safely? I think I might try to send the paperwork to you.

I've been trying to email the Apostille to the Ministry Vet to get the go ahead, but the emails kept bouncing back saying *the quota for the email account has been exceeded*😳, got there in the end and she's given us the go ahead! Andrea is up for the 22nd June as well, although she has an appointment for her second Covid vaccination on the same day and I need to confirm it with Rachel at Thompson.'

We chatted about the properties that Trisha designed interiors for. One had been built by a Greek merchant in 1874 with spectacular views over the town and looking towards the "Sleeping Lady" mountain range. One photo of the lovely scenery, blue skies and glittering sea were quite a contrast, as I looked at them sitting in my shed on the allotment sheltering from the wind and rain. I mentioned that (last I heard) Lawrence Olivier's old flat on Brighton seafront still had the labels on the drawers and shelves of his walk-in wardrobe. I had a vague idea that Shirley Bassey used to have a property in the same mews, but that could have been an urban myth. Trisha's work was fabulous and it was so lovely to see life breathed back into those classic properties.

I emailed Rachel and found that the next transport date which would work for us would be 29th June, I also asked if we could include Vincent on the bus to get him to Martin. The pick-up point for this trip was to the East of Athens, so we'd need to work out how we would get the cats there from Poros.

Dave: 'Hopefully the new date for the Ministry Vet visit on Thursday 24th would work better for Andrea, too. I'm also waiting for confirmation from the Ministry Vet that Andrea can go on the 24th ... and that they will be willing to do Health Certificates for both Teddy and Vincent at the same time.'

Trisha: 'It's all doable.😺 I just heard that the UK are saying no trips to Greece unless it's an emergency. Is that correct?'

Dave: 'If I used every word in my head to describe the UK government then your phone would melt! More mishandling on their part means that a *Delta Variant* of Covid is now on the rise here and I wouldn't be surprised to see another lockdown: at least regionally.

The scenes at Heathrow are unbelievable. Thousands of arrivals all crammed together. No enforced separation of green light arrivals from red (they've got two terminals! It's not rocket science to use one for low risk and one for high). Quarantine rules are a joke. So, the government are quite happy to continue infecting the UK with variants.

Their rationale on travel from UK to other countries seems equally bizarre. Holiday travel is pretty limited (Portugal seems ok for some reason, but several other countries don't want arrivals from the UK anyway). I think controlled business travel, like Thompson is currently okay.'

Trisha: '🙈🙈🙈'

Dave: 😂 '... and not one wise monkey amongst them. I wish Jacinda Arden was our PM ... or Nicola Sturgeon ... ah well.'

Trisha: 'About posting stuff to me. I do sign at the post office. I just picked up a parcel and signed for it. So maybe post restante.'

Dave: 'Interesting idea. I'm just writing to Martin. He'll need a friendly solicitor in his pocket to get the Adoption Papers certified for the Legalisation Office and the Apostille. If we're going to get Vincent on the 29th June bus I'll need to move things along swiftly, but I can do most of it.'

Trisha: 'Lovely, you are an angel 😇. I informed Martin that you have been doing all the work for Teddy and cats. Robert has offered to drive the cats to the pick-up point.'

Dave: 'That's quite a long drive – he is clearly a friend to treasure.'

22.5.21

Trisha sent me a photo of Teddy playing with rolled up fabrics while I was checking the allotment for wind damage from the previous night's storm. We talked about the wildfire raging near Corinth, which sounded dreadful. I asked her to send me copies of Vincent's Pet Passport so I could get on with his paperwork.

The bus departure date had been moved forward another day to 30th June, but we should still be inside the ridiculous 10-day Health Certificate validity period. Time was ticking – and we still had Martin and Vincent's Apostille to obtain.

We now had a departure date of 30th June and an arrival date of 3rd July: both were entered on the calendar with a frisson of excitement.

25.5.21

I sent Martin and Trisha an update and I also sent a letter to Trisha just to test the postal service to Greece before sending the documents.

Trisha: 'Thank you for the update. What a mission!' 🙀🍷

Dave: 'Sure is. Just walking home from the allotment in high winds and freezing cold wearing 5 layers. I've got Long Johns under my trousers like a cross between Max Wall and Lee Marvin in *Paint Your Wagon* 😂. Any idea when I might get Vincent's Pet Passport details?'

Trisha: 'I'll message Litsa as I don't have access to the clinic.'

Dave:' Thanks, Trisha. I hate to hassle her and please apologise to her for me. I wouldn't ask if we didn't have the time constraints. I still haven't heard from the Ministry Vet ... I think all the vets went on strike last week over a proposed mass neutering program, so that might explain it. We must buy those nice bottles of wine for Litsa and Nikos.'

As far as I could make out from the news reports, part of the new bill about animal rights and protection included proposed legislation (due for public consultation around this time) that would make animal neutering mandatory. I had no idea of the exact wording, but it seemed that it might not just be aimed at the welfare of stray animals, but could also affect pedigree breeds/breeders. One example that was singled out was the Cretan hound – said to be Europe's oldest dog breed – with claims that the new law could bring about their extinction. I found it hard to believe there wouldn't be a degree of finesse in the legislation, but many seemed to believe this was the case. Animal protection groups talked about the daily discovery of boxes of kittens and puppies being found dumped in rubbish bins. Apart from the rare breed opposition there was the age-old concern of some Greek men that sterilisation equated with the denuding of manhood. I wondered if the vets might have been striking partly in solidarity with the preservation of rare breeds, but possibly also out of some concerns as to who was going to pay for the mass neutering and the enormous amount of extra work it would involve for them.

27.5.21

Teddy in a basket

Vincent in a flower pot

Trisha had managed to get passport photos for both of the cats. Teddy sat still for her, but Vincent kept hopping about from pillar to post. She would be sad to see them both go as she is very fond of gingers, as are we.

My trial letter still hadn't arrived at Trisha's local post office, but I decided to send her the print-outs of all of the documents. However, I wasn't going to risk the hard-won Apostille going in the post. A copy would have to do.

The Ministry Vet popped up out of the ethers having been on sick leave and sent me an email. She confirmed the date of the appointment and their office hours of 9:30 to 12:30. With regards to the fee, that would be 30 euros, but it should be paid via a dedicated "Paravolo" website page which was only available in Greek. I can read a little bit of Greek, so I clicked on it to take a quick look.

I was greeted by an internal server error!

I asked Rachel if she had any advice about this: 'Hi, Dave. Usually at the appointment to get the certificate they will give you a slip of paper which has the details of the fee to be paid. It can only be paid online by someone who has a Greek tax number. It doesn't have to be paid in advance, unless they are doing it differently there!'

So, I let Trisha know where we'd got to.

Dave: 'I've had a message from the Ministry Vet. She's included a link to click on to pay the Health Certificate fee, but the link doesn't work (of course it doesn't 😂!)'

Trisha: 'Rebecca is thrilled. You didn't really think the link would work, did you? I don't expect things to work here, that way I'm happily surprised when they do. It could turn one to drink!'

Dave: 'It turns me to furious digging on the allotment.'

I wrote step-by-step guidance for everyone and emailed that, along with digital copies of everything else, to Trisha so she could get them printed if my copies didn't show up in the post.

As I was planting out our courgette plants on the allotment a message came through to say that Vincent's microchip pinged on the reader, so we had that number to work with now.

30.5.21

Trisha: 'I just sent an email with Vincent's mug shot for his Pet Passport matched to the size of Teddy's. Does it look okay if you print it?'

Dave: 'I love it, and yes it prints at the same size.'

Trisha: 'Okay, I need to go to a different print shop as the main one has a problem with their colour printer. I'm off to Piraeus for Monty, who is a large Maine Coon 😻to have an operation. I have him, my husband, a computer, 4 suitcases, litter and litter tray and a spare cage to pick up abandoned Siamese kittens in Piraeus. Think I will jump off the planet.'🙃

Dave: 'Good luck with everything 👍. I'll send Teddy's paperwork by post tomorrow and hope it arrives ok, but not the original Apostille, the MV will have to be content with a PDF print out.'

Vincent's "Mug Shot"

Chapter 10

Elektroniki Palaver

June 2021

I have studied many philosophers and many cats. The wisdom of cats is infinitely superior: Hippolyte Taine

1.6.21

I was busying myself painting a second coat of white masonry paint onto the walls at the front of the house, prior to getting the path tiled (and pretending I was using asvesti in the Greek sun), when a message came in.

Trisha: 'Litsa has collected the mug shot of Vincent "Corleone".' 😻 I made it to Piraeus and have dropped Monty off at the vet to have his teeth out. He's a very large boy.'

Dave: 'He is a big boy. Must've worn his teeth out with all that eating.'

Trisha: 'I bought Teddy a new Green collar today and a Greek eye to go on it.'

Dave: 'Aw, lovely. We've just bought a cat activity tower for him.' 😺

3.6.21

Litsa sent me Vincent's Pet Passport details so I quickly completed and forwarded his Adoption Papers and Authorisation document PDF to Martin, along with a guide on how to get the Legalisation Office of the FCDO to process them for an Apostille. I let Trisha know and asked if she could contact the Ministry Vet to tie up a few loose ends.

Trisha: 'I will try to find out. Vincent was caught with his head in the food bag last night while I'm in Piraeus. Monty is recovering in our studio apartment here, he has the tv remote and is watching the wildlife channel with my husband.'

Litsa continued to help Trisha with Vincent's details (and was also trying to reach the Ministry Vet to get the correct website address for the payment). Martin confirmed his place on the bus with Thompson – hedging his bets that the Apostille would be back in time, although his solicitor was still yet to certify the papers. There was still no sign of either my letter or package of paperwork at the Post Office in Poros and last entry on the Greek ELTA postal tracking site showed my parcel to still be at Athens airport airmail centre, so I sent them an email asking for advice.

9.6.21

Trisha: 'Teddy and Vincent are packed ready to go 🎒🧳🕶🕶🕶🕶. I did tell them the sunglasses may not be necessary.'

Dave: 'Ha-ha, they won't get as much use out of their shades here as they do there, that's for certain. If we could get the documents ready, signed, and in Andrea's hands well before 24th it would give us a safety margin. If we relied on getting the documents to her that very morning and there was another strike that would be that. Whereas, if she's already got the documents we'd still have 4 days to get them back to you.'

Trisha went into Poros town to Gregory's print shop and the heavens opened, soaking her with more rainfall than they'd had all winter, rivers running in the streets, so she went barefoot. She sent me a message with his email address and I sent him all the documents ready for printing.

Gregory's shop – *Memory of Greece Bookstore and Souvenir* – is one of those splendid Greek emporiums stocking everything from toys, books, beachwear and sunscreen to drinks and cigars, plus offering a very helpful print service. He was to prove indispensable.

10.6.21

Trisha sent me a photo she'd just taken from her house of a long line of boats out to sea. She had no idea what they were doing. I'd been keeping up with some Greek news and had heard there was going to be a ferry strike so they were probably in solidarity with that. It further underlined the need to get those documents into Andrea's hands well before the Ministry Vet appointment date. We spoke on the phone and went through all of the documents printed by Gregory, checking that they were all there and in the correct order, stapled together and placed in each cat's individual folders ready for the MV appointment.

Litsa reported that she still wasn't getting a response from the offices of the Ministry Vet and Trisha couldn't get hold of the head of vets. It was probably due to that day's Transport and Public Sector strike.

We'd bought Teddy a new pyramid-shaped cat cave bed so I sent Trisha a photo of that. She said she'd like one for herself and sent me a video of Teddy purring mightily. Sue and I watched Teddy's video several times as we sat in the back garden on a still, balmy summer's evening watching the swifts whirl around catching insects, issuing "screes" as they went. Beautiful to behold and the epitome of summer for us.

11.6.21

Trisha: 'Okay, I got through to the Ministry Vet and I know more or less what to do with this Paravolo thing, but I need to find a Greek person to help me with the payment. She said she would help me if I get stuck. I'm on my way to Nikos' office to meet Litsa and it's raining again.

Dave: 'Oh dear – that's a little unseasonal of it! I'm loitering in the nursing home garden for 20 minutes sorting out the flower border I've planted up ... unless it also rains here, which looks entirely possible. Anyway, I'm on the end of the phone if you need me.'

Litsa emailed me Vincent's completed Registration certificate so I forwarded it to Gregory for printing. By the time I got home, about 15 minutes later, Litsa had gone round the corner to Gregory's shop, picked up the printed certificate, got Nikos to sign and date it, and emailed a photograph of it back to me. Quite Amazing!

14.6.21

Trisha let me know that she had spent quite a lot of time with a Greek friend trying to pay the Ministry Vet fees, but without success. Despite finally managing to access the website, various drop down menus made no sense whatsoever and each one had to be completed before you could reach the actual payment stage: Elektroniki Palaver indeed.

The following morning Litsa was on the case. I phoned Trisha and she passed me over to Litsa who explained that she had been able to get onto the website page to register the Paravolo and it had (thanks to having a special code) in turn, generated a payment form which she would send me a copy of. I suggested that Trisha paid it as soon as possible and tried to get some proof of payment in case the Ministry Vet asked for it.

The Paravolo payment form (administrative fee details) wasn't just a bill – nothing so simple. It had an administrative fee code, details of the Public Authority/fee category/fee type (the result of the mysterious dropdown menus), the amount, a payment code, a VAT number, the payee's name/father's name/mother's name/date of birth/phone number and email, plus the details of the bank account to pay it into!

Now the only thing we were missing was the Apostille for Vincent's Adoption Papers. Andrea had a printer so she could print that out her end at the eleventh hour if necessary and Trisha could send everything else to her in advance.

I updated Rachel and she informed me that I also had to photograph every page of the Health Certificates and upload those to IPAFFS, as well entering the Health Certificate numbers issued by the Ministry Vet (British bureaucracy has its fair share of anal-retention, too) ... I gurgled hysterically for a few minutes ... it had been another bumpy ride, but progress was being made.

16.6.21

Adrianna

Octavia

I sent Trisha a photo of Dorian visiting me on the allotment and she sent back photos of two of the street cats she feeds, Adrianna and Octavia.

Trisha had had a busy morning. The lady in the Post Office had been completely nonplussed by the Paravolo payment form and had scratched her head for some time before suddenly realising how to process it. She issued Trisha with the payment confirmation to "The General Secretariat of Information Systems of Public Administration – Ministry of Digital Government". There's a mouthful of bureaucratic mumbo-jumbo for you. Then she visited the Marinos Office at the harbour to ask about sending a parcel of documents in a jiffy bag via the ferry. In the olden days you'd just hand it to the ferryman, maybe give him a tip, and generally it would turn up the other end. Things had moved on. It would cost 3.5 euro each way and would have an official print-out attached. There was a midday hydrofoil to Piraeus the day after next and Andrea would be able to collect it.

Trisha: 'Robert found this little one, still alive, in a flower pot. He's hand-feeding her and she's responding well. She's called Lulu and just opened her eyes today. He is fine about the date and time to take Teddy and Vincent to the pick-up point.'

Dave: 'What a remarkably generous and kind man.'

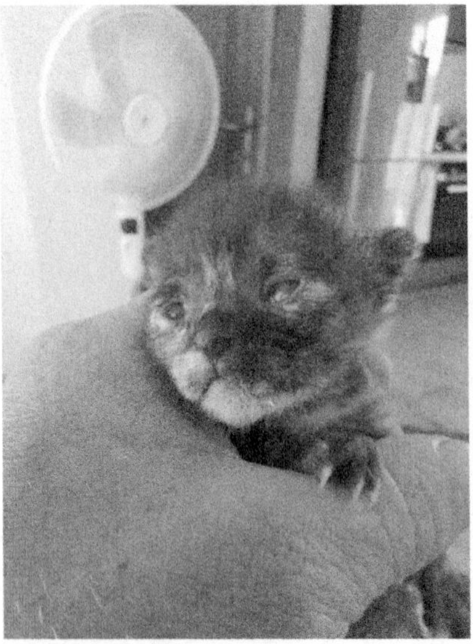

Lulu being hand-fed by Robert

17.6.21

The drop off point for delivering Teddy and Vincent to Thompson turned out to be nearby to where Rachel lived, so I sent Robert the exact coordinates. It would mean driving right around the Saronic Gulf and back – frankly heroic – and I told him as much, as well as thanking him in advance for his kindness and invaluable help.

Vincent admiring the view

Trisha: 'Just back from feeding Athena and the church cats. The ever-curious Vincent is admiring the view.'

Dave: 'Wow, I'd join him and stare at that view for hours.'

Trisha: 'Vincent and Teddy are friends so they will be good pals for the journey to England.'

18.6.21

Trisha: 'The package with all of Teddy's and Vincent's documents has been labelled and paid for. It's on the ferry and heading for the mainland.'

A couple of hours later another message arrived to say they were safely in Andrea's hands. I swiftly paid Thompson the balance of the transport fee and breathed a sigh of relief ... for Teddy, anyway. I still had Vincent's Apostille to wait for.

19.6.21

Trisha: 'Here is Teddy's collar for travelling with the heart, protective eye (μάτι) and name tube with your telephone number and mine.'

Dave: 'Aw, that's lovely, thank you xxx. We're just prepping some fish, squid and prawns, plus a Greek salad ready for Karen and Andy who are coming for dinner tonight to help celebrate my 59th. They are our local chums who are also friends with Cordelia in Athens. Could you send this photo to Cordelia and send her love from Brighton?'

Dave, Sue, Karen and Andy

Trisha: 'It's your birthday! 🎂🥳Happy birthday. My husband sends you happy birthday too. I'll send it to Cordelia now.'

Dave: 'Thank you. Yeah, gemini ♊.'

Trisha: Me too. Just had a reply from Cordelia: "Awww lovely! Bless them! Karen and Andy are wonderful. When is the kitty travelling?".'

20.6.21

Dave, Çiğdem, Sue and Martyn

Triantafillos playing harmonica

While we were celebrating my birthday, which I also share with our friend Çiğdem; along with her husband Martyn and our friend Mel, Trisha sent a video of her husband, Triantafillos. He was on the balcony overlooking their garden and the beautiful blue sea, wished me "Chronia Polla" and played Happy Birthday on his harmonica followed by "Never on a Sunday" (from the Greek romantic comedy film) as Trisha panned her phone across the bay. It was such a touching gesture and filled my heart with joy, it also elicited a round of applause from our friends.

Dave: 'Efcharisto para poli, thavmasios. The lady in red has the same birthday as me. We are in their back garden. Çiğdem works for the NHS and (although Covid has stopped it for the present) she also sings in a local choir called "The Jam Tarts". Her husband, Martyn is a retired English teacher, author and poet, and he used to do a comedy stage act as a Brighton landlady called Mrs Hoover.

21.6.21
Martin was due back from Spain over the weekend so I updated him on progress. He was in quarantine for 10 days: but there was still no sign of the Apostille and the deadline for payment for Vincent's place on the Freedom Bus was fast approaching. He was, understandably, concerned that he could lose the entire transport fee if the issuing of the Health Certificate was compromised without the Apostille. If everything came together, we agreed to meet up at the pick-up point in the UK when Teddy and Vincent arrived.

22.6.21
Having poked at the hornet's nest, Martin received a text telling him that the Legalisation Office were still working on his Apostille application and the Apostille wouldn't be complete until after the date of the cats' departure!

I took some deep breaths and came up with a contingency Plan B.

I asked Martin to sign another set of Adoption Papers (dating them exactly the same as the originals) and email copies to me, which I forwarded to Andrea to print and include with Vincent's documents.

Teddy's documents would be fine, but we needed options for Vincent's.

1/ I asked her to explain to the Ministry Vet that Covid issues had delayed Vincent's Apostille, but copies of the emails and postal receipts proved that it was being processed and we promised to send them the Apostille as soon as we received it if they would kindly sign off the Health Certificate in good faith.

2/ Phone the Head of Vets, explain the situation, and that Teddy's documents showed our commitment, to try to get her approval.

Time would tell.

Chapter 11

Ministry Vet Day
(Into the Labyrinth of Bureaucracy)

24th June 2021

If a cat spoke it would say things like 'Hey, I don't see a problem here': Roy Blount Jr.

07.00 (UK time – 2 hours behind Greece)

I'd set the alarm to wake me up so I could be available from the time of Andrea's arrival at the Ministry Vets' offices.

07.40

Dave to Trisha: 'Andrea should be seeing the Ministry Vet about now. I'm by the phone in case of problems.'

08.24

Andrea to Dave: 'All will be alright. We are still working on it here at the Ministry. They have been reasonable about your missing paper, you will email it to them. Details of further tests by the vet etc required before leaving Poros are enclosed in files that I will return to Trisha. The huge difficulty here is Brexit. All procedures have changed and become so strict and all are new to them. I sit quietly here as 2 of them struggle on their PCs to move forward with the online form filling, I guess in English? Their willingness to give us what we need is apparent, but the online bureaucracy is killing them. So, it comes down to the Ministry Vets making their own systems work for us to win this battle.'

08.26

Dave to Andrea: 'Wow, well done. Yeah, having to do this last stuff online at all is bonkers; all they need to do is stamp all 4 pages of both Health Certificates and issue the reference numbers. I feel sorry for them that Brexit has given them all this extra work ... it's given all of us extra work ... for what? Yes, the cats' vet needs to do a final check and sign off that page of their Pet Passport before they can travel.

Thank you so much, Andrea.

Virtual hugs through the electronic ethers.'

08.28

Andrea to Dave: 'They don't have a choice!'

08.30

Dave to Trisha: 'I could hug Andrea! Looks like they've accepted our proposal of completing the Health Certificates for us and then Martin sending the Apostille to them by email as soon as he gets it! Apparently they're really struggling with their own online bureaucracy!'

09.10

Then I got a phone call from Andrea:

'Now got 3 MVs working on it.'

(We now had 3 Ministry Vets clustered around the computer screen like the opening scene from Hamlet ... muttering not entirely dissimilar incantations as they prodded the recalcitrant electronic cauldron. I let out a small, hysterical laugh.)

Andrea: 'Don't laugh, they are doing everything they can!'

Dave: 'I'm sorry, it's just the absurdity of the situation.'

Andrea: 'They are asking have you done your IPAFFS?'

Dave: 'Yes, the UNN is on the top right of Health Certificate as generated by the IPAFFS application.'

Andrea: 'Too much information!'

(It took them a while to find the Health Certificate among all the other paperwork they asked for ... I could hear constant rapid discussion in Greek in the background throughout the call between all three Ministry Vets and Andrea. They managed to find the UNN as I'd advised and moved on to the next bit.)

Andrea: 'Their online system is asking for the "Imerologio taxidiou" Travel Journey Log to show exactly which countries the Pet Transport Company are passing through, which towns/cities and at what times. A 5-page travel journal. They want all the details from Poros to the UK, each stop and each border.

I will not do this again. I did it before for 7 cats and they accused me of cat trafficking because no one could have that many cats!

The Ministry Vets have said they will not do Health certificates for cats from Greece to the UK again!'

Dave: 'The travel details are part of the IPAFFS and therefore covered by the UNN.'

Andrea: 'They have to have the "Imerologio taxidiou" Travel Journey Log!'

Dave: 'Okay, I'll try to phone Rachel at Thompson and find out if they have it.'

I phoned Rachel:

Thompson had only ever been asked for a Journey Log once before in all the times they'd done the trip. It is not an official requirement, but she would try to contact Lynda and get the information to the Ministry Vet.

09.12

Andrea: 'The Ministry Vet is saying they can't progress with the online system without the Journey Log information. I can't spend all day there plus they close the office at 12:30 (10:30 UK time)!'

09.21

Dave to Andrea: 'Rachel is contacting Lynda (who owns the company and drives the bus) to sort out the Travel Journal. The Travel Journal is not an official requirement and Thompson have only ever been asked for it once before. I've given Rachel your number, too.'

09.24

Dave to Trisha: '... problem – the Ministry Vets (3 of them working on it now) want a Journey Log or "Imerológio taxidioú" from Thompson – dates and times of each border crossing etc.

Luckily I have Rachel's mobile number – she said they've only ever been asked for this once before and it is not an official requirement, but she will contact Lynda and try to sort it.

If it's not done quickly we may lose our window with the Ministry Vets and Andrea. My heart rate is really quite spectacular!'

09.30

Trisha to Dave: 'Oh for God's sake ... I will wait for news.'

09.40

Andrea to Dave: 'While hoping for the journal, which countries are they going through? I can hear the form is asking for that.'

Dave: 'Greece, Italy, Switzerland, France, UK – as entered in the IPAFFS.'

09.42

Andrea: 'What time will the cats be handed over in Poros?'

Dave: '3pm.'

Andrea: '29th?'

Dave: 'Yes. More information coming ... Robert picks up the cats from Poros 3pm on 29th. He will drive right round the Saronic Gulf to Kalyvia to deliver the cats to Thompson Pet Travel. Thompson leave Greece on 30th.'

09.48

(I Logged into the IPAFFS and sent a screenshot of the Transporter details and the countries)

Dave to Andrea: 'This is a screenshot of the relevant section of the IPAFFS ... arrival at Kalyvia by Robert is 6pm on 29th.'

09.51

Andrea: 'No access to IPAFFS here. They need this travel journal! 5-page form.'

09.54:

Dave: 'I know, I was just proving the countries are as entered on the system. Rachel is trying to sort it out. This is Rachel's telephone number (sent in the message).'

09.56

Andrea: 'What am I supposed to do with her telephone number?'

9.58

Dave: 'In case you need to speak to her. If all else fails then as a last resort: I think it may need a call to the head of all vets and ask her advice.'

10.03

Andrea: 'I will not be a smartass and do that. I have 3 professionals in front of me working for over 3 hours trying to sort out our case. If they can get through without more details they will! They are still trying.'

Dave: 'Okay, I'm sorry. It's not their fault and I really appreciate they are doing their best with the stumbling block of this ludicrous online form. Other Ministry Vets just enter the number, stamp and sign the forms and that's that. These good people are clearly having to do it by the book, possibly because they are used to processing so much livestock for transport from the port?'

10.05

Rachel to Dave: 'Hi Dave I've just sent Andrea a photo of the journey log.'

Dave: 'Wow, amazing! Nice one, Rachel. Could you send it to me as well as a back-up?'

10.05

Dave to Andrea: 'Photo of Journey Log from Rachel should be with you.'

Andrea: 'Where?'

(It sounded like Andrea hadn't received it, so my belt and braces approach of getting a copy from Rachel was lucky.)

10.06

Dave: 'Copied in here:'

'Hi Andrea,

Here is the first page of the Journey Log. We don't usually complete it because it's not relevant for pet transport – it's for horses and livestock, I believe. I haven't filled out the other pages because they are just completely irrelevant. It says about having a vet here at departure and arrival which is completely unnecessary. Hopefully this is acceptable as it has been to the only other Ministry Vet who has asked for it. Let me know if you need anything else.'

10.13

Dave to Rachel: 'Just took a moment to read the travel log – fast work, Rachel! Well done! Thank you so much, you total star!'

Rachel: 'Hope everything goes well.'

Dave: 'I think Andrea is close to meltdown, but it sounds like the Ministry Vets are genuinely doing their best ... they've been at it for 3 hours 13 minutes and counting!'

10.15

Rachel: 'Well, I'll be here if anything else is needed.'

10.16

Dave: 'Thanks, Rachel and lovely to speak to you ... albeit in hair-raising circumstances xx.'

10.30

Andrea to Dave: 'Ok, it's going through!'

Dave: 'Phew, thank goodness. I can't thank you enough for all you've done, Andrea xx.'

11.04

Andrea: 'Done. And on the Flying Dolphin to Poros. Exhausted, no more chat please. TRISHA informed. Vets said check all, anything wrong can be corrected tomorrow. NOT BY ME! Am still in shock, never again, but wish the boys a painless journey. GOOD LUCK WITH ALL.'

11.08

Dave to Martin: 'She's done it! I've been on the phone/WhatsApp to Andrea and Thompson since 7am. You wouldn't believe what's been involved. I am definitely going to write a book about this: Sue suggested it. You'll need to send copies of the Apostille and Adoption Papers to the Ministry Vet when you get them – I'll explain how when it arrives.'

11.15

Dave to Rachel: 'Well, we started 9am Greek time (I got up at 7am) and ... she did it! The paperwork is on the ferry back to Poros. Hopefully they stamped and signed the right bits – I'll find out later when I get copies from Trisha for you and the IPAFFS.

Thanks again,

Dave
xxxx.'

11.51
Rachel: 'Perfect! Glad to hear it x.'

11.56
Dave to Rachel: 'Andrea is utterly exhausted and will never do it again. The Piraeus Ministry told her that they will also not process Health Certificates for pets travelling from Greece to the UK again. (Nice one Brexit, hopefully they will calm down in time as Trisha still has at least 5 more cats to send to the UK.) We've been super lucky. I'll let you know when Trisha has got the documents back safely and I've finalised the IPAFFS and sent the document copies to you.

Thank goodness I got your number last week. I think I might suggest to Trisha that she gets a group like GAR to register the other cats she wants to send in their name and go that route with you ... anyway, that's for another day xx.'

12.01
Dave to Trisha: 'Andrea has been our champion today! The Ministry Vets themselves were totally on our side, too. It took 4 hours, but we got there. So many phone calls and WhatsApp messages! Could you let me know when you have the returned documents safely in your hands? Wait until you get everything home and then see if you could take nice, clear photos of each page of the Health Certificates. I'm going out for a delayed birthday lunch at the pub my stepdaughter manages ... Sue's offered to drive as I'm a tad washed out.'

12.11
Trisha: 'Got the stuff back!'

12.19
Dave to Martin: 'Documents safely back on Poros.'

15.32
Dave to Trisha: 'Hiya, just back home. When you get a moment could you take nice clear photos of each of the 4 pages of both cat's Health Certificates,

please? I need to upload them to complete the UK IPAFFS, send copies to Rachel and then verify IPAFFS and pay the UK Customs Agent. Thanks, me dear x.'

16.03

Trisha: 'Okay. I am out at the moment trying to sort out some poorly kittens. This is a bad story. Phoebus had an eye disease with blood pouring out of his eyes, but he is super now.'

Dave: 'Oh god, that horrible eye disease … I've seen that in Greece before. Have you got the appointment with Nikos tomorrow to sign off the Final Exam page in the Pet Passports?

Trisha: 'It's all in hand.'

21.04

Trisha: 'Looks like cats going to the UK is a no go according to the Ministry Vet I have to use. That's really bad news for my Greek cats that urgently need homes. It will affect couriers unless the rules are made more lenient. Andrea doesn't want to do it again, the stress has made her feel quite unwell. I don't know anyone else that could do it.'

Dave: 'I think many of the other Ministry Vets are still amenable, it might be that we were unlucky and the Piraeus office is used to commercial exports on a large scale so they wanted to go through the process in extreme detail. Hopefully they will calm down, given time, and help with the other cats'

Trisha and I had a long chat on the phone that evening. Not just about the next stages, but about Trisha's 30 years living in Greece, being married to a Greek man, having to prove herself in her role as interior designer and eventually winning the trust and respect of her clients. We talked about how the islands all seem to have slightly different characters, like villages in the UK. How different nationalities favour particular islands for their holidays. How she often gets castigated for trying to rescue and care for abandoned cats. She's done remarkably well in those 30 years. She must be a very determined woman. She said that Teddy purrs all day. Vincent likes to sit by a small gap in the wall where cockroaches occasionally emerge and he bops them and throws them out of the house: she'd miss them both when they set off on their journey.

Chapter 12

Cool for Cats

Late June 2021

A kitten is, in the animal world, what a rosebud is in the garden:
Robert Sowthey

25.6.21

The morning after Andrea's Ministry Vet visit, Trisha sent me photos of all of the Health Certificate print outs, which seemed to be in duplicate despite the pages being numbered 1 – 8. If only they could have just entered a reference number for each cat on the Health Certificates I provided, stamped each page and signed the last one, it would have saved them 4 hours work. I guess they had to do things by the book on their own system, even though it appeared to be incredibly confusing and at least partly based on the old Traces system.

Trisha was in a muddle with the order of the photos so we tried again.

Trisha: 'I would not be a good spy …'

Dave: 'I used to be 007 licensed to "drill" 😂.'

Trisha: 'Imagine secretly going into a room whilst a party was going on in the other room. Shuffling around the secret documents and taking pictures of all the wrong ones!' 🙈

Dave: 'That's modern art, that is 😂😂.'

Five hours later I went back into the online IPAFFS system. It would only allow me to upload one document so I combined the Health Certificate photos from Trisha into a single PDF and tried that … it worked and I now had both cats on "Submitted" status. A couple of lines had been incorrectly crossed out by the Ministry Vet and there was concern that DEFRA would reject them, but with hundreds of submissions every day I kept my fingers crossed it would be okay. Rachel at Thompson Pet Transport reassured me in her usual wonderful way: I am usually a pretty calm chap after years in a high-stress profession, but I had become so emotionally-invested in adopting Teddy.

Trisha: 'Wow, you are a wizard! I am meeting an old client tonight, we built her philosophy retreat on the mainland about 5 years ago. She is forcing me out for a drink 🍷🍷.'

Dave: 'You deserve one!'

Trisha had taken on five more adopters for her cats in the previous two days; fortunately they were bound for Paris and Holland so they wouldn't fall foul of the Brexit-generated bureaucracy as their new homes would still be within the EU. It had taken some doing to find those new homes, though. With the difficulties in getting cats and dogs to the UK from Greece it meant that other countries within the EU were facing a situation where supply was starting to outstrip demand.

27.6.21

Dave: 'Hi Martin. I've produced a guide for Trisha and Nikos ready for getting the Pet Passports signed off after the pre-trip clinical examination. I'm not sure if Thompson need a copy of your Adoption Papers, but I've sent them what we have (I think it's only relevant to the Ministry Vet and the issuing of the Health Certificate). To date, over 40 people have been involved in getting our cats to us - epic! Let me know if/when your Apostille arrives and I'll let you know who to send it to and all that jazz.'

Martin: 'Thanks for all your work, Dave. It wouldn't be happening without your efforts. You have had to be incredibly tenacious. All things being well I shall be seeing you at the collection point next Saturday.'

Dave: '🤞🤞 I really look forward to meeting you, Martin. I'll keep you updated. You can follow the cats' journey and progress on the bus on Facebook.'

Martin: 'This is my cat, Lara, who also came from Trisha. I followed Lara's progress on Thompson's Facebook page a couple of years ago when they brought her over for me. Her current favourite place is the airing cupboard. Looking forward to meeting you, too.'

28.6.21
In preparation for the last hurdle, Teddy and Vincent's vet needed to sign off their pre-trip Clinical Examination. The Ministry Vet had placed a Post-it note in with the Pet Passports saying that there were three further things to do ...? We knew about the final Clinical Examination, but now they seemed to be insisting on antiparasite and anti-echinococcus as well. Even though the worming treatment was legally only required for dogs we got that done as well – plus some more Spot On – and everything was signed, stamped and completed. We were finally ready for departure!

Max the tiler had just finished laying a new front path and he'd made a superb job of it. We'd been meaning to get it done ever since we moved, some 26 years ago. We thought of it as the equivalent of the "Red Carpet" for Teddy's arrival home. Max told me that he had just recently adopted a dog from Macedonia. He'd been through a similar rigmarole, but the issuing of the Health Certificate sounded considerably more straight forward than the complicated system in Greece. His new friend's name was Peanut, a Šarplaninac (formerly also known as the Illyrian Shepherd Dog) and she was a perky little soul who kept him company while he laid our path – except while he was laying the concrete base, in case her paws made it looks like the Hollywood Walk of Fame. He said she was one of 9 pups adopted from Macedonia and the new owners had set up a Facebook group so they could all stay in touch. In between laying the base for the path and finishing the tiling, Max had taken a little break down in Devon. While he was there he met up with one of the other adopters and one of Peanut's siblings on the beach. The dogs briefly sniffed and then spent ages tumbling over each other with delight.

That evening I received an email from Rachel.

Rachel: 'Hi Dave, we have a slight problem. The air conditioning stopped working on the van on the way back on the last trip and we thought it would just need re-gassing. However, after it was taken to the garage they said it's the compressor which has blown! They initially said it would be ready for us to collect tomorrow, but now he is struggling to get the part and said he "hopes" they will have it by midday tomorrow. If he does get it then the van will be ready tomorrow, if not we will have to delay the trip by one day. If that's the case then as the cats are coming from an island and everything is planned, I think it's best they still come here (so if the van is ready then everything goes to plan), but if it doesn't go to plan then there is an animal hotel next door to us where you could book in Teddy and Vincent for the night, would that be okay? I'm really sorry for the change of plan (maybe). Let me know your thoughts! Thanks.'

Dave: 'Okay, the transport from Poros to you is all ready to roll, so I think it would definitely be best to get Teddy and Vincent to you and, as you say, use the cat hotel overnight. We can be flexible with collection at the UK end. Looking at the weather in Greece it could be a very warm trip so definitely good to have the air con powered up. Dave x.'

Rachel: 'Thanks for understanding! Yes, we have had 40 degrees here the last few days so definitely needed.'

I contacted Martin to let him know and to check he was happy for us to make a provisional booking at the cat hotel, in case. Naturally, he was in full agreement and happy to cover Vincent's bed and board. I let Rachel know and she contacted the cat hotel, coming back to me to check if the boys could share a "room". I asked Trisha who thought they were generally fine in a large room together, but maybe separate confined areas would be best as they might be getting a bit stressed.

I could hardly believe it was the eve of departure. Trisha would miss them, but I reassured her that she'd be getting regular updates.

Trisha: 'Martin said he could not have done it without your support and help.'

Dave: 'Very kind of him ... it seemed logical, albeit with some added stress, and at least Teddy and Vincent will hopefully make it over before the Ministry Vets implode.'

Trisha: '🙈🙈🙈'

29.6.21

Bags packed and ready to go

09:17am

Dave: 'Hi Martin, provisional booking made for the boys' hotel: one "room" each. Rachel will pay the hotel and we can give the cash to Lynda when we pick the boys up. If the arrival date into the UK changes I'll go back into IPAFFS and correct that. I'll keep you in the loop, old bean.'

Martin: 'Ok. My solicitor has returned the request from the legalisation office. Still waiting for the Apostille.'

Dave: 'Ha, oh well ... one day. By the way, Royal Mail and ELTA tracking show that the copies of all the documents I sent to Trisha just turned up at Poros Post Office. I just popped into my local Post Office to send a parcel to my aunt. They wanted to know how long it took for my documents to get to Poros (tracked and signed). I said they arrived at Athens Airport sorting office in 48 hours, but took a further two and a half weeks to reach Poros (too late for Nikos to sign, so Trisha reprinted everything). They thought that was quite good! Apparently they reckon that Greece puts all external post into 2 weeks quarantine before sending it on!'

Martin: 'Somehow that just doesn't surprise me.'

Dave: Ha, yeah. Mind you they've managed Covid pretty well in Greece ... I just hope the forthcoming relaxation and tourists bringing in variants doesn't hit them hard.'

"Morning, here I am with my new collar, name tag and evil eye"

09:30

Trisha: 'Teddy is a good boy, Vincent prefers to play with his collar. Just had this message from Rebecca who originally found Teddy back in October 2020. She is coming to Poros in 2 days so just missed him. PS – She has always called me Lara, as in Lara Croft.'

Rebecca: 'I WISH TEDDY A VERY, VERY SAFE JOURNEY TO UK ... I hope he has a wonderful life with his new family ... I will miss him so much ... 😞... Lara Croft you have done an absolutely fantastic, fabulous thing ... from your heart, of caring and bringing Teddy up in his first year of life to a just gorgeous purring none stop Teddy Poros💕 ... with silky shining fur ... take care and have fun Teddy ... I have a tear in my eyes here in Gibraltar 🇬🇮. Love you, Teddyxxxxxxxxxxxxxxxxxxxxxxxxxxx😻'

Dave: 'Aw, bless her.'

Trisha: 'All ready for pick up with Robert. All 26 pages plus passport for Teddy and 21 pages plus passport for Vincent (minus his Apostille). Collars on. They have had Spot On and breakfast. I will give Robert 2 sachets of *Felix* plus water bowls.'

Dave: 'Fabulous, thank you so much, Trisha. We've got a room each at the cat hotel reserved in case they need it while the air con is being fixed – might be worth mentioning that to Robert, but Rachel and Lynda will meet him there and advise/update. Does Teddy have a preference of cat food flavours? Wet, dry and Dreamies?'

Trisha: 'He likes all of that. *Felix*, *Sheba*, *Whiskers*, *Dreamies* party mix ... I have been giving them all Purina for urinary health, because Rubin was rushed off to the vet with a blocked tract. That way, if he hijacked the other plates he would be ok 🙀🥴.'

Dave: 'Okidoki, we'll probably pick up some *Natures Choice* wet and *James Wellbeloved* dry as well.'

Trisha: 'Oh that's far better than what we have on the island.'

Dave: 'Not the cheapest, but has very good ratings. If you get the chance to take a photo of them in the car and setting off it would be a poignant moment for the book ❣️'

Trisha: 'Yes, will do. I am getting nervous, Robert is on his way.'

Dave: 'Be excited for them: positive emotions are lovely. We've come a long, long way to get to this point 😘.'

Trisha: 'Yes, I know, but it's always difficult putting them in the cage to see their little faces.'

Dave: 'I totally understand. We've met so many cats in our travels to Greece, it's always hard to say farewell and that's just after a fortnight's holiday!'

Trisha: 'I have had them 8 months 😢.'

Dave: 'You'll see Teddy again one of these days, I'm sure xx.'

Trisha: 'They are going to be so happy with you and Martin.'

Dave: 'They sure are 😻.'

Trisha: 'It's getting so difficult now with my 20 plus cats as well as the street cats, some ups and downs, trying to concentrate on my job. I think if I was rich I would give up work and just concentrate on cats and hubby.'

Dave: 'Difficult to know what to suggest. I think all of the Greek animal welfare people are struggling to keep pace.'

Trisha: 'When I eventually get to England I will definitely visit.'

Dave: 'Of course.' 🐈 🍷 🍴

The Journey Begins

13.30 UK (3.30pm Greek time)

I had a phone call from Trisha.

She was, naturally, very upset to see the boys go. She put Vincent into his transport basket first and then Teddy into his. Teddy's basket was brand new, but she hadn't noticed a problem with the plastic front which was broken and Teddy sprung out and she couldn't catch him. Luckily Teddy didn't go too far, so Trisha dashed into town to buy another basket, got back and successfully caught Teddy, finally getting him into a safe transport basket, although apparently he wasn't overly keen.

She looked at their little faces as they were loaded into Robert's car and realised she didn't really want to let them go. Robert reassured her that she was doing exactly the right thing and they set off on the first leg of the long journey to their forever homes. Due to the broken basket incident they missed the ferry to Galatas and had to wait for the next one.

Most of Trisha's cats were inside/outside cats, but Teddy and Vincent had spent their lives in the house, occasionally sitting on the rock at the edge of the room with a view out over the sea. They were always there when Trisha came back from work, the first to greet her. Covid, lockdown, not being able to work, the stress of the new – seemingly insurmountable – bureaucracy, plus her husband's poor health had meant Trisha had been through a tough time and she felt like those little ginger boys had supported her throughout. She was always sorry to see her charges set off on their travels to a new life, but Teddy and Vincent had been with her for longer than most destined for adoption, so their departure was like a cork out of a bottle of pent-up emotions for her. We talked for a while as I reassured her that both boys would have a lovely life with us and with Martin. It really was the best thing for them and she still had a house full of cats to look after, let alone all the strays to feed and neuter.

14:18

Rachel: 'Hi Dave, we are having to delay by one day as the van is still at the garage, any idea what time the cats are due to arrive here so I can let Chris know? Thanks and sorry for the inconvenience! Also means collection will be the 4th July at 10am.'

Dave: 'Hiya, the boys are on their way. They left Poros about 3-3:30 Greek time so should be with you from 5:30-6 onwards if you could make sure you're around. It will depend on traffic as well. Robert also has all the paperwork, which I guess you'll need to double check. Yep, I figured collection would bump forward to Sunday 4th; I'll let Martin know. Trisha had a bit of a wobble when they left. They were two indoor cats who've been her companions throughout lockdown, as well as during her husband's ongoing health problems, plus being with her much longer than normal due to all the bureaucracy. Anyway, I talked to her for half an hour or so and she seemed a little happier by the time we finished: she knows they're going to good homes. Let me know how it goes after Robert's been. If you need to get him I think his wife is travelling with him as it's a long haul, so you've got their mobile number.'

16.17 (18.17 Greek time)

Robert called to say they were at the given coordinates but there were several gated houses so they didn't know which was the right one. I gave him Rachel's mobile number and said to call me back if they didn't have any luck within the next 5 minutes.

16.35

Robert phoned me back to say they had found Rachel and successfully delivered the cats. I told them how grateful we were to them for making the long journey right round the Saronic Gulf. Robert and his wife, Brenda, said it was a pleasure and no problem at all and asked which of the cats we were getting and which day we would collect them in the UK. Once again, I thanked them profusely and mentioned that I was writing a book about it as it had been such a palaver – I promised them a copy and wished them a safe journey back round the Gulf and home to Galatas.

16.38

Rachel sent me a photo of Teddy and Vincent in their transport crates, in her bedroom with the air conditioning on. Seeing that photo was a huge relief. Rachel just had to wait for the owner of the animal hotel (Chris) to finish a meeting before she could come and take them overnight.

I forwarded that photo to Trisha and Martin and let them know they had made it on the first stage of their journey.

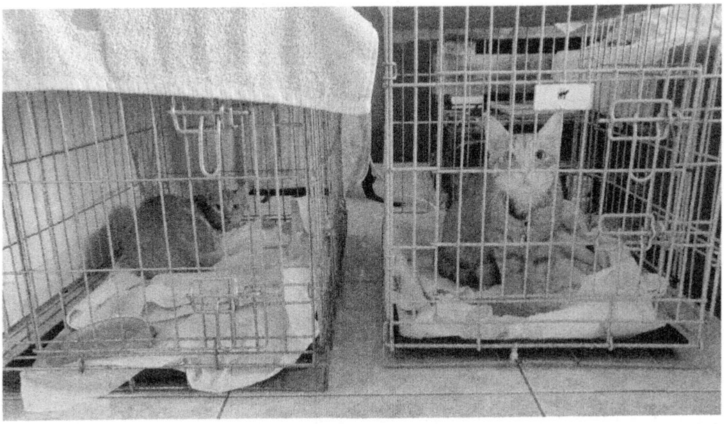

17.30

Martin: 'I think Vincent is wearing the collar. On the right of the photo?'

Dave: 'Yeah, Vincent is unmistakably the chap on the right with the blue collar.'

Martin: 'Very stressful for them. Worthwhile in the end.'

Dave: 'True on both counts, but better than starving to death on the side of a mountain. They will have long and happy lives with us.'

Martin: 'They will.'

18.12

Rachel: 'Chris is going to take the cats now, I think it will be better for them anyway as I can't let them out here.'

Dave: 'Great. Yeah, it'll be good for them to have a little stretch. There's a fair wedge of paperwork, but I guess the important bits for you are the Pet Passports and the Health Certificates?'

Rachel: 'Yep! That's all we need so unless there's something in there you want, do you mind if we leave it behind? We take a lot of paperwork with us as you can imagine.'

Dave: 'I would kinda like mine back if you don't mind. I fought so many duels over every bit of it I'd like to keep it in Teddy's folder. Martin's probably less bothered as I did most of it for him.'

Rachel: 'Okay, no problem at all.'

Dave: 'Thanks, Rachel: maybe a bit nerdy, but wow, there were some battles to get that stuff.'

Rachel: 'Ha-ha, that's fine I completely understand!'

I sent a message to Martin and Trisha to let them know the cats were on their way to the cat hotel where they could stretch their legs in larger compartments.

30.6.21

Trisha: 'Morning, Dave. Will collect letters. Robert and Brenda are really special people... 💕. Just going to feed the 5000.'

Dave: 'Robert and Brenda really went above and beyond in taking the cats to Rachel, and with such grace and good humour. Hope meals on electric wheels are gratefully received. Also hope you're feeling okay today. If I can help in any way let me know. I'll let you know every stage of the journey from my end.'

Trisha: 'Thank you. I am still a bit jelly-like today. I rang my best friend in the UK last night, because I was so upset. I think, as you say, the cork popped. I missed the boys this morning 😢.'

Chapter 13

On the Road

July 2021

Kind old ladies assure us that cats are often the best judges of character. A cat will always go to a good man, they say: Virginia Woolf

1.7.21

Early in the morning Nena was at the Freedom Bus with the dogs travelling from Greek Animal Welfare, so she was able to meet Teddy just before he boarded. The little ginger boy who we'd spent so much time over. He banged his head on the cage roof when they were trying to transfer him, but luckily no harm done.

Rachel: 'Lynda and Frank left this morning about 6:30am, air con is working perfectly. Teddy is a bit afraid, he doesn't like the crate, Lynda will make friends with him in the coming days I'm sure!'

Dave: 'Thanks, Rachel. Great to know they've set off. I'm told Teddy is quite a shy little chap, but as you say, he'll warm to Lynda. It must seem so weird to him ... he's only ever known Trisha's home. I think he has a strong sense of self-preservation! Thanks for everything you've done to help, Rachel. You've had the patience of a saint and I couldn't have done it without you. Love on ya, Dave and Sue xx.'

Rachel: 'Aww, yeah he will be okay, he has no idea what's going on and the amazing life he will have! You're welcome, it's amazing the amount of patience and determination you had to deal with everything, but you got there and it's a wonderful thing you have done for Teddy x.'

Lynda's First Update from the Thompson Pet Travel Facebook Page

'...and we're off!!

Good morning to all you lovely people who have opened your hearts and homes to a wonderful Greekie ❤❤.

Frank and I left Athens at around 6.30 this morning with some of our crew already on board. Yesterday we took delivery of pussy cats Teddy and Vincent, Teddy wasn't too happy with being handled last night, but he ate all his dinner and he's a lot better today (but quite vocal 😁) he was just a little afraid. Vincent is really laid back and taking it all in his stride. 2 lovely Pointer types for Pointer rescue called Maple and Milly. Also arrived yesterday, both gorgeous with that famous gentle and affectionate nature.

From Messini shelter came Jack K and Athena. Jack has been many years in the shelter, he's not a young boy but he's so so sweet! Athena is a gorgeous, friendly youngster, not the least worried by her latest adventure ❤. Also arriving yesterday was Percy the Pug! He's also very easy going, calm and collected. He's well-travelled and he looks like he's really enjoying the ride!

Lastly is little Puppy Robbie and Lucy the Kokoni, they travelled by ferry yesterday from Crete to Piraeus and then by pet taxi to us at Kalivia. They came with Robbie's siblings who are staying for a little while so they all had a really big area yesterday to run around in and settle after the first leg of their journey. They're absolutely lovely pups, they hadn't met Lucy before but they all adored her and she was so kind with them all, she's such a sweetheart ❤.

We're heading for Larissa now and will arrive at 11.00 (our time) to collect Hermes the pussy cat and Anestis the dog. I'll let you know how they are a little later. After that we're going to Halkidiki and then to our good friend Olga's lovely pet hotel in Thermi, Thessaloniki where she very kindly lets all the kids run and play and have a good leg stretch before we head to Igoumenitsa for our overnight ferry to Brindisi.

We will keep you posted on our progress and take lots of photos so you can see your gorgeous kids and find out how they're all doing. ❤

I hope like Percy, you enjoy the ride too! Xx'

I posted a comment: 'So happy to hear you are under way, Lynda and Frank. Teddy is a shy little chap, but hopefully he will settle down for the journey ahead; pleased to hear he hasn't lost his appetite though. It feels amazing to know he's on his way and I have to confess to having a tear in my eye to think that he will soon be with me and Sue at last.
Big love and καλό ταξίδι, Dave and Sue 😻xx.'

Lynda's Evening Update from the Thompson Pet Travel Facebook Page

'All passengers Present and Correct!!

We collected from Julie at Halkidiki 3 gorgeous little sibling pups - Coco, Bruno and Ziggy, dear little babies. Also little Rosie, she's very pretty, and such a tiny little girl. A little nervous but already she's wagging her tail as are the brothers! Lastly from Julie was sweet little blonde Hobi!

Then it was off to our final pick up at Olga's, it was so hot – 44 degrees so all the kids virtually had a complete bath with the sponge to make sure they didn't overheat! Although Easter actually needed a bath as she had been playing in a mud bath and it had all dried on her! We thought she was brown and white until she had a bath ... all the brown washed off!! 😁.

Crema was next on the bus, a little bit shy but she seemed perfectly happy to walk into her travel cage and settled down very quickly.

You can relax now Jean, Lotty is on the Freedom Bus!! She got a lovely cuddle from Olga and Alex who've been caring for her and then joined the crew!

Last but definitely not least, Jake, a beautiful Rottie who turned up in the street outside our friend Roula's house, he wasn't in great shape and I'm told he was being bullied by the cats! He cried when they came near him. So between Marina, Olga, Roula and Alexandra, he's been cared for and loved and is now in great shape! He's just as soft as he was when the cats scared him. He's a cuddly baby, full of love for everyone. Lucky boy 💚💚💚

Sorry to go on about the weather, BUT it hit 47 degrees about an hour and a half ago!!! A truck's cooling system blew up on the same road to Igoumenitsa that we're travelling. Stella's temperature did rise, too, but not to any dangerous level. We just kept our speed down so as not to put any extra pressure on her. That's the hottest I've ever seen it here so far. And it was 7 in the evening!

It's cooled down now to a balmy 41 😅. The kids are all fine, being kept nice and cool in the back, oblivious to just how hot it is outside. After their walk they're all either sleeping or just laying down. There's no noise at all! Ziggy was a little vocal for a while but he's fast asleep now too!!

We didn't take photos at Olga's it was too hot for the kids to be outside any longer than necessary to do their ablutions so we had to just focus on them and couldn't keep them outside longer than necessary, I have to say I did get very red faced myself so we went into the office where it was cool and they gave me and Frank some gorgeous, fresh and very cool watermelon ... that hit the spot!

So now we have about another hour and we'll be at the port waiting to board our midnight ferry to Italy.

It's great to have everyone aboard Stella Blue now, all safe and sound and sleepy ... lovely 🩶🩶🩶.

I posted a comment: 'Today has been a testament to your planning and your care and empathy for your passengers in really challenging conditions. Thank you. We're thinking about you every step of the way.'

The weather reports in the press for that day gave an indication of how extreme the conditions had been, thank goodness they had the new (and improved) air conditioning system up and running.

'One of Greece's most visited tourist destinations, the Acropolis, was closed in the afternoon due to rising temperatures. The country suffered intense heat on Thursday as temperatures exceeded 43 degrees Celsius (109 degrees Fahrenheit), the hottest of the year. Authorities warned the public to stay indoors if possible. People have been told to stay inside if possible while air conditioned halls have been made available to the homeless, elderly and other vulnerable sections of the population. In Athens, the Greek capital, a high concentration of north African dust turned the sky grey.'

Dave: 'Hi Trisha, they set off earlier this morning, so both boys are on the bus and have started their journey. Vincent is taking it all in his stride as you'd expect. Teddy's a bit scared of the travelling cage on the bus and is quite vocal, but he ate all his dinner which is a good sign. Lynda will keep reassuring and talking to him, so hopefully he'll settle down. I'm so glad to know they are finally on their way. I had a bumpy night last night thinking about them. I've got a tear in my eye myself this morning ... it's been such a long and arduous rollercoaster that I can hardly believe it's actually happening at last.

We're off to our local pet shop to stock up later on (they haven't seen us since February 2020 when we lost Simba). Then when we get home I'll put Teddy's cat tower together and begin distributing the many cat beds around the house. I think we'll keep the spare bedroom doors and dining room door closed for a few days so he isn't overwhelmed by too many new places in his new environment.'

Trisha: 'Ah, such good news. I thought Vincent would be more relaxed than Teddy. I am still amazed that other people managed to get their cats and dogs on board.' 🤔

Dave: 'Apart from fixing the air con they also installed new secondary fans so they can safely run the cooling system at night/when parked up, serendipity! It hit 47 degrees outside at one point so they've been careful not to push the bus too hard. The passengers are in the right place with their new air con working well.'

Trisha: 'Serendipity indeed! I have to collect the 4 kittens with the bad eyes this weekend, 3 of the blind kittens here now have homes lined up in Holland. Amazing no one else will help. Would you be willing to talk to Rachael who wants to adopt 4 of my cats? Thank goodness Evi of PAWS has said she will look after little Pompom if I sort out the Pet Passport and vaccinations for Paris, then Maria is coming back in 6 weeks when kitty is old enough and will take him in the cabin to Paris.'

Dave: 'I will certainly help if I can. It'll depend on the Ministry Vet.'

Trisha: 'Here is a ditty. I was doing the main house on my own for the philosophy client. I went to the work shop of an old boy who was a wrought iron railing maker. Yassas, I said, would you make some railings for my client. Oh yes, he said, and proudly showed me photocopies of his work. So we arranged to meet at 10 o'Clock at a local coffee shop on Saturday. It was Monday. On Saturday I went to the coffee shop and waited and waited. I called, but no answer. So I left. A week later I saw him working in the shop. Zzzzzip, zzzip, flash 💥

'Yassas, meh thimase (Hi, you remember me).'

'Nai kopela mou (Yes my girl).'

'You were supposed to meet me on Saturday.'

'Hmmm, yes,' he said,' but I retired on Friday...' 😂

Dave: 😂😂 'Fabulous ... essence of Greece!'

2.7.21

Lynda's Update from the Thompson Pet Travel Facebook Page

'Good afternoon from a sunny (still) Italy! Apologies for the delay with today's update! The kids had a lot of time off the bus today once we arrived at our first Italy walking area. Their walks yesterday were purely functional due to the extreme heat and they were glad to get back into the cool. Today it's hot, but normal hot, only 38 which feels just right ... 🤔 They really needed their time so we're behind our normal schedule but we have a contingency built in so we're fine for arrival time.

Teddy and Vincent on the Freedom Bus

The kids were fine this morning, even the pups had just had a pee in their cages! It took no more than 20 minutes to clean and change the few that needed it. We had no problems at all with customs, in fact it went better than usual and I have to say that our experiences with Italian customs are always positive. They're generally very relaxed and they chat to the kids when they inspect the van and are always nice to them. This time he asked us to open the door, I slid the side door open and he stood and looked at the dogs and looked up and down and round. Then he turned to us with that general Italian gesture, a circle made from thumb and forefinger and just said 'Very, very good'. We felt so proud, I know they face some real horrors at the conditions some 'transporters' have their dogs and cats in. He just seemed so pleased and the kids did an awful lot to influence that! They were laying down, front legs crossed in that classic Greekie way looking so chilled and relaxed. No one even barked at the stranger looking at them! Well done kids 💚💚💚.

I know everyone is keen to see the pics so I'll keep this short and post the pics first, then I can tell you a little more about each one of them later. But I can tell you that they're doing brilliantly well, not a sound is coming from the back as they're all sleeping very soundly after their walks and time out, it's done them all good.

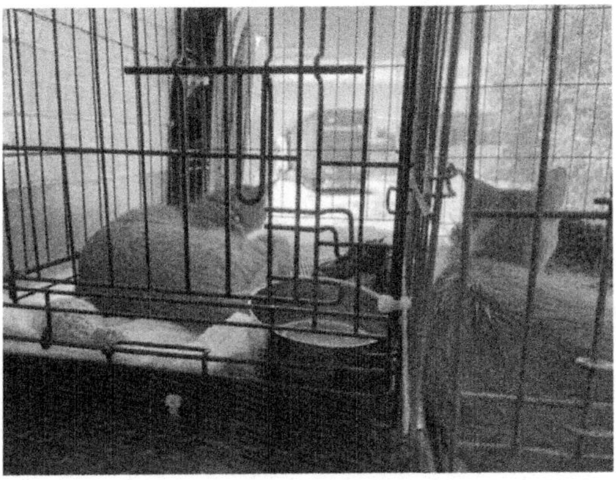

Teddy and Vincent in Italy

The kits of course can't come off but they're always at the back with the doors wide open so they can see out at least. Just before we were leaving a truck decided to park behind us which would have blocked their view, usually no one parks where we are because it's away from everything and isn't really a parking area for big vehicles. At least it was when we were done, but just when I was taking pics of the kits!

Last bit I have to tell you is about the mini tornado!! We felt such a jolt on the van 2 times really quickly then we saw it going across the field! Frank tells me it's called a 'Dirt Devil'. Then we saw another one but it was just starting. It was really high and it was spinning the dirt so fast. It must be to do with these extraordinary weather conditions ... never a dull moment on this bus!! 😂😂😂'

Sue posted a comment: 'Thank you Lynda for the pics and updates; cannot wait to meet Teddy (and Vincent) in 'Person' very soon.'

3.7.21
Lynda's Update from the Thompson Pet Travel Facebook Page
13:30 UK time

'Good morning! Only one more day to go before you meet your beautiful kids (and for Percy until you're reunited with your Mum who can't wait to see you again). They are so quiet and calm, Bruno sometimes has a little bark for 5 minutes when we set off again, either after the walks or in the morning, but he didn't bark at all this morning, there's not a peep from anyone right now, even Teddy, who does like to make his presence known! He's so funny, he talks to me 😺. He's in my direct line of sight when I turn around to ask him what he would like. He stops and then chatters on again looking at me all the time, he stops when I speak and then answers me (I wish I spoke cat 😸). He's so good now, he's mostly asking for affection, he purrs his little head off now that he's all relaxed. Lots of head bumping and cuddles, and his appetite is huge! He puts his paw through to Vincent's and tries really hard to actually scoop up a paw full of his food! He has breakfast and dinner and I swear he'd eat twice the amount if he could! Definitely a chilled boy now 😸. Vincent is also very chilled, purring, and loving attention, he's just quieter about it! He loves to watch everything that's going on in the bus, he's a thinker as well as a softy. Hermes the blind cat is struggling a little, it's really difficult for a completely blind dog or cat. They have no idea where they are, there are no familiar smells and the people they know are gone. They gave him his own toys and we put them on his bed with him but he's very quiet. He likes being stroked now, he wasn't too sure at first, understandably. But he's getting lots of reassurance and is slowly coming round. Hopefully he'll eat a little today. 🖤

The puppies are amazing little kids, they really can't walk on leads outside so they get the chance to run around free inside the van with pads covering the floor. They're quite happy then to do the necessary 😁😊. Ziggy is probably the most shy one, but he wags that little tail of his now when it's time to come out or it's dinner time! Rosie and Hobi are the most confident of them all, they're so full of fun and love a proper cuddle! Mind you they all really like a close in cuddle, it's really difficult for us to do this for them, I mean, spending all this time cuddling pups, having little puppy kisses on your nose smelling puppy breath (I love puppy breath) nibbling your earrings, yeah it's so tough it's just got to stop! 😂😂. So Ziggy, Bruno, Coco, Hobi, and Rosie ... just keep doing what you're doing, tomorrow you're going to cuddle with your real families, brings tears of joy to my eyes just thinking about it! As we only have one drop off point tomorrow, you can come earlier to collect your babies if you'd like to? You can come at 8.30, just let me know on this post if you're going to come at that time please 😊.

Easter is really strong on the lead when she first comes out! She's spotlessly clean inside so she generally needs a pee and a poo! Once she's done that it's a bit easier to ask her to stop and then walk again, if she pulls stop again and so on. She's just a very lively, curious full of life lovely kid 🖤. Her neighbour Crema (who I called Easter in the photos! 🙄) is also spotless inside, she's very calm and such a sweet and kind girl. Next door to Crema is lovely boy Jack K, he's so nice. Right now he has no idea that shelter life is over for him! He's no longer just one of hundreds of dogs. His behaviour is very typical of a long term shelter dog. He's quiet, he does exactly what we ask of him. He very calmly comes out for his walks, he does everything outside (yet another spotlessly clean kid) and when it's time to go back in he steps on the van and walks into his travel cage also very calmly. So many shelter dogs do this, it's like they've lost a little bit of themselves, so they just do what's asked of them, I think to myself that they're thinking 'ok, so this where I live now, I live on a van, people are nice to me, I get fed everyday ... that's ok I guess'. But Jack has no idea just how much his life is going to change!!! I wish I could tell him that he has a family now who will love and cherish him for the rest of his life. He's never going back to shelter life again!! Once he's got the hang of his new life being forever, he's going to be the happiest dog alive 😁🥰🥰🥰.

Believe it or not, I started this post at 10.30, but between driving and we've just finished another walk, that's about two and half hours and that was quite a quick one as we need to walk them again before the ferry AND try to get on the 19.50 one instead of the 21.20. But if we don't we don't, we'll still be there overnight ready for everyone (except Nancy who's going to collect Crema and Easter tonight hence we want to try for the earlier one) to meet your kids tomorrow morning. Liz, your 2 babies (Milly and Maple) are really coming out of their shells now. They're doing much better with their lead walking too! They're very loving, just like pointers and pointer mixes like these 2 are! I believe Milly is the mum of Maple? They're very different in colour but both have very similar personalities. Such sweet girls 💜.

Big Jakey, what can I say! He's truly the big soft bear that you both said Marina and Olga. What a gorgeous lad, and also as you said Olga, he doesn't even pull on the lead!! He's such a big strong Rottie, he could take me for a walk if he chose to, but he quite happily goes wherever you want him to. Great rescue girls, what a life he'll have now with you Karen!! 💜💜.

I'm going to post this now because I need to go in the back and let the pups have their crazy play (and poop) time on the floor. I'll post again a bit later with an update on the rest of these beauties!! Xxxxxx

Don't forget to let me know if you'd like to come at the earlier time? Just post it on this thread.' 💜

I posted a comment: 'We aim to be with you 8:30 – 9am Lynda. Thank you so much for the update on Teddy. It's such a joy to know he's happily chatting away (we need to brush up on our Greek cat speak). Great to hear that he has a healthy appetite, too. We went to our favourite old pet shop on Thursday and stocked up well, so he will eat like a king! We're getting the house ready for him and can't wait to lavish all our love on him.'

I updated Trisha and she sent me a photo.

Trisha: 'Giving them meds and cleaning eyes ... my husband helping. I have the 3 blind 🙀🙀🙀 and one that can see.'

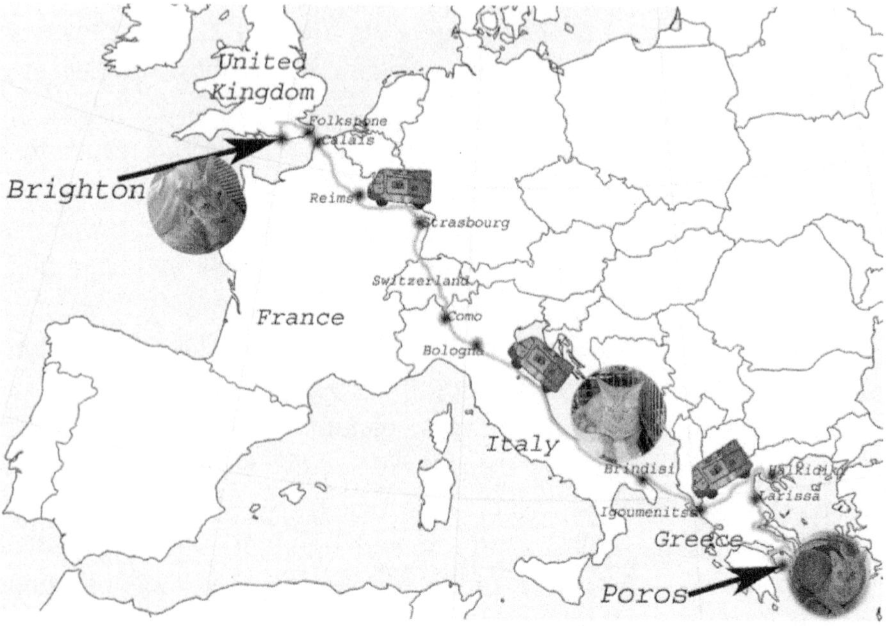

Chapter 14

Teddy's Independence Day

4th July 2021

I regard cats as one of the great joys in the world.
I see them as a gift of highest order:
Trisha McCagh

It felt like the night before Christmas, the night before going on holiday and the night before a music festival, all rolled into one. Just managing to sleep in between bursts of excitement. I woke up again around 6am, just as it started to pour with rain.

At 7:30 we were on our way, like the NASA recovery team heading to the astronauts' splashdown location.

Intermittent showers and fog on the way to the pick-up point didn't slow our progress too much and we arrived on time. We couldn't immediately see the Freedom bus, but Rachel sent us an aerial shot so we could spot it. Then I saw a familiar figure walking towards me across the car park: it was Martin who'd just arrived. So good to meet him for real and be able to update him on the whereabouts of the bus.

Lynda and Stella Blue, the Freedom Bus

It was lovely watching the other people meeting their new canine friends, especially the reaction of the puppies and dogs themselves and the look on the faces of those with children.

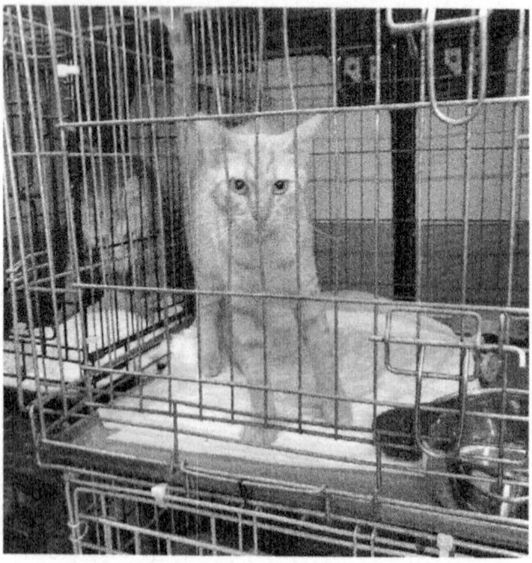

We jumped on the bus to meet Teddy and Vincent, taking turns in gently poking a finger through the crate bars and letting Teddy give them a good sniff before giving him a little tickle behind the ears. We had to hold back tears of joy at finally getting to meet him.

Dave and Martin

Vincent was transferred from the transport crate to his pet carrier while Sue took a photo of Martin and I together. He described his home and how it was a quiet area where Vincent would be able to sit and observe the world sliding by – Vincent loves sitting and watching, taking it all in. Martin had a fairly long return journey ahead of him so we bade farewell – such a charming fellow, Vincent would have a splendid life ahead.

Teddy, however, was less than keen to leave the bus. Frank and Lynda did their absolute best to get him from his crate into our carrier several times, but he wasn't having any of it. Probably due mainly to his dislike of cages, but also in part due to the design of our pet carrier. It was a plastic top-loader with a transparent front door, which had been perfect for our previous docile old boy (Simba), but Teddy had other ideas...

Eventually, when all the other dogs and Hermes (the blind cat) had set off on their onward journeys, we had to make a decision as to how we were going to get Teddy back with us to Brighton. Lynda and Frank, with their characteristic care, patience and understanding decided that the best (and only!) thing that would work would be for Teddy to stay in his metal animal crate for the homeward journey. Frank steadily undid the fixings and links on all the surrounding crates and carefully removed a couple so they could lift Teddy's straight out of the bus and into the boot of our car. We also draped one of our old blankets over the crate to lessen Teddy's stress. I fixed a couple of bunjee straps to prevent the crate from shifting around while driving and he was all aboard for the last leg of his epic journey. We thanked

Lynda and Frank profusely for their kindness, they are such amazing people. The animals in their care were all given individual attention and support throughout the long journey, completely safe and happy in their expert hands. We asked about returning the crate, but Lynda said they are always updating and replacing them and not to worry about getting it back to them. After all they had done for Teddy the least we could do was send them some money towards a replacement.

The journey back to Brighton was smooth and we carried Teddy in his crate into the kitchen and closed the inner door. We opened the door of the crate while Teddy sat in the far back corner and eyed us suspiciously. After about 30 minutes he cautiously made his way out of it, but then whizzed under the kitchen table and on top of the radiator where he sat hunkered down for the next hour or so.

I sent a message to Lynda and Frank, thanking them again for being superstars. I commented on how joyful it was watching the new owners meeting their new furry friends; Percy the pug even did a little dance on his hind legs at his reunion.

I also let Trisha know about the day's events and that all was well.

Trisha: 'What a palaver. Teddy hated the cages. Did he have his collar? Great photo of you and Martin, so glad you got to meet. Love the T-shirt.'

Dave: 'No sign of his collar, it's a shame after you preparing it so beautifully, but most importantly he's home now and won't be going out for a while: we do have a spare new collar. I'm currently out the front wrestling the cage into wheelie bin liners to keep it dry and then I'll put a message out on the local animal charity sites to see if they could use it. Sue's in the kitchen trying to entice Teddy off the radiator with *Dreamies*. Vincent is currently hiding behind Martin's sofa.'

Later on Martin sent a photo of Vincent exploring his new territory and also commented: 'Percy the pug was a joy to behold.'

Later that evening Teddy left his post on the radiator and found his way up onto the top of our fridge/freezer where he kept an eye, allowing the occasional tickle and lots of encouraging noises from us. We let him be for a while and went into the living room to have a sandwich. About half an hour later there was a metallic crash from the kitchen. Sue went to investigate. The lid of the stainless steel butter dish was on the floor and Teddy was under the table looking all innocent, whilst licking his paws. Whether you believe the old saying or not, he had effectively "buttered his own paws". He had come down from the fridge and had a good old tuck in to the food we'd put out for him. He spent the next few hours stretched out on the kitchen floor purring contentedly.

Teddy on top of the fridge

That night as checked on him again and he was curled up in his new pyramid cat cave under the kitchen table, full of food and finally the adrenaline of the past few days was subsiding enough to let him get some sleep.

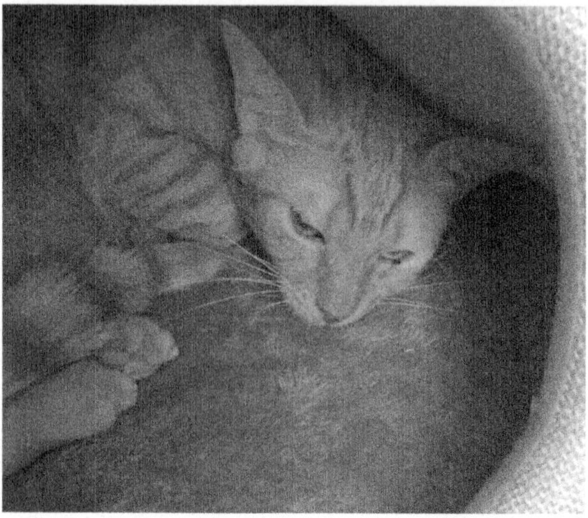

Cats gravitate to kitchens like rocks gravitate to gravity: Terry Pratchett

Chapter 15

Settling In

July 2021

I have been told that the training procedure with cats was difficult. It's not. Mine had me trained in two days: Bill Dana

5.7.21

Dave: 'Teddy is eating like a king! He's Just tucking into some more "Teddy Brek" having made ample use of his litter tray.' 😹❣❣❣

Trisha: 'Ha-ha. Thought the litter trays weren't so full.'😂

I sent Trisha a little video of Teddy, as his purr was reinstated, and she forwarded it to Rebecca.

Rebecca: 'THAT HAS MADE MY DAY😻💕. Just absolutely fabulous!! From Dustbin to Coastal Resort UK 🇬🇧 and the purr is even louder, just great to see, thank you. Watched the video five times already! Xxx'

Trisha: 'Rebecca is here, back on Poros, thank goodness.'

Much of Teddy's day was spent dozing on top of the fridge freezer, offering a good view of proceedings in the kitchen.

The plan was to use a sort of feline advent calendar, introducing him to one new room every few days as he gradually became familiar with his territory.

So, on his second evening, fuelled up on half a pouch of chicken and turkey dinner and lots of stroking and tickles, his first door-opening revealed the hallway and stairs. With very tentative, wide-eyed, cautious exploration he made a few brief sorties from the safety of the kitchen along the hallway and back again. With a sudden burst of confidence he set off up the stairs like "Sherpurr" Tenzing, letting us know his progress with plenty of meowing and vocal commentary.

Back in the kitchen (having conquered the northern slopes of Burnham mansions), there was a good run all the way from the kitchen right down the hallway after a mouse toy and we got to see his Usain Bolt impersonation. A quick drink of water was followed by a thorough and lengthy wash, supper, and a long sleep.

Martin and Vincent

I sent Martin some photos and asked how Vincent was getting on. The picture he sent back said it all.

6.7.21

First Teddy Brek at 6am, second at 9, followed by a game of ping pong football with some skilful returns and catches. A headlong leap into his cat cave, a big meow ... and weee ... his hitherto untouched catnip toy flew out of the entrance swiftly followed by a ginger blur. Listening to Ken Bruce's Pop Master on the radio we hoped for some Greek-themed questions about Vangelis, Nana Mouskouri or Cat Stevens that Teddy could help us with. Another little explore of the hallways and then up onto the corner of the worksurface where he sat and looked up for a while, thoughtfully. He stood on his hind legs, reached up with his left paw, and rested it on the photograph of our previous cat, Simba: it was almost like he was paying his respects, but more likely just wondering who this other cat was. Then another long snooze through the afternoon.

Kitty TV (the washing machine) and on his way to investigate the shelves

An early evening snack and then he was agog at kitty tv, aka the washing machine, followed by advent door no. 2: the living room. Teddy strolled across the mantlepiece above the fireplace and sniffed at the flowers before leaping up to the top shelf in the corner with the ease of an Olympian and began testing various ornaments for their response to the forces of gravity ... so we did some hasty rearranging and a bit of packing things away in bubble wrap.

Freshly-grown cat grass was deployed and nibbled on immediately. Nooks, crannies, shelves all given the once over, with the hilariously-predictable exception of the newly-installed cat activity tower. However, back in the kitchen he tried out a big, soft cat bed for the first time and was soon fast asleep, upside down, looking as comfy as it's possible to be.

Trisha: 'Is Sue relieved now that Teddy finally got home?'

Dave: 'Hugely so! There can be no lovelier thing in this world than winning the trust of a little animal. We opened the door to the living room for him to explore this evening – then packed the more delicate ornaments away in bubble wrap 😂. He's checking out every square inch! Although, the one thing he hasn't investigated yet is the cat activity tower.' 😂

Trisha: 'Teddy is one lucky kitty to have you as his parents. Rebecca is nearly in tears. If you had seen him up the mountain so frightened and trying to eat an old dry bone. Rebecca is now scared to cycle up there in case there is another, but unfortunately we can only do what we can.'

Dave: 'It's so hard isn't it? Many a time we'd wished we could take a Greek kitty home from our holidays ... now we have the perfect Greek Ambassador. Our training is coming along nicely: we should make highly-acceptable staff.' 😂

Trisha: 'I think you should have an honours degree🥈🏆 in Greek cat adoption, after all Martin would never have adopted Vincent without you.'

7.7.21
While Teddy was happily watching various Brighton types mooch past on the street outside and with Martin's Apostille finally arriving in the post, I caught up with some messages I'd been meaning to send.

Watching Brighton life outside

Dave: 'Hi Robert and Brenda,

Thank you so much again for your wonderful help in getting the boys all the way to the drop off point. Teddy is home with us and Vincent is home with Martin. We collected them on Sunday. Teddy is gradually settling in and catching up on sleep. Vincent had his paws up on Martin's sofa in no time😻. Love to both and if I get that book written I'll try to get a copy to you. Dave and Sue Xx'

Robert: 'Hi Dave and Sue.

It was a pleasure to help. I saw the photo of Vincent, the journey clearly wasn't too traumatic for him. I hope Teddy enjoys his new home and thank you to you for adopting him. If you are ever in this neck of the woods you are welcome to visit. Robert and Brenda.'

*****

Dave to the Ministry Vet:

'Please find attached the Adoption Papers and Apostille for Martin and his cat Vincent, as requested. Sorry for the delay.

Thank you so much for your excellent help with the Health Certificates for Vincent and Teddy.

Both cats had a good journey from Greece to England and are in very good health, enjoying their new lives in their new homes.

We will always be very grateful to you and your team for your kind assistance in making it possible for them to come to us.

Best Regards

David Burnham'

Ministry Vet:

'Thank you dear sir. The documents are complete now.

I hope you have a nice time with your new company.

Best regards'

10.7.21

Today was Teddy's 1st Birthday (or thereabouts).

We sang him 'Happy Birthday' with a candle on a tin of special fishy treat, which he polished off in one go.

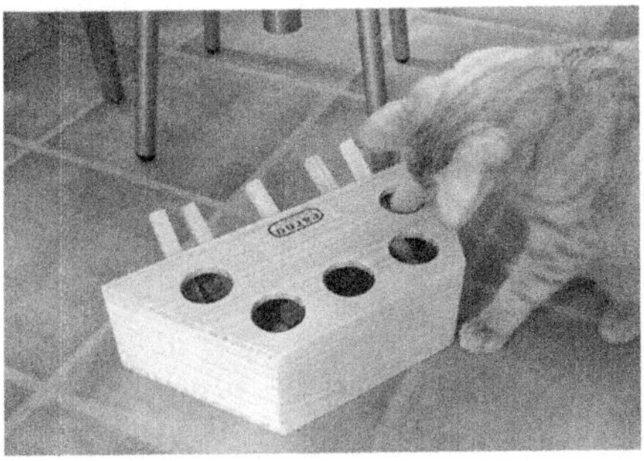

Presents of a new wooden, pop-up, Whack-A-Mouse toy and new raised, tilted cat bowls met with approval.

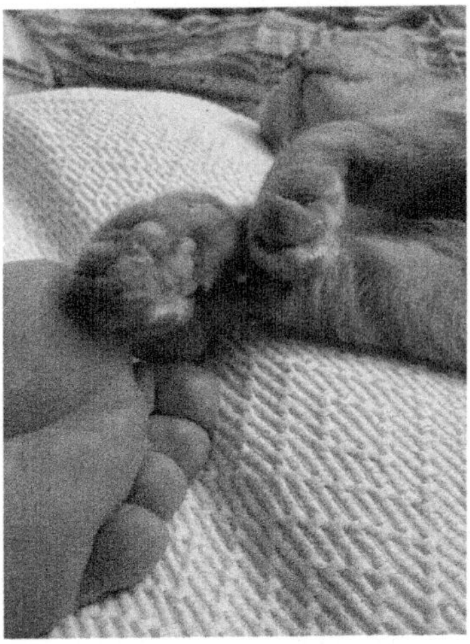

"Mixed Beans"

After a busy day of games, treats and tickles we settled down on the sofa to put our feet/paws up in a bunch of 'mixed beans.'

11.7.21

By the following Sunday, one week on from being a frightened little soul hiding on top of the kitchen radiator he was a happy boy, curled up between us on the sofa. I lifted his bowl up and popped a handful of crunchies into it, as I started to bend down again, he stood on his hind legs like a meerkat, reached up to place a paw on my hand and gently guided the bowl down to his food area.

A local cat charity called Kitty in the City Cat Rescue provides a warm refuge for street cats and they were delighted to receive the cat crate as a gift.

In the strange way that things sometimes come full circle. I got talking to a new carer at my mother's nursing home. It turned out she was from Greece, not only that, but her grandmother is from Poros where Teddy is from and her grandfather is from the nearby town of Galatas on the mainland: it's a small world.

Our training was coming along nicely ... as his ever-willing, ever-loving staff: no need for a kitty white board and marker pens or a PurrPoint presentation.

Cats are connoisseurs of comfort: James Herriot

Teddy

Chasing the Gods
Up on Mount Olympus
Defying the odds
Out for the count
Ginger furry shrimp puss

Tiny teeth and just a bone
His hourglass running out of sand
Only heath to call a home
Rescued by an outstretched hand

From shrimp to prawn
A saint his loving nurse
His spark reborn
From faint to constant purrs

An epic journey awaits
You're really not sure of the dates
The second hand dances
The minute hand strolls
The hour hand glances
And the calendar rolls

Our country escaped imagined locks
As we battled with bureaucratese
Releasing monsters from Pandora's Box
To dot the i's and cross the t's

With the wheels back on your destiny
Your lucky star to riches from rags
The look on your face would suggest to me
The time had come to pack your bags

You travelled on Stella Blue
Passenger on the Freedom Bus
Driven by the greatest crew
They brought you home to us

(Dave Burnham 2021)

Chapter 16

Ticket to Ride

(The other passengers on Teddy's journey on board the Freedom Bus)

"Meow" means "woof" in cat: George Carlin

I put a post on the Thompson Pet Travel Facebook page to see if the owners of any of Teddy and Vincent's fellow passengers on the Freedom Bus would like to tell their own pets' stories and I had some lovely responses.

Hobi

We are huge dog lovers and used to have two wonderful cross-terrier rescues, pre-children, called Brandy and Pebbles. We rescued them from the Bermuda RSPCA and they were our pride and joy! I could tell you some stories of their adventures, but perhaps another time! We lost Pebbles to diabetes at the age of 15, soon after the birth of our second child. She was a wonderful bouncy dog, part Australian cattle dog, part terrier. We miss her even now. In 2007 we returned to the UK with our two young children and Brandy came with us and had to quarantine for 3 months. That was very tough. When we finally got him, we were all absolutely overjoyed! He didn't like the UK as much as Bermuda (I wonder why!) but was happy to live out the rest of his life here with us until he turned 17 and his organs started to shut down. Parting with him was the hardest thing we have ever been through. He was such a special dog and we loved him completely.

We couldn't bring ourselves to adopt another dog at that point, but the house was so empty without animals, we gave in to our children who were desperate for kittens and adopted Boris and Sacha from the RSPCA. Little did we know how much we would adore them! Boris is a beautiful ginger who is now a senior citizen, and Sacha was our beautiful black tabby. A few years ago we also adopted Minx a white tabby from Cats Protection. Two years ago we lost our precious Sacha to oral cancer which was sudden and terrible, but fortunately we still have Boris and Minx.

We have always wanted another dog but our busy lives wouldn't allow for it with young children, busy jobs and cats. Life with cats just worked better, although we so missed the love of a dog and the wonderful walking adventures. Fast forward to two years ago and the start of lockdown. Husband's job became a permanent work-from-home and we had had our names down at numerous shelters in the UK but to no avail. Unfortunately as soon as you mention 'cats' you are not eligible for many adoptees. We were all becoming very despondent.

Then one evening this last May we were taking a walk along Shoreham Beach when we met the most STUNNING dog called Dahlia – a kind of white setter/hound with the softest face imaginable. Chatting to her owner he told us they had just got her from a wonderful organisation called CARAT run by an amazing lady by the name of Linda Titchbird. Well you don't forget a name like that, so when we got home I googled Carat and filled out an adoption application immediately. Very quickly Linda got in touch and said she would like to do a home visit on Saturday. The whole family was beyond excited! Saturday finally came and we had a lovely visit and Linda showed us pictures of three possible gorgeous Greek doggies. All quite young. Two were larger and beautiful, and there was also a little fluffy puppy. Linda gave us the backgrounds of all three doggies and lots of pictures, then left us to have a big think. Well it didn't take us long to decide that our two kitties were more likely to accept a pup and, with the summer holidays approaching, with the time on our hands to train a pup we chose the little fluffy cloud and named him Hobi.

We only waited about a month for Hobi's arrival, and Linda and Julie from Hal shelter sent us regular updates and pictures of him during that time. We started to talk to his sister Rosie's owners on Whatsapp, too, along with some of the other 'puppy parents'. Linda was amazing at preparing us all for the new arrivals. Such practical and wonderful advice, along with reality checks along the way. It was brilliant to be able to talk together and discuss any concerns or questions we all had. Linda always had answers and we learned so much about Greek pups and what to expect – it was a real education.

So finally the day of departure came. Such excitement! And then delay due to poor Lynda and Frank's van needing a new air conditioning unit. Lucky that was done though, as they had such a long and very hot journey ahead of them, in record breaking temperatures! I can't begin to tell you how amazing Lynda and Frank were with their updates and pictures for all of us anxious puppy parents. She called them 'the kids' and spoke with such affection for them all, it was clear that they were being so well loved and cared for the whole way.

Then at last, SUNDAY MORNING arrived! We were up and out! On the journey we got a quick text from Linda saying that Hobi and Rosie had runny tummies! When we arrived at Cobham Services we saw the van quickly and drove up. As we got out of the car, we could hear some sad cries – it was Hobi, sad because Rosie had been taken out of the van! Poor Hobi! And then poor Frank having to clean out Hobi's crate again!

Then very soon after, Hobi appeared first with Lynda (See pic) then with Linda who brought him over to us. What a fluffy blonde ball of cuteness he was to behold! He didn't know what to make of the grass but it smelt really good. Then we held him and he snuggled right into my neck. The journey home in the car he settled right between Sam and Leah and was calm and happy as anything! He has been a joy ever since. He LOVES the beach, people, children, the car, comes when he's called, sits and stays to order, sleeps all through the night, doesn't shed, doesn't even chase the cats! Quite honestly Hobi is the best dog in the world and we have only had him for three weeks. He's made so many lovely doggie friends already and we can't imagine life without him.

Our thanks go to everyone who has made it possible for us to adopt him. You are all amazing and your work and dedication for rescuing these animals is incredible. I look forward to reading all about Teddy's story and the other special little passengers too! We wish you the happiest of lives!

Written by Gaynor – 27.7.2021

Lucy's Story

They say that life is a rollercoaster and it has been for me, and I am still only 17 months old.

There was I being good, doing what puppies do, on Crete my island of birth, when suddenly, I found myself in a car and then being thrown out of the car door onto the roadside, abandoned to fend for myself. I don't know what I did wrong, however, in a moment, my life was turned upside down.

Fortunately for me the car behind was being driven by a woman called Camelia, with a connection to Greek Animal Rescue. I was lucky as she almost ran me over! Fortunately, she stopped, picked me up and took me to the vets for a check-up.

I was then fostered for 4 months by another kind woman called Niki and I lived in her house with her dogs.

Then, one day out of the blue, I was off on my travels again, however this time not in a car to be abandoned, but to hitch a ride with other dogs and cats on what I was to find out was called The Freedom Bus.

Unbeknown to me I was heading on a journey to my forever home in a country called England. Whilst a little nervous to start off with I soon got use to my accommodation on the bus and I was fed, watered and walked regularly as I made my way from Greece, overland through Europe to England.

Lynda and Frank of Thompson Pet Travel were really kind to me and my fellow furry travelling companions, who I got along with really well. We had regular stops to stretch our legs and relieve ourselves, together with fresh food and water along the way. There was also air-conditioning in the Freedom Bus to keep us all cool.

Thompson Pet Travel also provided updates and photos to my new family as we travelled across Europe, which they loved.

On the evening of Saturday 3rd July 2021 after crossing the English Channel on a ferry, The Freedom Bus arrived at the Services on the M25.

We had an overnight stay before meeting our new families for the first time the following morning. We were all getting really excited and found it difficult to sleep that night.

Where would our new homes be? What would our new families be like? Would there be other furballs in our new homes? What would our walks be like? So many questions, which would soon be answered.

At 8 am on the morning of Sunday 4th July, my new family arrived, who I was later to find out were called Belinda and Nick.

Belinda and Nick walked me around the grassy area near the Freedom Bus, along with my other canine travelling companions, so we could get to know each other. They seemed OK to me and I was sure that they liked me.

After a while, it was time to say goodbye to my Freedom Bus friends and I headed off to Belinda and Nick's car for the final leg of my journey to my forever home. Belinda knew I was a bit nervous of cars, so she sat beside me in the back all the way. She even gave me some treats.

2 hours later and I was in Bournemouth. I went inside my new home and met Olive The Cat. She told me that she was in charge, however that was OK as she has been there for 14 years. She said that if I was good and didn't chase her, that we would become friends quite quickly, so I made sure that I was good and not too bouncy around her.

After 3 days with my new family, I overheard them saying that they were going to adopt me. Woo hoo, amazing, fantastic, woof woof, waggy tail, as I love my new home.

Anyway, I cannot believe it has not even been a month since I moved in, it has just been the best month of my life. I get to play in the garden and I have been bought lots of new toys, my favourite being Pig who I throw all over the place.

I have a few daily walks with both Belinda and Nick separately, however we also all go out together regularly. On my daily walks I meet other dogs who I am becoming friends with and also meeting lots of people who think that I am lovely.

It is incredible, I have been to the beach a few times already. Bournemouth has a huge sandy beach and I run around, albeit on a training lead as I need to learn recall. I dig holes in the sand, chase other dogs and if I am feeling brave, dip my toes into the sea.

We also go to the countryside and walk through the forest and by the river.

In the evening, I settle down in my lovely snuggly bed, with my toys and Belinda puts on the radio on low volume for me and I sleep downstairs, to allow Olive her night-time space upstairs.

I have met Belinda and Nick's grandchildren Jake and Erin, and they love me and I love them.

Belinda and Nick cannot believe how good I am and I have been to the pub, a restaurant and café with them and have been no trouble at all.

All in all the last month has been amazing and I cannot wait to see what other adventures I go on with Nick and Belinda. I heard them saying about going away and staying in a dog friendly hotel at some point... I cannot wait.

I keep wagging my tail in disbelief that all this has happened to me in such a short space of time.

So, a huge thank you to Camelia, who found me. To Niki, who fostered me. To Donna for putting Belinda and Nick in contact with Greek Animal Rescue. To Gillian who suggested I would be good for Belinda and Nick and finally to Lynda and Frank of Thompson Pet Travel for getting me to England.

I hope that my furry travelling companions have had as good a start in their forever homes as I have in mine.

Lots of love and tail wags, Lucy x

(Written by Nick Fewings: 26.7.2021)

Diego (formerly Robbie)

Hi Dave!

Robbie (now, Diego) was one of the puppies from Betsy, the "mama in chains" who was found on a farm on Crete island, she was chained up with no food and dirty water. Robbie, along with his two siblings were found ridden with ticks and a belly full of worms. Thankfully the volunteer who found them convinced the farmer to let Betsy and her puppies go, he was reluctant to let them leave as he had used Betsy as a doorbell for nearly 8 years. Both Robbie and Betsy were lucky to be adopted in the UK. However his two siblings (GiGi and William) are still in a shelter in Athens looking for homes.

He's absolutely thriving now and loving his new life ♥ we feel so lucky to have such a sweet, friendly and clever little Greekie

Written by Hanna

Percy

We went to Greece for 3 days in August (Sifnos and Crete) and we are now back in London. Percy is coming back with Thompson on Saturday. Poros is really nice and close to Athens too. So about Percy's trip in June and July: We took Percy to Athens with the plane on the 3rd of June and he came back to London with Thompson on the 4th of July. His overall trip with Lynda and Frank was very pleasant and Percy was really happy when he saw us. Lynda was regularly posting updates and photos on Facebook of all the passengers (cats and dogs) with a unique description on each one of them. Even when I was a bit worried that Percy looked unhappy (he always has this face) I was texting Rachel and she was providing me with updates and extra photos. They were really looking after the dogs and cats and Percy seemed to get along really well with the rest of them as well as Lynda and Frank.

Percy is coming back with them again this Saturday and I am sure he will have a great experience again. 🙂

Written by Sofia

The Halkidiki Pups: Ziggy, Bruno, Coco, Rosie and Hobi

Hi Dave,

The story of the 5 Halkidiki pups on the van.....

An emaciated and exhausted young female hunting dog, barely more than a puppy herself, arrived on the front steps of a house in Halkidiki one night, where she laid down and gave birth to 3 little puppies, later to be called Ziggy, Bruno and Coco. When the homeowner came out in the morning she found mum and pups and called Julie Tsiakmakis, a Geordie lass who has run Halkidiki Animal Rescue for more than 20 years. Julie immediately came to the home to see the little family. Of course, new born puppies cannot be brought into a dog shelter for fear of disease, so the householder kindly agreed to feed the mother dog and keep her safe until the puppies were old enough to be vaccinated. Julie provided quality food for the mother dog and left her in the care of the householder.

'Mother Theresa' with the pups and Bruno on the right

Coco and Ziggy

A short while later, Julie had just made another of her regular visits to the mum and pups when she found another puppy, only a few days old but left behind by her feral mother who had moved on with her other pups. As the young mother of the pups was recovering well and putting on weight she took the abandoned puppy back to the house and introduced her to the mother dog, who immediately adopted the orphaned puppy as one of her own.

Once the puppies were old enough to have their puppy parvo vaccination they were moved with their mum to a quarantine room of their own at the shelter that Julie runs. Only a few days later Julie found 4 newborn hunting dog puppies dumped on the mountain in a plastic bag, so she brought these puppies back to the shelter, too, and introduced them to the mother dog....who again took the puppies as her own straight away, bless her soul! From then on we called her Mother Theresa....

These are the 4 pups Theresa took on after they were found dumped in a plastic bag on the mountain.....and the BIG pup in the background is the little white orphan!!

In the village below Julie's house live an elderly couple who keep their pair of small dogs in appalling conditions. Left in an exposed outside pen with little or no shelter, the dogs desperately crave a kind word or a caress. Julie had tried for years to convince the couple to allow her to sterilise the dogs to spare them from an endless cycle of breeding, but they enjoyed giving their unwanted puppies to their friends as gifts and refused. Naturally, after giving away so many puppies twice a year they eventually ran out of friends to give them to and asked Julie to take the two remaining puppies from the most recent litter which they were unable to give away, so she agreed but only on condition that the female dog was sterilised. So....as you might have already guessed....two more little lost souls, Hobi and Rosie, came to join Mother Theresa's ever-expanding brood!

Hobi and Rosie

Our charity, Caring for the Animals Trust (CARAT) has supported Julie since soon after she established her shelter. Once the puppies were old enough to begin their passport preparations we advertised them for new homes in the UK. Of course, such cute and friendly little bundles were snapped up by the first suitable families that we home-checked ... and were lucky enough to share their journey on the Freedom Bus with Teddy! Since arriving in the UK the pups have met up with their friends again for playtimes.

Bruno

Coco

Ziggy

Rosie

Hobi

Mother Theresa

And Mother Theresa has found a wonderful home with a family in Germany ... where she will never have to raise a puppy again! We think she really earned her early retirement...

Kisses to Teddy!

Kind regards,

Linda: 27.7.2021

Vincent

Most of Vincent's story has been told in conjunction with Teddy's, but I thought you might like to see a photo of Vincent as a tiny kitten and also the ginger Tom who is thought to be Vincent's Dad. The other photo is Vincent at home in Martin's house in late July 2021.

Vincent on the left of the three kittens "Probably" Vincent's Dad on the right

Vincent in his new home

Part Two

Other Greek Tales

Chapter 17

Skiathos

(1997/1998)

It takes a lifetime to discover Greece,
but it only takes an instant to fall in love with her:
Henry Miller

The first holiday Sue and I took together to Greece was to the Island of Skiathos. Our arrival in a new country was exciting in itself, but the approach to the island's airport was nothing short of dramatic. It has pretty rugged terrain so a sufficiently flat area was created by reclaiming land between Skiathos and a small adjacent island. Planes fly really low to approach the airport - effectively at sea level - giving passengers a spectacular view, followed by some pretty serious reverse thrust and braking on landing to deal with the comparatively short runway. Needless to say, and as cliched as it seems, as the plane came to a halt and turned to taxi away from the impressively adjacent sea, everyone in the cabin broke into spontaneous applause.

Arriving in Koukounaries we were greeted by beautiful pine trees on the hills (the bay of the Stone Pines giving the village its name), a long, golden crescent of sandy beach adjacent to a lagoon and the scent of the pines and mountain thyme in the air. The small road to our studio was lined with lovely oleander and bamboo rustling in the breeze and our first floor wooden balcony overlooked a grove of olives and figs. (It was the first time I'd witnessed a saw being used for pruning huge, prickly, thick-leaved palms, but it made perfect sense.)

Sitting in a taverna that evening eating wonderful Greek food in a delightfully ambient temperature, under a stunning moon, with gentle chatter and happy laughter around us and the beguiling stridulation of the cicadas, it already felt like we'd come home.

The next day about lunchtime we had one of those *meet and greets* with the travel rep'. She was a cheery young Welsh girl who welcomed us to 'Koo-koo-narry-ess', taught us a few words (eff-harry-stow, yassas and yammas) and brought round a choice of orange juice or wine while she went through the trips and outings on offer.

Later that afternoon, while on Koukounaries beach, we became aware of a voice calling from some distance away. As he got closer we could see an elderly gentleman trudging along the sand with a large cool box and several bags, calling out 'Plum', with increasing desperation. We waved at him and were presented with a substantial bag of plums (a bargain and paid for in drachmas in those days). They were absolutely lovely and probably from his own garden. A few hours later a different voice approached, this time a younger chap on a well-laden donkey selling pastries and donuts. We wondered if he might be "Donut, Son of Plum" as he trotted down the beach like a baker on his way to a quoits convention. When we got back to our studio I noticed a clicking noise from underneath my flip flops, which turned out to be a seed from one of the pines. Like a nail, it had embedded itself so firmly in the rubber it took some effort to extract it with my Swiss Army knife: thank goodness I hadn't gone barefoot until I'd reached the beach itself.

Having a proper chillout for the first few days we explored some of the other local beaches (Skiathos has over 60 around her coast). Krassa beach just across the headland had some impressive rock formations. There are effectively two beaches in this area also known as "Big Banana" and "Little Banana" beach. Originally named after the crescent-shaped sweeps of sand, Little Banana took on a different meaning as we swapped beaches in the late afternoon. We've nothing against naturism, but in those days at that time of year it seemed to attract a relatively elderly, quite portly, clientele who took great pleasure in parading up and down the shoreline, or else basking on the rocks like crinkly lizard people. Suppressing our giggles, we imagined they probably thought they looked like Greek gods (possibly true, but it would be Silenus in their case). I believe the beach has sunbeds on it these days, so enjoyment of the sun probably has a less exhibitionist quality.

Following a tip from one of the neighbours at our studio we found a small, quiet little beach below an inactive/derelict hotel. That was a glorious four or five hours and as the sun's strength subsided I tried a little, modest disposal of the swimming trunks myself. I took care not to overdo it in areas that rarely saw the light of day, but I have to say (in the immortal words of Steve Martin in *The Man with Two Brains*) 'The breeze felt good!'.

I think it was Vangelis, manager of Stamelos taverna, who told us about Mandraki beach. Vangelis was a charming fellow who was really accommodating when we explained we were mostly vegetarian, taking us into the kitchen and proudly displaying the range of options available to us. We returned there regularly both years we stayed on Skiathos and were always met with the same warm welcome and managed to learn some more new Greek words. He'd begun the enterprise in the late 1970s, building a bar around the trunk of a tree; 20 years later it was a splendid, thriving taverna also offering some accommodation. Anyway, he told us that Mandraki was his favourite beach and we could find a path at the edge of the lagoon which would take us on a 20-30 minute walk through a pine forest to reach the beach. It was a glorious walk, peaceful, pine-scented and blessed with birdsong and considerately-signposted at various points. As we exited a small clearing we passed through some lovely sand dunes to find a fabulous bay and unspoiled beach spread out in front of us, flanked by rocky promontories, waves gently lapping at the shoreline. Amazingly we had it to ourselves!

Walking along we found a rudimentary wooden/bamboo construction and a fabulous sculpture built from flotsam and jetsam. We later discovered that the beach had long been a favourite with the hippy community and the alternative vibe had carried on. The sculpture had a sign announcing it as the "Blue Man of Mandraki" and Sue sat in front of it for a photo.

I had started writing my novel, *Flux*, so I plonked myself in the doorway of the makeshift cabin and got scribbling – the photo borrows something from Robinson Crusoe. We'd bought a frisbee in a local mini-market and played with it in the sea until, during one enthusiastic leap, my beach shorts were tugged off having filled with water: that, and the occasional inquisitive small fish finding its way inside, led me to favour speedos for years afterwards.

We had a day trip to Skopelos and Alonnisos in 1997. Entering the town bay at Skopelos was fabulous. Houses skirted the semicircle of the harbour and clambered up the hillside in amphitheatrical tiers, thinning out towards the summit crowned with trees. We had a few hours to explore and it was captivatingly photogenic, including meeting some beautiful cats. Sitting in one of the harbourside tavernas, a combination of the crystal clear waters around Skopelos, watching the fishermen unload their catch and the smells coming from the kitchen, was the moment when several years of vegetarianism slipped ... a plate of superb calamari marked our rebranding as "pescatarians". I don't know what impact the success of the film Mamma Mia had on Skopelos, but hopefully the island has retained the charm we encountered.

Alonnisos was a much quieter, sleepier place. Very charming in its own right and our first experience of what Greek island life must have been like before the advent of mass tourism. We didn't have long to explore, but the traditional stores and buildings (those that had survived an earthquake in the mid-1960s) exuded a tremendous depth of charm and tranquillity. We ate lunch at a small traditional kefenion and the owner wrote the bill in pencil on the paper table cover. This island also gave us our first sighting of one of the extraordinary agricultural transport vehicles that we've since spotted in many parts of Greece, we've heard of them being referred to as "Makanaki", but also as "Trikykla" or tricycles. There were a large number of cats around as well; some in better health than others ...

In 1998 we had a day's outing on a boat from the jetty in Koukounaries. It took us to Lalaria beach, which is only accessible by boat and without beach shoes we braced ourselves to walk over the stony beach, but it was well worth it to see the eroded archway and imposing cliffs. As we reached the Northern tip of Skiathos we could see the remnants of a medieval site high up on the rock. The Kastro had been the main settlement of the island for some 500 years – which is often the case for these naturally secure positions on the Greek islands.

Our studio in Koukounaries had a wood-clad interior and the aforementioned balcony. The shower was "characterful" and about halfway through our second holiday there (incredibly we were allocated the same room!) the shower hose fell apart in my hands. I was going to report it to the holiday rep', but she wasn't about and we were heading into town that morning. While pottering about the backstreets we came across one of those general purpose stores selling just about everything and I picked up a replacement for a handful of drachmas. It was easy to fit; I never bothered to mention it, seemed like a friendly thing to do.

Most evenings we'd sit on the balcony with a glass or two of wine or ouzo (my new favourite drink) before venturing out for dinner, usually playing a few games of backgammon. Once in a while an overly-enthusiastic throw of the dice would see one of them bounce through the railings onto the tiled roof jutting out above the ground-floor studios. The odd collection of kitchen utensils in the studio included a fish slice, which proved just the job for recovering the escapee die. We also had the odd visitor, such as a large, black, flying, wasp-like insect with a pair of long sacs dangling on cords either side of its abdomen: I've no idea what it was, but we nicknamed it the "Bolas Wasp" after the Gauchos boleadora lasso. We got chatting with a new neighbour, John, a retired policeman on a solo trip as his wife didn't like the Greek heat. He was good company and we'd often share an ouzo or two with him in the evening. However, his very generous measures of the tipple resulted in us not actually making it out for dinner once, although there were snacks in the room to nibble on so hunger was averted. Our breakfast entertainment was provided by the arrival of a chef gathering figs from the tree in the grove below on a more-or-less daily basis. He was always dressed in full whites that only just stretched around his generous midriff, with his huge black moustache quivering as he filled his wicker basket with the fruits of his labour. As the days rolled by his quarry became increasingly challenging to gather. We assumed he must have been doing this for years and the passage of time was steadily raising the odds. On our final morning he was clambering up into the branches as they creaked and groaned like the mast of a tall ship, edging his way out to the furthest limbs, gasping and puffing as he plucked at the remaining fruit whilst avoiding plummeting to the ground.

The local bus into town pretty much started at Koukounaries, but by the time it reached the main town, and the end of the route, it was stuffed full to bursting. Somehow, on most journeys a little boy managed to play his accordion, rattling a polystyrene cup for loose change.

The Chora had charming old backstreets to explore and the more cosmopolitan harbourfront where taverna owners would try to inveigle you in. Papadiamantis Street ran right through the centre with the bank, post office, police station, souvenir shops and tavernas along the way (the street being named after the island's famous poet and also includes his house, now a museum). An old Yaya (Grandmother) looked down on the street from her balcony as we walked by with the other tourists and we wondered at the changes she must have seen to her home town over the years. We were dressed in holiday shorts and t-shirts, enjoying what to us seemed like a warm summer's day (it was early September), but we quickly became aware that many of the locals were bundled up in pullovers – feeling the cold – an indication of the temperatures they'd been used to in July and August. The old fishermen's harbour was a great place to watch the catches being unloaded and sold, with the routine of daily life continuing as it had done for many years.

Back by the sea the Bourtzi (meaning "tower" relating to its days as a fortress) separates the fishermen's quay from the more commercial harbour. It's an islet that you access by a causeway and has a statue of Papadiamantis, plus a cultural centre hosting an annual Aegean festival. It was a great spot to stop for a drink under the pines watching the coming and going of boats and ferries. We sat there one afternoon and watched a plane coming in to land, flying low over the sea. As it roared past us at eye level there was a sudden increase in engine power and it climbed steeply back up, circled around and came in for another try, landing on the second attempt. We'd wondered what it would be like for a pilot making their first attempt at landing at Skiathos: well, that answered the question.

We saw some posters for an outdoor cinema and tracked it down. I think they showed *Shine* and *The Big Blue* when we went. It was a fabulous experience, sitting out under the stars, the film projected onto a large, whitewashed wall. Director's chair-style seats were paired with a little table for food and drinks between them, it was lovely to have a beer or an ouzo during an alfresco movie, plus there was a welcome interval to nip to the loo or the bar. This being September and towards the end of the season, the canvas was beginning to give way on some of the chairs. Once in a while there'd be the sound of a loud rip and someone would go through the seat ending up with their legs in the air, to a round of applause from the audience.

Being a bit younger in those days, one evening after dinner, we strolled round the harbour to one of the little nightclubs and spent an hour or two having a wiggle on the dance floor. We'd been keeping an eye on the time as we didn't want to miss the last bus back to Koukounaries. These were the early days of our Greek holidays. Now we are very familiar with the gradual attrition of the islands' bus service timetables as the end of season grows nearer, but not so back then: arriving at the bus stop, we could see that on the timetable pinned to a lamp post the last bus to Koukounaries had been firmly crossed through. After a short time wondering what to do, a taxi responded to our waving and drew up.

'Where do you want?' he asked.

'Koukounaries,' we replied.

A brief exchange between the driver and two young Greek gentlemen who were already in the taxi reached a positive consensus and a rear door swung open. One of the guys was a chef and had just finished work; they tried to engage us in a conversation about football, but our knowledge of *the beautiful game* has always been less than rudimentary, so – after a brief conversation about Manchester United and how we'd be happy for Panathinaikos to win – talk swiftly progressed to the outdoor cinema and how we were enjoying our holiday. They paid the driver and got out near Troullos and we were soon back in Koukounaries. It's common practice for Greek taxis to pick up other passengers, as long as the licensed number of passengers isn't exceeded, although you shouldn't expect to split the fare.

We had a meal at Stamelos on our last night with John, our neighbour from the studios, and Vangelis gave us a bottle of ouzo to remember him by. Such a lovely guy.

At the airport the next day we discovered that the baggage handlers and ground crew were on strike, so the aircrew checked us in and then had to load the bags onto the aircraft themselves! (I think they worked for Thompsons or some similar charter flight company and they obviously wanted to get home that day as much as we did.) In those days you could check-in your bags and then go back outside the terminal building to the "airport taverna" and enjoy a last pre-flight drink or snack in the sun. The airport PA/tannoy system extended to the taverna, so when your flight was called you could just stroll back into the terminal building to board ... those were the days. Although, on this occasion we had to keep strolling right through the terminal and across the tarmac to the plane, as the transfer bus driver was also on strike (not that it was any great distance). We took off and looked down as the plane circled over the Island of Skiathos and as it steadily disappeared below us, felt a huge level of sadness about leaving. Sue even shed a few tears; it seemed Greece had won a special place in our hearts.

Skiathos: Mandraki beach, Sue and the Blue Man of Mandraki, Dave "Robinson Crusoe"

Skopolos town and cats

Alonnisos "Makanaki"

Skiathos: Sue with Vangelis at Stamelos taverna

Cat in the Chora

Chapter 18

Lesvos

(1999)

Lesbos vibrates like a spiderweb with the names of high antiquity – the greatest of all being Sappho:
Lawrence Durrell

It was around the time we were planning our next trip to Greece when we came across Matt Barrett's Greece Guides: greecetravel.com.

It's a fantastic website packed with information, tips and itinerary advice and for over 20 years has always been our first stop for finding out information about new islands for over twenty years now, in conjunction with various books we've picked up. There's also a very friendly and informative Facebook group: Matt Barrett's Greece Travel Guide.

Lesvos sounded like a great island to explore so we headed across the Aegean, settling on the resort of Anaxos in the North West. Our first sunset and meal were spent at the nearby Sea Side Restaurant, warmly welcomed by its owner, Charlie ... more of whom later.

The following day was my birthday so we caught the bus to Molyvos (Mithymna), a charming harbourside village, with houses built from local stone clinging to the hill connected by narrow, cobbled streets, topped by a magnificent Byzantine castle (replacing the original which was said to have been taken by Achilles in the Trojan War).

As we strolled down the slope towards the picturesque harbour we passed two ginger cats on the cobbles looking quite healthy and happy. Octopuses swung on ropes drying in the sun in front of a classic caïque fishing boat with its characteristic lights used to attract fish at night. We had lunch at the Captain's Table with its magnificent views and a great menu. We returned a couple of times during our stay for magical evenings with a splendid bazouki player sitting at a nearby table serenading the diners (we sent him a 'tip' in the form of a small bottle of ouzo to show our appreciation, as was the custom). With the fishing boats bobbing gently in the harbour and the castle floodlit on the hill above, various cats mooching amongst the tables, along the cobbles and sitting in an adjacent tree by the animal sanctuary, it was a perfect setting.

On the evening of my birthday in Anaxos we watched a lovely sunset from the beach as it cast an iridescent pink glow around a half-submerged small boat – which it turned out had belonged to Charlie (we nicknamed it the *Titanic)*. Later, while having dinner at his restaurant our fellow diners joined in a chorus of "Happy Birthday" as Charlie appeared with a baklava, complete with a large, pink candle. As the evening wore on his father (who was pretty elderly and had enjoyed a few drinks) decided to call it a night, clambered up onto his *Papi* moped and set off at some considerable speed for home. Suddenly, there was a cartoon-like crash as he rode straight into the chalkboard that was propped outside Charlie's taverna. Not to be deterred, he gamely remounted his steed, but his son tugged him off it to avoid any further catastrophe and drove him home by car. We stayed at our table, partly because there was some more wine to see off, partly chatting to our fellow diners and also as we still had a bill to pay. Charlie soon reappeared and with just the three of us remaining he brought out a bottle of ouzo – oh dear... We protested feebly saying we didn't want to keep him up, but he assured us that he had to stay open late during the season just in case any late customers drifted in and anyway, he was going to watch his favourite sport on TV and wanted us to join him. Sue and I aren't really into sport (other than once a year watching tennis from Wimbledon), but he'd been so hospitable that it seemed churlish not to follow him as he disappeared behind the bar clutching our generous measures of ouzo. We then spent one of the most surreal nightcaps ever, sitting with our new friend in his "office" drinking ouzo, with the sound of the waves lapping on the beach behind us and the incongruous juxtaposition of watching Sumo Wrestling from Tokyo on his satellite TV.

We decided to hire a car for a week or so to better explore the island. Our first outing was to Skala Kalloni. Lesvos is shaped a bit like a travel neck pillow and the enormous bay at the centre has Skala Kalloni at the middle of the island. Famed for its sardines, the water is remarkably shallow for some way out from the beach. We watched the activity for a while at an old boat-building shop near the harbour, a master craftsman steadily working on one new caïque and one restoration.

It might have been the moment that, watching an age-old tradition and admiring their elegant contours, I developed a lasting fascination with Greek fishing boats: over the years I've taken scores of photos of different boats, probably second only to those of Greek cats. Sadly, it seems that over the last 15 years or so, caïques have gradually been reduced in number. In an attempt to reduce overfishing in Mediterranean waters, the European Union has been paying fishermen a comparative pittance to give up their licences and their little fishing boats. The rather barbaric deal is apparently for compensation only to be signed off at the instant of the boat's destruction, so they are forced to watch their beloved old vessels smashed to pieces (often bulldozed) in front of them. It seems to me that they are destroying not just the tradition (both the fishing and the skilled boat-building), but also – in my mind – works of art and cultural icons. I wonder how the thousands of lost little caïques stack up against the impact of the giant trawlers of the many fishing fleets that patrol these waters? I would think that the small boats would be a far more sustainable way to fish and support many more families.

"If you take Greece apart, in the end you will be left with an olive tree, a vineyard and a boat, which means that with these items you can rebuild Greece": from the poet Odysseas Elytis.

We settled in a taverna by the square and ordered what was becoming our standard, late-morning, Greek holiday beverage of choice: a frappé, metrio meh gala – iced coffee, medium sugar with milk. Nothing better. As we revelled in our invigorating frappes one of the locals plodded over to meet us. He was handsome, friendly and certainly not camera-shy: Ioannis was a magnificent pelican. His bill was topped with glorious blue marbling, with yellow and red stripes running down its length, an ochre pouch swinging beneath. He eyed us up thoughtfully for a while, assessed that we weren't in possession of any sardines and pottered off to look for richer pickings.

Mono Ipsilou is thought to have been the epicentre of the volcanic activity that created the Petrified Forest at Sigri and we drove past it on our way there, passing a wind-power park with turbines up on the hill (the Greeks were pioneers of this particular form of green technology, which we were unfamiliar with in those days). The lava flow from the eruption engulfed prehistoric vegetation millions of years ago, which later became exposed by erosion to create a "Fossil Park". It was extraordinary to examine the vividly-coloured remains of an ancient forest, one trunk with something like an 8-metre circumference and some with annual growth rings just visible.

Sigri itself had a beautiful little church (Aghia Triada) down by the harbour and an 18th century Turkish Fortress. The fishing village derived its name from the Greek for "safe harbour".

We spent the afternoon at Skala Eressos: a long, sandy beach nestled at the foot of some impressive mountains. It had a wonderfully laid back feel to it with some fabulous bars and tavernas built up on stilts to level them against the slope of the beach; their terraces looked like a superb place to watch the sunset. The birthplace of Sappho felt like it had a lot to offer and were we to return to Lesvos at some future date, it would make a brilliant base.

Having developed a taste for Plomari Ouzo I had to visit the town itself. The road slowly wound its way down the hill and we parked up to have a mooch about. The old olive oil factory on the seafront was in some disrepair, but there were impressive clocktowers, traditional buildings and mansions. We tracked down one of the ouzo factories, but unfortunately it was closed. I peered with interest through the window and could see intriguing metal vats and a long table with what looked like bottling equipment, perched at the end of which was one of the biggest fire extinguishers I've ever seen!

It took us a couple of attempts to find the Roman aqueduct at Moria. On the second pass through the village I noticed, just in the nick of time, a tiny little sign really high up on the wall of a corner shop by a narrow turning off the main road, so I swung the hire car onto the side track. A little way along the track we found the aqueduct, which is a really impressive construction.

Thought to have carried about 100,000 cubic metres of water each day over 20-30 Km it relied entirely on gravity to maintain the flow. Much of it was made from marble blocks, which may explain how six complete arches are still standing, despite the ravages of time – and earthquakes. Walking towards it, there was a rustle in the undergrowth and a two-foot long, ring-headed dwarf snake wriggled along the base of one of the aqueduct stones. That and a sign drawing attention to falling stones (ironically flattened into the parched vegetation) suggested it might be time to move on.

Lesvos is famed for its healing mineral springs so we decided to drive up the East coast on the way back to Anaxos. We came across Loutropoli Thermis – divine spring of the Goddess Artemis – and stopped to have a look around. To one side of the gloriously derelict, slowly-decaying Grande Old Hotel Starlitza Palace was a peach-coloured building housing the new therapeutic baths. Although they weren't actually open at the time, further exploration revealed enormous header tanks feeding the baths. I'd had a small, bothersome patch of eczema on my right elbow for about ten years. I could go for long periods without even knowing it was there, but in the previous few months it had flared up a bit. I checked no one was about and waggled my arm and elbow about in the rusty orange-coloured water for a few minutes – more in hope than expectation – much to Sue's amusement. As I write this, twenty-two years later, that little itchy eczema patch hasn't worried me once since our visit to Lesvos. Coincidence? I really don't know, but if it works don't knock it.

On the road to back to Petra (the village adjacent to Anaxos and on our route home) we came across a taverna by the turning to the village of Stipsi and decided to stop for lunch. The cutest little black and white kitten came bouncing over and we gave him some morsels of our lunch. He was very grateful and quietly came to sit at the table with us. Such a sweet little cat.

That evening we walked the length of the beach and found a charming little family-run taverna at the far end. As we enjoyed our meal under the stars, the sound of the waves tickling the shoreline and the stars twinkling overhead, we heard a few gunshots and loud cheering that sounded close, back down the road. A steady flow of cars were competing for parking spaces, disgorging their well-dressed occupants who then headed for a large taverna where a crowd was gathering. We wandered past later to see a wedding reception in full flow, the bride and groom dancing in the middle as guests took it in turns to walk forward and chase them round as they pinned money to their clothes. It was lovely to see a proper Big Fat Greek Wedding for the first time and a joy to witness some Hellenic nuptial mayhem as we floated by.

Towards the end of our time on Lesvos we were in our room showering after a day on the beach when it suddenly started to get very dark. As we watched through the balcony doors the small island of Agios Georgios vanished as the grey rain clouds approached. Within seconds it was bucketing down and after about half an hour we were rolling up towels and stacking them at the bottom of the doors like sandbags to stop the rapidly rising water – overwhelming the balcony's drainage – from flooding the room. An hour or so later the sun had returned so we decided to stretch our legs and walk over to Petra for dinner. Quite shortly after setting off, a large dog decided to join us on our walk and trotted alongside us. We were about halfway to Petra when more clouds began to build and we felt the first few drops of another rain shower. A sign by a small turning announced a café bar in that direction, so we decided to take a detour and find shelter. The dog followed us down the side road, but then suddenly veered off into an adjacent field which was full of sheep. The shepherd looking after them was less than happy about this intruder and started to shout and wave his arms about in our direction. My Greek was pretty thin on the ground in those days so, the next thing we knew he began hurling rocks at the dog and there was a worrying thud and a yelp as one struck its rear end and the poor old hound quickly scarpered. We picked up the pace as we did not want to be on the receiving end of any similar treatment. The shepherd continued to shake his fist and shout at us, so we decided to leg it as it seemed he thought it was our dog! There was no way of knowing what might have happened if the dog had reached the sheep and of course the shepherd had to protect his flock. We were a bit shaken up by the incident but the whole situation could have been avoided if the dog's owner had taken their responsibilities more seriously.

We just made it to the café as the rain got heavier and met another couple from Germany, also sheltering from the downpour. We bought a round of drinks each as we waited for the rain to abate. I was impressed by their ability to speak Greek and it transpired they'd been coming to Greece for over thirty years. Thanks to a handy map on the café's wall they pointed to all the places they'd visited, giving us some good recommendations. As the rain eased they offered us a lift in their hired jeep. We were clambering in when we caught sight of the dog from earlier, lying under a tree. He stood up when he saw us so I went over and patted him on the head, glancing at his flank. There was a mark where the rock had struck, but no wound to speak of and he seemed okay otherwise. As we drove off he turned to head back up the beach, which was a relief.

The charming couple we'd met in the bar dropped us off and we climbed the steps up to the "Church of Sweet Kisses" at the top of the large rock – from which Petra gets its name – and admired the view for a while. Strolling around we came across the 17th century Vareltzidaina House with its impressive, engraved wooden balconies (Sachnisini), built to increase the inhabitable space of the building. As we ate dinner on the seafront some of the clouds remained and we were treated to a most spectacular golden sunset.

We spent our last evening at Charlie's taverna along with a lovely Austrian couple who, it turned out, were huge fans of Rowan Atkinson's *Mr Bean* character, particularly the seaside/beach scene where he attempts to change into his swimming trunks, which our friends recollected with considerable glee:

"...and he puts the under-trouser on the over-trouser and then takes the over-trouser under the under-trouser..."

Several drinks and hours of laughter into the small hours marked the end of a fabulous holiday.

Oh, and Charlie's boat did eventually sink.

* * * * * * * * * * * * * * * *

Although it happened sixteen years after our visit there, I'd just like to mention the refugee crisis that began on Lesvos in 2015, which accounted for over half of the asylum seekers who transited through Greece that year. The pressure on the Island continued to build as the number of refugees rose, overwhelming the makeshift camps, as an over-stretched system for dealing with the migrants struggled to process asylum requests. It all came to a head in 2020 when a terrible fire broke out at the Moria camp during a Covid quarantine/asylum rejection protest and in the face of on-going targeting of refugees by far-right groups. Due to its geographical location, Greece found itself in an impossible situation, with limited support from other European Union countries, as they tried to aid and protect peoples displaced from their homes by war, persecution and conflict. The people of Lesvos have been helping refugees for many years, such as those escaping the civil war in former Yugoslavia, but the escalation in recent years – exacerbated by the attitude of the Turkish State and the lack of support from EU member states – has severely tested the *philoxenia** of Lesvos' inhabitants (*the welcome extended to strangers is intrinsic to Greek culture). The situation impacted on tourism causing even more pressure in the wake of the recent austerity measures. Currently it seems that Europe is increasingly turning to new methods, such as AI-powered lie detectors, drones and sound cannons to prevent the influx of displaced people, but surely this is dealing with the symptoms rather than the causes?

If you are thinking of visiting Lesvos please don't let the refugee situation put you off going. The camps are located away from tourist areas and the locals will be so very happy to see you. If you want to do something other than supporting the local economy by visiting, then there are various organisations helping on the ground there:

Aterias – Starfish Foundation: provides practical help for vulnerable people on Lesvos, both refugees and locals - asterias-starfish.org

Dirty Girls of Lesvos: wash clothing, blankets, sleeping bags and other materials so that they can be reused rather than being trashed and wasted - dirtygirlsoflesvos.com

Have a look around on the internet for other groups providing help and support.

* * *

When I first took on an allotment in Brighton one of the fellow allotmenteers was Eva Voutsaki. Eva originates from Crete, just outside Chania where her parents have a farm, hence her interest in gardening. Her father calls his vegetable growing area his "Lahanokipos" or "Cabbage Garden", which I really like. Eva teaches photography and design at the University of Sussex and has published a book of her own photographic work called "Traces Within": *The format for Traces Within was based on the idea of drifting through memories, the intention was to create a book with no obvious beginning or end and allow the viewer to drift through the photos.*

In 2015 Eva flew to Lesvos to help where she could and she subsequently wrote a piece for Protagon.gr: The website features opinion pieces, analyses and reports on politics, business, society and culture. It is known for being popular among intellectuals. She kindly gave me permission to reproduce that piece here and you can visit Eva's website at: www.evavoutsaki.com

Eva Voutsaki
NOVEMBER 5, 2015
Go out and shout I went to Lesvos too!

I have found time to write. Days now, months, years I have tried to understand what is happening. I think, I meditate, I reflect and I wonder about Greece, about the whole world. Difficult questions and even more difficult answers.

About a month ago I also went to Lesvos on my own for three days. I decided at the last minute, booked tickets and before I knew it I found myself on one of the Greek islands where history is written and not written, unfortunately. Or rather, history repeats itself. The Greeks who arrived in '22 were refugees and those who are coming now are also refugees. The man who leaves to escape the madness of war is not an economic immigrant. No war ever made any sense. I left the legal aspects and explanations and went in.

I talked to locals; most of them seemed deeply shocked to me, in a meteoric depression. I let them laugh when they could. The pain they have seen in the eyes of others has haunted their souls forever: how could it not? For ages after I returned to my daily life, I dreamt almost every night that I was back on Lesvos, helping. I woke up anxious. Often a drink of water wasn't enough, even holding hands could not always still my disquiet. The locals are divided into good and bad. Those who help and those who not only do not help, but curse those who do. The couch potatoes, the fascists, the con men, the black marketeers, the inbreeds of the Turkish traffickers. Good and Evil will fight forever and ever.

In general, however, the island is full of volunteers: Danes, Norwegians, English, French, Portuguese, Americans, Australians, Spaniards. I even met someone from Brazil and saw an Icelander in a video. An entire chain of people has been set up on the internet. They exchange views, encourage, ask, comment. All of them are necessary to rejuvenate potential and give the locals some time to rest.

I often think of Katerina and George from Agalia. George's description of the situation and the messages I exchanged on the internet with Katerina were instrumental in my decision to go to Lesvos and this tribute to Papa-Stratis. *(*1)*

Years in the struggle of humanity. Since then Iraqis and Afghans started coming, and from Syria which was once a safe country.

I often think of Spanish lifeguards: proud Catalans. How much longer will they last? And yet they endure. Their gaze haunted. How can they forget the shipwrecked ... the children? They arrived in September when they learned about Alan. *(*2)*

They fought and they are fighting: the more children and babies, mothers, brothers and men are lost, the more stubborn the Catalans will be. They are the ones with the yellow t-shirts and the red raincoats. Colourful in this grey.

I often think of the baby I held in my arms for a while that night: it was not crying. The other children were shouting and screaming, I was trying to hug them, too. Many people embraced us. I was looking to find his mother, to give him back to her. It all lasted four minutes. Crying, screaming, panic, tension. Emotions change very quickly, but the wound does not heal so quickly.

Those who come should go to psychologists, psychotherapists. Mostly children. There is always hope for children.

Tearful and cultured in what I write, does it make a difference? Am I also looking for my five minutes of fame? In any case, history will prove that I, like many, as an artist and volunteer, was just a civilized crow, feeding on the flesh of dead children, on the flesh of consciences. Refugees are difficult to understand. It is difficult to justify sleepwalking Europe and the even more so, the insane Greek government.

All this haunts me. Before going to Lesvos, I watched Al Jazeera videos and cried. Now I am waiting for the next video of Eric from Lesvos and I curse everyone and everything with him. *(*3)* Governments, journalists, opportunists, the swindlers, the weather, the rubbish, the shit, the big NGOs. Watch these videos and when you go to Lesvos or Kos or Leros or Kalymnos or Eidomeni or Athens you will always find the refugees somewhere. It is a touring troupe. They offer a spectacle in Europe, a target for us the sensitive and a scapegoat for the unconscious. Do not take pictures with them. Ask them their name, remind them that they are human. That alone. Get organized. Go out and shout.

(*1) Agalia is a Greek NGO operating on the island of Lesvos and in 2016 the jury of the Council of Europe awarded them 2016 Raoul Wallenberg Prize, for "outstanding achievements in providing frontline assistance to thousands of refugees irrespective of their origin and religion." Founded by Father Efstratios – known as "Papa-Stratis" who passed away in September 2015 – Agalia has continued to gain steady support as its devoted associates pursue the Father's endeavour.

(*2) Alan Kurdi was a three-year-old Syrian boy of Kurdic ethnic background who made global headlines in September 2015 when he drowned, along with his mother and brother, and was found lying face-down on a beach near the Turkish resort of Bodrum. He was among a group of refugees escaping Islamic State in Syria, attempting to reach Kos.

(*3) Eric Kempson – a long haired ex-Safari Park manager from Portsmouth and his family – became the unlikely first responders to the tidal wave of humanity coming across the sea from Turkey, scanning the sea every morning for incoming boats, overloaded by the smugglers. www.facebook.com/thekempsons

Sue and Eva on the allotment in Brighton

Lesvos, Molyvos: Ginger cats

Molyvos: Bazouki player at the Captain's Table and Skala Kalloni: Boat building

Ioannis the pelican and Roman aqueduct at Moria

Loutropoli Thermis mineral spring and Kitten at the taverna by the turning to Stipsi

Chapter 19

Naxos

(2000/2002/2015)

When I left thy shores O Naxos
Not a tear in sorrow fell
Not a sigh or falter'd accent
Spoke my bosom's struggling swell.
Yet my heart sunk chill within me
And I wav'd a hand as cold
When I thought thy shore O Naxos
I should never more behold:
Lord Byron

The first time we went to the lovely island of Naxos we flew overnight to Athens and caught the X96 bus to Piraeus at around 4am. It was impressive to see so many young Greeks still coming and going at the various nightclubs en-route to the port as the bus hurtled along the relatively quiet roads. The Blue Star ferry was due to depart at 7:30am, but we were allowed on board well before that, stowing our luggage in the relevant section for Naxos. Arrival there included our first experience of passengers crowding together waiting for the ferry's ramp to descend, accompanied by the deep rumbling sound of the engines and a continuously-repeating, basic, electronic version of The Cuckoo Waltz. As the ramp slowly opened we caught our first tantalising, dizzying glimpses of the Chora sliding by as the ferry swung round to dock. Once it was safe, the foot passengers disembarked – to anyone who's watched this from a distance it resembles the birthing of a hundred little spiders all trundling their wheelie cases or carrying rucksacks.

We had booked our accommodation through the local travel agent, Naxos Sun Holidays, and were met at the port by the charming manager who drove us to Plaka and Paradiso Studios. On the journey there she told us a little about the island and asked about us and where we'd previously been to in Greece. Our apartment was on the first floor with a substantial balcony overlooking newly-planted vines and the fabulously long sandy Plaka beach, with a view of Paros across the sea – where we would watch a sequence of fabulous sunsets.

On our second trip to Naxos we flew to Santorini, stayed overnight and caught the afternoon boat. We once again arranged the accommodation with Naxos Sun Holidays, but were extremely saddened to be told the news that the manager we had met had lost her life in the dreadful MS Express Samina ferry disaster of September 2000. Her lovely sister Lida had taken over the role of manager and again met us at the port, taking us back to Paradiso Studios.

The beach seemed to go on forever, from Agia Anna, along the magnificent stretch of Plaka with its sand and dunes, on to Mikri Vigla and Kastraki. We walked along the beach to Mikri Vigla and settled in a little taverna for some lunch. A nearby couple, who were clearly well-known to the owner, called him back over after he'd taken our order. The man complained that his beer wasn't cold enough and the woman said her tzatziki didn't have enough garlic in it. We weren't sure if they were joking, but a few minutes later the owner reappeared, banging down a bottle and a plate on their table. The bottle of Mythos beer had been frozen solid with the ice pushing its way up past the neck and the plate contained a big mound of raw garlic cloves. 'Endáxei?' he laughed. They also saw the funny side.

Sitting at a table under a large tamarisk tree on a warm evening at the Paradiso taverna we looked across the sea at the lights of Paros, twinkling like fairyland in the distance. A group of young men arrived and sat a couple of tables of away. One of them produced a guitar and began to sing. Joining in with Pink Floyd's *Wish You Were Here*, singing under the stars, after a lovely meal and some local wine in hand it felt like a perfect moment.

One early evening the wind got up and we watched the owners of a beach bar lashing their palms with ropes, like Christmas trees tied up ready to sell. By the time we'd had dinner it was verging on a tempest so we ducked into the bar on our way back to the studio. Several others (tourists and locals) had also taken shelter and we stayed until late drinking Metaxa with them. The following morning we had absolutely no recollection of what we'd talked about, but the sound of laughter was still ringing in our ears and the wind had subsided.

Taverna Manolis on Maragas beach became a favourite with us, possibly in part because our evening pre-dinner promenade was invariably met with a glass of wine thrust into our hands as we walked by. We got to know one of the waiters, Elias, who worked there in the summer season and then as a 'dancer for the ladies' back in Athens in the winter. Manolis regularly had live music – the usual combination of guitar and bazouki – and one evening as we watched a young Greek woman dancing with her family we became aware of an American chap at a nearby table who seemed quite taken with her: 'Aphrodite lives!' he cried out several times. Elias could sense that her father wasn't best pleased at this admirer's enthused exclamations, so he decided to divert his attentions by introducing him to us.

John O'Keefe was a playwright of some regard in the States and had lucked out with several months' funding from the American government to write the script for a play, choosing to find his inspiration on Naxos. He was certainly a live wire who wore his heart on his sleeve and we left Manolis late that night after a fascinating and highly-entertaining conversation. Our paths crossed again just before we were due to travel back home and it seemed that John had spent a little too long in the sun, losing track of time as he wrote, resulting in his white bits turning lobster pink. We'd bought a sun brolly for use on the beach so he was delighted when we gave it to him for his future protection ... a donation to the arts, as it were. I believe from an American friend we met on Milos some years later that John is still working in the Bay Area of San Francisco and has had a considerable number of his plays produced at significant American theatres over the years. He's also published books and received multiple accolades for his work. We sometimes wonder if the play he penned on Naxos was a success and if he still has that beach brolly...

The first two holidays were mainly spent relaxing, swimming and writing, but we did venture out a bit by bus and boat (it wasn't until 2015 that we hired a car and did a bit more proper exploration). We visited the Vallindras Kitron Distillery in Halki, a small pottery, the Kouros statue at Apollonas and, of course, the famous Portara. On one trip we passed a field with an enormous mound of potatoes and if I remember correctly Naxos is renowned for that crop, both for the Greek consumer market and for seed production: 'Naxos is where the heart of the potato beats', said the chef overseeing the 2017 World Record breaking heaviest batch of fries.

Sitting above the Chora is the Kastro. We walked up the wide stone steps (worn smooth by centuries of footsteps) and beautiful archways to reach the entrance to the Della-Rocca family house on the north side of the fortress. A posh-looking little ticket bearing their coat of arms gained us entrance and, as luck would have it, our own personal tour guide. She showed us around the rooms of the Venetian aristocrats with their original furnishings and we looked out on a fabulous view of the town and Portara below. She also produced a book of photographs, some of which showed those worn, sloping, stone steps we'd climbed up on the way there, covered in snow. You can imagine how treacherous they would be when covered in ice, let alone the incongruity of those images when viewed in the heat of the summer.

The Portara is said to be the gateway to the unfinished Temple of Apollo. It's an impressive structure on the Palatia Islet and when we first visited Naxos in 2000 the area was open for anyone to explore. It was said that if you walked through the Portara then you would be sure to return to Naxos, so we did just that, hand-in-hand, and sure enough have returned twice to date. The massive marble doorway is the emblem of Naxos, can be seen from Paros and was the first subject I painted in pastels.

On our next visit in 2002 we booked with Vassilopoulos cruises to take a trip on the *Dionysos Express* to the Mikres Kyklades: Koufonissia, Shinoussa and Iraklia. It departed at 10:00 from Agia Anna. We were sitting up on the top deck enjoying the sun and sea breeze when Sue whispered in my ear, 'Do you recognise those two?' I turned and recognised the American couple – who had been carrying a large package of pottery in the queue at the port on Sifnos whilst waiting to board the high-speed ferry to Piraeus the previous year (shortly after the 9/11 attacks so we had lots to talk about). When we arrived at Iraklia we decided to have a swim on the town beach and found ourselves sitting quite close to them. I couldn't let the opportunity go.

'Hello, there,' I called over to them. 'Did you get that pottery back home from Sifnos okay?'

Understandably, they seemed a bit phased by this at first, but after we re-introduced ourselves they told us they had decided to have another Greek holiday and had happened to settle on Naxos. The amazing coincidence of being on the same boat trip was pretty boggling. They had managed to get their pottery back in one piece to Brussels (where they were currently working for the UN) and thankfully their friends and relatives were all safe following the terrible Twin Towers attack of the previous year.

The little islands were delightful and would be the perfect place if you were seeking utter tranquillity and escape. Returning to Agia Anna around 19:30 we found a local seafront bar and had a drink and a chat with our American friends before heading back to Plaka for dinner. To date, we haven't bumped into them again on any Greek islands, but you never know! It's a small world.

Our 2015 trip to Naxos started with a flight to Mykonos. While waiting in the queue at the airport we got talking to a lady and her daughter and we decided to share a taxi as they were also catching a ferry. The driver asked us where we were going to (Naxos) and seemed happy that the 'new' port was the place to be. I also asked the person in the ticket office at the port just to double-check that the Naxos ferry went from there, showing her our Seajet2 tickets. (Our lovely friend, Wendy, had brought the tickets to us in the UK on her most recent trip from her home on Paros). The tickets don't actually show any departure information, so I thought it was best to check. I was told that it was the correct port. We had an hour or so to wait for the ferry, so we bought a couple of cooling frappes, found a shady spot (sitting on the concrete bench of the waiting area) with a good book and watched as the other ferries came and went. As the time for our departure drew near, the port seemed to have become eerily quiet. I walked over to a guy I recognised from one of the ticket offices and asked if the ferry was coming ... only to be told we were at the wrong port! If you're ever travelling to the islands by ferry from Mykonos do be sure to check and double check which port they depart from – as having both the 'new' and the 'old' ports in operation is seriously confusing. Noticing that I'd gone a bit pale, he made a quick phone call. All the taxis were long gone (and these are few and far between on Mykonos at busy times, taking people to their destinations on the island), but he shouted over to a large, moustachioed gentleman in a blue t-shirt several sizes too small for him who beckoned us over. He had the last mode of transport available: a three-wheeler Piaggio Ape! These small, open-backed vehicles are really designed to carry people's luggage, not people. Despite that, he hurled our bags in the back and motioned for me to clamber on top of them. Sue, meanwhile, was invited to sit next to him in the, ostensibly, one-man cab. Desperate times called for desperate measures and with the time ticking down before our ferry departed, off we went in a cloud of exhaust fumes. As he swung the vehicle precariously round bends and up hills, racing for the old port, I clung on to the low sides of the cargo bed for dear life. Suddenly, the passenger door next to Sue in the cab swung open and she almost toppled out onto the road! Quite calmly, the driver leant across her to slam it shut. Also, because of the tight squeeze in the cab, each time he turned the steering column his left elbow made contact with Sue's chest, 'Sorry, Madam!' he kept apologising ... at what seemed to be very regular intervals. After about what might have been 10-15 minutes of fine honing of our circus skills (but seemed like longer), we came to a sudden stop in a cloud of dust in front of the departure area of the old port, just in time to hear an announcement:

'Ladies and gentlemen. We apologise for the late arrival of the 14:50 Seajet2 to Naxos, we hope to have you on your way in 30 to 40 minutes.'

Over a hundred faces turned to look at the dust-covered lunatics falling out of the Piaggio, completely delighted and relieved by the news of the delayed ferry! I pressed ten euros into the driver's hand for somehow getting us there and Sue planted a kiss on his blushing cheek; after thanking him profusely we sheepishly joined the other passengers to wait for the ferry, which duly arrived to our enormous relief.

The taxi from Naxos port drove us right to the far end of the dirt road behind Plaka beach to reach our studio, Marine Dream, where Maria and family made us feel very welcome. I'd chosen it for its location and we had a lovely room with a small balcony overlooking the sea. During the day the birdsong was like music, along with the happy buzz of bees around a magnificent callistemon shrub below our balcony with views across the fields behind the studio and fishermen passing by in front. The evening sunset over Paros was beautiful and with such low light pollution the stars, moon and even the Milky Way were impressive. It was a bit of stroll to the nearest taverna, but it helped to work up an appetite. Maistrali was the closest: a family-run taverna where you were invited into the kitchen to see what was on offer and experience some delightful home cooking. Similarly at Voula, a little further along. There seemed to be more flowers, birds and insects than I recalled from our previous trips, but maybe that was because it was June whereas we usually visited in September.

We did some proper explorations of the Chora on this trip. We'd come to love the designs of old Greek front doors and there were plenty on offer in the winding backstreets, as well as a plethora of enticing old covered archways and Cycladic architecture, with one church looking like a curvy, icing-covered cake. Old feta tins adorned whitewashed steps, planted with basil, pelargoniums and small olive trees, hanging baskets swung above a narrow street filled with bright petunias, and shimmering bougainvillea clambered up walls and over balconies. One tumbledown ruin had lost its roof, but a fig tree had taken root and grown up inside it until its leaves replaced the area where the tiles once were. A creative blacksmithing lab called *Ironworks* contained some remarkable pieces. It was next to the entrance to the Archaeological Museum, which we also visited. The museum had a collection of superb Cycladic art, mosaics, pots and vases, as well as some Roman glasswork that could be a forerunner for the iridescent work of Loetz.

We met many of the local cats and admired some of the remaining caïques in the harbour as well as revisiting the Portara, now roped off from tourists, but still magnificent. We came across an interesting sign on the way back to the bus stop by a day trip sailing boat, as well as comfort, sailing lessons and assorted equipment they also promised that you could enjoy swimming slippers for the caves and “Noodles for Swimming”; how splendid.

This time we hired a car. Mike’s Bikes was on the Plaka beach road so it seemed the easiest place to go to. We were greeted by the owner:

‘Ah, hello, you are English,’ he observed.

‘How did you know?’ I asked.

‘Your knees and Monty Python,’ he replied. ‘How can I help you?’

‘We’d like to hire a car for a week, please.’

‘Okay, I only have one at the moment. It is the Matiz Chevrolet.’

We agreed a good price for the week and swiftly completed the paperwork with a perfunctory recording of any existing scratches and bumps.

‘I will drive carefully,’ I said, taking the keys.

‘You, my friend, I am not worried about,’ he said, ‘it is the local goats behind the wheel we must watch. My friend will explain the car.’

The owner wandered off to talk to a couple who wanted a quad bike and a shy fellow who spoke very little English looked us up and down and pointed to the car.

‘This is your car. The gas goes in here … the key goes in there … umm, thank you, goodbye.’

Off we went.

A visit to the Temple of Demeter near Ano Sangri was well overdue. A lengthy path edged with hibiscus and oleander took us from the car park to the sanctuary itself. Constructed from Naxian marble it's a proper little monument and one that we found particularly appealing as the offerings made to Demeter weren't of animal or human origin, but vegetables and fruit, squashed into pits so the juice could run along a channel. Our kind of deity, Demeter: I might have to build a little offering area on the allotment to help ward off blight and keep the badgers off our sweetcorn. On the way back there was a fabulous view of the Chora and Portara from Galando.

We passed the imposing Tower of Agia (built around the 17th century and becoming the holiday home of the noble Kokkoi family) on our way to Apollonas. Sue decided to stay in the taverna with a frappe this time (as we'd seen the Kouros together in 2002 on a day trip), but I set off up the steep steps out of the village and up the hill. I passed some lovely little gardens on the way, mainly full of flowers, but one with courgettes, tomatoes and red onions, plus a cicada who posed obligingly to have his photo taken. I reached the road we'd come in on and crossed it to continue my ascent up into the ancient marble quarry. As luck would have it I had the place entirely to myself and the opportunity to marvel at the big old 10 metre Colossus of Dionysus. You can clearly see his head, beard, arms and feet, so after all those days/months of carefully chiselling away, those Archaic stonemasons must have been mightily miffed to discover it had a crack running right through it – although some think it might have been okay, but whoever had commissioned it didn't stump up the readies ... or maybe they just bottled it as getting that hulking great thing down off the hill would have been a huge undertaking. The Kouros reminded me of "Gort" from the 1951 version of *The Day The Earth Stood Still* – if you've seen it you'll know what I mean, particularly his angular chin. Resisting the temptation to call out 'Klaatu Barada Nikto', I made my way back down to the hill to re-join Sue.

That evening, I showed Sue the photos I'd taken of the Kouros over dinner back at the Paradiso taverna. As I gazed across at Paros, just I'd done 13 years previously, I casually mentioned that the twinkly lights of Paros seemed a bit fuzzy (as if there was a sea mist or something). Sue then passed me her distance glasses.

'Ooh, that's so much better,' I told her.

'You've been driving us round the island!' she said. 'I think you need to go to the opticians when we get back, meantime you'd better wear these.'

Hey ho, Anno Domini. I cut quite the dash wearing Sue's purple-framed specs for the rest of the holiday.

We had lunch on my birthday at Lucullus Taverna in the Chora. It's said to be the oldest taverna in Naxos, established in 1908, The interior decor is wonderfully traditional and there was a cool alleyway outside with tables for lunch. We were given an olive tapenade and bread to go with wine while we considered the menu. We had a gorgeous shrimp ramekin in tomato juice, ouzo and feta cheese sprinkled with lavender petals. French fries and the 'Feast of vegetables' with two types of lettuce, tomatoes, carrot, glikomizithra (sweet Naxos cheese) and a dill and vinaigrette dressing: orea.

We spent the afternoon on Plaka beach and I spoke to my parents on the phone (as I always did if we were away), before taking a seat in a funky beach bar and having a beer as my phone pinged with birthday messages from friends.

The following day we took a daytrip on the ferry to visit our old friend Wendy, on Paros.

Continuing our exploration, we took the car up past the windmills of Tripodes and up into the hills. Stopping in Filoti the views were breath-taking and the little backstreets great fun to explore. On up to Halki (once the capital of Naxos) with its big neoclassical mansions and colourful alleys. We found the imposing tower of Gratsia – its surrounding wall as impressive as the building itself and, although we couldn't find it, a drawbridge somewhere – as well as some fabulous remains of what might have been an olive press or a mill. The window ledges and gardens burst with colour and the village nestled amongst olive groves (Naxos is said to have several hundred thousand olive trees.) We had to revisit the Vallindras Kitron Distillery where they make the local liqueur from the leaves of the citron tree (pronounced with a hard "C") using traditional methods and the 1862 copper distiller (part of which resembles an armoured *Clanger*), huge fermentation bottles and a colourful array of various products for sale.

We climbed on to Apiranthos on the slopes of Mount Fanari with its marble paving, shaded taverna seating, stately archways, beautifully-carved bell tower of Panagia Apeirathitissa and spectacular views. Byron loved it so much he said he would be happy to die there: we, however, settled for a collection of memorable photographs.

Naxos: we'll be back one of these days.

Naxos

Theseus' loss was Dionysus' gain
Ariadne's crown Borealis framed
The guardian of Zeus
So it was said
Kouros reclines on a hillside bed

Like Kubrik's monolith the Portara stands
Long ago we walked through it
Hand in hand
Now we are returned
to Byron's favourite land
To stroll the shoreline and silvery sand

Hora's alleys and arches
A twisting maze
In the climb to the Kastro's former days
Every corner a picture at which to gaze
Then down to a kafenion to sit and laze

Up the hills we weaved and wove
Til' a jewel in Tragea
'Mongst the lilacs and groves
In Halki the Vallindras Kitron still flows
As the fame of the Olive and Fish grows

Below Mount Zas rising like a mighty fin
Views from Filoti
Pretty as a pin
To Apiranthos' marble-paved streets
On which the rays of Helios beat

(Dave Burnham 2015)

Elias, John O'Keefe and Dave at Taverna Manolis on Maragas beach

Chora: cat and caïque

The Portara at the Chora (pastel painting by Dave)

Temple of Demeter near Ano Sangri and the Kouros at Apollonas

Dave and Sue on Plaka beach celebrating his birthday

Distiller at the Vallindras Citron Distillery in Halki

Chapter 20

Sifnos

(2001)

You have your brush, you have your colours,
you paint the paradise, then in you go:
Nikos Kazantzakis

Sifnos was the first of the smaller islands we'd visited. Having read about it on Matt Barrett's Greek Island Guides website it sounded right up our δρόμος (street).

We stayed in a studio apartment at the beach resort of Platys Gialos to the South East of the Island. The long, sandy beach was metres away from our room, so several days were spent under the shade of a tamarisk, venturing into the water for cooling dips. I was writing my novel at the time (*Flux*) and days on the beach were the perfect environment. Most days my scribblings were interrupted by the little beach cat who would take advantage of our small stock of opportunistic cat crunchies and then curl up on my lap. I was more than happy to sit and gaze out to sea while the little ghataki had a snooze.

We explored the island by public bus.

Vathy is a lovely sheltered harbour and we spent a long, lazy lunch in a taverna right on the beach watching the ebb and flow of holidaymakers, plus occasional yachts arriving and leaving, which kept us entertained: there was one in particular. Having dropped anchor in the bay, the occupant set forth aboard a small inflatable dinghy. The yachtie was of a rather substantial build and their weight set the dinghy at quite a jaunty angle, with the prow and stern raised at about 40 degrees, with the outboard motor propeller acting more like an electric frappe whisk. However, stately and steady progress was made to reach the shoreline on the beach, where they disembarked with some considerable difficulty. Unfortunately, we didn't witness the return journey, but assume they made it back on board the yacht without incident. As the afternoon wore on we studied the map and Sue figured it should be possible to walk back to Platys Gialos, which was situated just around the nearest headland. This seemed like a good plan at the time, rather than taking the public bus all the way up to Apolonia in the centre of the island to change to another bus back down to our village. As we set off I spotted an elderly Greek gentleman in his garden, so showed him our map and asked if he thought there was a footpath. He pointed up to the hill behind him and nodded with a wry smile, which in retrospect I should have interpreted as: 'Yes, you could walk from here ... although, I wouldn't and I don't know why on earth you'd want to.' Undeterred in our happy naivety, we set off up the road towards the hill. The footpath started by a bend in the road, where a goat shepherd gave us a cheery wave as we noticed the massive knife swinging from his belt. The low mountain path was a delight, a mini adventure into the heart of a Cycladic island. As the path became a narrow track, we saw piles of rocks with dots of blue paint helpfully marking the route – presumably left by previous adventurous walkers. I should mention at this point that we had in mind a gentle stroll back of about an hour or so, and we were wearing our beach attire, flip-flops on feet, with no food or water on us. A couple of walkers appeared around the bend coming towards us from the opposite direction. We waved and greeted them, but they regarded us with a look of incredulity and seemed less than chirpy as they trudged past. A light breeze picked up as the sun edged towards the horizon and we heard distant gunshots echoing around the mountain-side as someone took pot-shots at what remained of the wildlife. Continuing onwards, we came across a small bay below us with a church: Agh. Georgios, with a priest arriving on a small boat. This was theoretically the halfway point, but the helpful piles of painted rocks had disappeared and the track was almost impossible to make out with criss-crossing paths. There was little to give us any clues about which direction to take, with the exception of a few goat droppings. A decision had to be made. Whether to press on and risk being stuck on the hill in the dark without water (yes, I know, we won't do it again, promise) or turn back immediately and retrace our steps before it was too dark to see anything. Another echoing shot around the hillside followed by barking dogs made up our minds. We turned on our heels. About an hour later we arrived back at the bend in the main road leading down to Vathy. It was completely dark by now and we knew we only had about half an hour until the last bus to Apolonia left the village at 9pm. We legged it as fast as we could down the road to Vathy, both of us covered in dust and gasping with thirst. With minutes to spare, Sue waited at the bus stop just in case it came early – promising to hold it for me – as I stumbled into a nearby taverna to ask the bewildered owner: "Σε παρακαλώ, ένα μπουκάλι νερό;" (Picture someone crawling out of the desert begging for water and you'll get the idea!) Luckily a 2 litre bottle of cold water was available to purchase and as the bus rolled up we clambered gratefully on board, resembling dusty desert rats. A few moments later a group of very smartly dressed middle-aged ladies boarded the bus on their way out for the evening. They eyed us with a mix of pity and amusement whilst nattering away for all they were worth, just like a Women's Institute day trip. On arrival in Apolonia we had a 25 minute wait until the last bus for Platys Gialos. Luckily there was a cafe bar next to the bus stop so a couple of pints of cool Mythos were ordered while we waited: by crikey, a beer had never tasted so good! Lesson learned though.

A few days later we visited Kamares, the main port. We spent the late morning on the rather attractive town beach, waiting for ferries to come in and rushing into the water to play wave-jumping in their considerable wash. A young couple had placed their towels and bags quite close to the water's edge (no tides in the Aegean) and were some way out swimming when a hi-speed ferry came into the harbour. We spotted it from our happy wave-hopping and I leapt out of the water to move their kit further up the beach before it was soaked – as we'd seen happen to another hapless couple earlier.

We found a psarotaverna by the water's edge for lunch and ordered one of the best fish plates ever, along with a small bottle of Plomari ouzo.

Some while later as we waited for the λογαριασμός (bill) a small chartered cruise ship docked nearby. A group of about 15 American tourists disembarked in a flurry and their overheard conversations seemed oddly distressed and out of keeping with happy tourists. We initially thought they might be talking about some kind of movie they'd just watched or a book they'd read. However, as they walked purposely past us we heard they were desperately seeking somewhere with a tv; specifically a news channel. We headed back to our studio and flicked on the tv in our room for the first time since we'd arrived. We watched with increasing horror as the Greek news reported the unfolding terrible events in New York and suddenly realised why the cruise group had been looking for a tv. The date was September 11th 2001.

A few days after arriving in Platys Gialos the 'boys' found us. There was a rustle in the undergrowth on the other side of the patio wall outside our ground floor studio apartment, then, *boing*. First to appear on the wall was a young cat, maybe 8-9 months, with distinctive black and white markings, swiftly followed by a pair of white cats with tabby-like markings on their heads. Sue found the crunchies box she always brings and they were soon tucking in.

The first cat had black, triangular patches over his eyes like a mask. We immediately christened him 'Lazarou' partly after the beach adjacent to Platys Gialos, but also after Reece Shearsmith's demonic circus master and collector of wives in the TV series *The League of Gentlemen* (of course, although essentially an otherworldly clown figure, interpreted as politically-incorrect now, especially in light of BLM, but a great character in its time, nevertheless). The next kitten we named 'Scooby' as he was always the first to arrive and loved his snacks, another we called 'Horace'. My father used to call me Horace when I was being cheeky as a child, I have no idea why, but it always made him laugh. Our cat treats had almost been hoovered up when one more fellow arrived. He had the unfortunate habit of arriving just-too-late to the party and often only got the last scraps of food. We called him 'Unlucky Alf' after Paul Whitehouse's character in the *Fast Show* (another favourite comedy show of ours at the time). They were lovely boys and would come and eat, play and purr with us most evenings during our stay. We think they must have had a home and were being fed, but they were always ready for another meal and some attention, which we were more than happy to give.

As the month of September progressed, the tavernas in Platys Gialos steadily began to close for the winter. On the same night as the 9/11 attacks we eventually wandered into one of the last couple that remained open. We took a table outside at the back on a concrete terrace overlooking the beach and a waiter came to take our order. Sue opted for the pasta and I explained: 'είμαι χορτοφάγος' (I am a vegetarian).

The waiter said: 'We will find you something', and mooched off.

Soon after the pasta arrived he plonked a plate in front of me and vanished back into the kitchen. A quick look and taste test confirmed that I'd been given three, giant cricket ball-sized meat balls! As everything was pretty weird that night, rather than complaining about my meal being anything but vegetarian, I came up with a plan. While no one was looking I wrapped them up in a large table napkin and dropped them over the edge of the concrete plinth – it was about a meter down onto the beach (and it was dark by now). We finished and paid for the meal then strolled back along the beach. As we passed below the plinth wall I scooped up the parcel of meatballs I'd just deposited. Back at the studio we found a plate, chopped up one of the huge meatballs, popped it by the patio wall and waited. We didn't have to wait long. With a sproing and meow one of the boys appeared: it was Alf! He couldn't believe his luck and tucked into the plate of meaty-loveliness with gusto. Having polished off a whole one, Alf looked up expectantly with a hint of a kitty belch. So the second meatball was proffered. Alf tackled it diligently, but about halfway through he had to have a little lie down. He rested his head on the edge of the plate. Every few minutes he would try and take another nibble at the meatball, before flopping back into a post-prandial reverie, like a feline version of Terry Jones' Mr. Creosote from Monty Python's *The Meaning of Life*. The other three boys turned up to polish off the remaining meatballs, but that was clearly a turning point in Alf's fortunes. A nice end to what had been a sad and difficult day.

The time came to head for home.
We decided to catch a bus back to the port – allowing plenty of time before our highspeed ferry's departure time of 10 pm. The bus rolled up and we loaded our cases into the luggage compartment and jumped on board. The bittersweet farewell of the, now familiar, scenes of our home for the past two weeks rolled past. It was particularly difficult to leave the lovely cats but we had an idea they'd be just fine without us. About halfway along the road to Kamares the bus coughed and spluttered and came to a shuddering halt. The driver leapt out, opened the engine cover and ferreted about within for a while before standing back and rubbing his chin. Climbing back into his seat he let the handbrake off and waited. We were just over the brow of a hill so the bus obligingly started to trundle down the road. It seemed unlikely to us that we'd make it back to Kamares by gravity alone, but it seemed a worthy attempt. Predictably, we came to a halt as we rounded a corner onto a level

surface. The driver hopped out again and made purposefully for the building located on the bend: it was a garage! Within minutes he was joined by a mechanic who was wielding a large spanner and sounded like he was experimentally clonking bits of the engine with it – that or auditioning for a role in *Stomp*. There were still a few hours before the highspeed to Piraeus was due to leave, but we were beginning to feel a little uneasy. The mechanic marched back into the garage. A few minutes later he reappeared brandishing a red and white cardboard box above his head with a big smile on his face; he and the driver were both laughing. It looked like we'd rolled up outside a garage in the middle of practically nowhere that just happened to have the one spare part for the engine that needed replacing.

About 40 minutes later we were sitting in a pizzeria on the seafront at Kamares. The pizzas were absolutely enormous, (as is so often the case in Greece – very generous portions!) so we asked for a 'doggy bag' and put the box in our hand luggage, thinking we might be able to snack on it later. Whilst waiting in the queue for the high-speed ferry at the port, we met a young American couple with large cardboard boxes tied together liberally with thick string. Apparently they'd been to the famous pottery workshops on Sifnos and were taking some examples home with them (they were based in Brussels working for the UN). Naturally, they were still in shock after the recent events in their home city of New York, and were awaiting news of friends who may have been in one of the Towers. We chatted while we waited and wished them well as we eventually boarded the ferry and they went forward to business class (something we hadn't considered before, but worth the extra cost for a longish high-speed trip) – this was the couple we randomly met again on a boat trip from Naxos in the previous chapter.

The brand new Eleftherios Venizelos Athens airport had only been open for about 6 months – it was built to cater for the huge influx of people expected to attend the Olympic Games hosted by Greece in 2004, and the old airport was seriously outdated. All the advertisement poster cases were empty as we strode down vast underground corridors and along travellators, with their stark clean whiteness and shiny steel giving the place an eerie, Sci-Fi feel. The whole effect compounded the strangeness we felt having become used to quiet Greek island life. The events of 9/11 had affected flights all around the world and we were advised to wait in a departure lounge along with a couple of hundred others. The air conditioning was going at full blast, so it was freezing cold in there; far too cold to sleep. So as the night wore on we felt a bit peckish and remembered we had some pizza in the doggy bag. At that point there were no food outlets in the departure area, so as we tucked into our left-over pizza we became aware of many pairs of envious eyes staring in our direction ... but that pizza tasted so good! Sometime around 3am our flight was eventually called and we finally boarded. The rest of the journey home was thankfully uneventful. We had planned to return to Sifnos and stay in Vathy in 2020, but sadly Covid put a stop to that.

Sifnos, Platys Gialos beach cat

Kamares fish taverna 9/11

Lazarou

Alf

Scooby and Horace

Serifos
(2003)

Enthusiasm is a wonderful thing.
In South America, they throw flowers to you.
In Greece, Greeks throw themselves:
Melina Mercouri

We booked our Serifos holiday with the travel company called Simply Simon. They specialised in destinations with what he described as 'a low alien count', or in other words, those without an international airport which require a bit more effort to reach. The transfers to and from Piraeus were left up to us to arrange, but the company were there for back up should we need it. We stayed in the main port town of Livadhi at Pension Eliza, not far from the seafront. Every evening around dusk the nearby trees would fill with the happy trills of what seemed like hundreds of roosting sparrows comparing notes on their busy day. Our neighbours at Eliza were a charming British couple in their early 80s who we got to know over several glasses of wine. They had been coming to Greece for a long time and were an inspiration for our continued travels. Although our main balcony was fairly inaccessible, one of the local cats came to visit the smaller area by the entrance to our studio.

The town beach was quite busy with a couple of tavernas that had tables right on the beach by the shoreline – these were rearranged by some high winds and large waves one night. We explored some of the nearby beaches following Simply Simon's directions along winding dirt roads and tracks with various "landmarks" along the way. Our favourite, though, was about a 25-minute walk to Psili Ammos (meaning 'fine sand'); we've come across a few beaches with this name on various islands and they're almost invariably wonderful. We spotted a praying mantis on one walk and there was a small cave at the far end of the beach in which somebody appeared to be living. We got to know the 'troglodyte' a few days later as he held court in a bar with a group of local youngsters. He was a genuinely entertaining chap and turned out to be an English teacher from Athens on his regular annual summer break to Serifos … he needed to reduce his living expenses so decided to try camping out caveman style, but had just moved back into more salubrious accommodation as his mother was flying out to join him.

Sue with a local Serifos cat

We caught the bus up to the Chora. It's a stunning village with small houses and narrow alleys sprinkled over the summit of the hill with windmills overlooking the port; a joy to explore. As we waited for the return bus we became aware of clunking thuds echoing up from the valley below. A shepherd was working in a patchwork of brown fields between a labyrinth of dry stone walls. He was busily dismantling the side of one wall, creating a gap between the fields and a set of steps. He then chased his sheep up the steps, through the gap and into the next field to graze, before setting about replacing the wall to keep them in. Fascinating to observe. It was a very hot afternoon and a little while later we saw him trudging up the hill towards us. We gave him a friendly 'Yassas' and were met with a grunt and a wild-eyed look as he loped past us wearing perished wellies and ragged clothes; he was entirely the same colour as the dust in the fields below.

After nearly two years since our stay on Sifnos in 2001, we decided to take the Highspeed ferry for a day trip to visit Kamares. We went wave-jumping in the ferries' wake again and back to the same psarotaverna/Ouzerie for another of their fabulous fish plates. On the ferry back we heard someone shout out, 'Delfini!' Sure enough, a pod of dolphins chased alongside and then in our wake for about 10 minutes: a glorious and wonderous sight.

Chapter 21

Samos and Patmos

(2004)

Today, to walk along the pebbled pathways of a traditional Greek mountain village or the marbled streets of an ancient acropolis is to step back in time: Laura Brooks

We were starting to get the hang of this Greek holiday malarkey, so decided to give the Dodecanese a whirl and booked our own two-centre trip to Samos and Patmos. Flying direct to Samos we stayed in the town of Pythagorio so we'd be ready to catch the boat over to Patmos the following day. At the eastern end of the harbour stands a modern bronze statue of Pythagoras positioned on the right angle of a huge triangle pointing up to its tip: adorned with symbolic elements of his theorem. I heard a story that Pythagoras didn't like fava beans, but it sounds like that was probably a myth brought about by the mistranslation of ancient Greek scripts. He believed in the transmigration of the soul into other living things and some ancient scholars had misinterpreted the texts as Pythagoras believing that fava beans therefore contained the souls of the departed, which could be lost through noisy farting if the beans were consumed! As time passed, some other scholars realised that the texts had nothing to do with beans at all, but were in fact another theorem all about angles.

As we pottered around the harbour we saw priests chatting with fishermen and some lovely caïques, with a few taken out of the water while being worked on. The Samos Spirit was due to depart early the next morning, but that year the meltemi wind was particularly enthusiastic so our ferry was cancelled and we had to spend another night in the hotel.

Our tickets had been transferred to one of the Flying Dolphin hydrofoils, but with the sea still choppy we took our seats and hoped for the best. We were about halfway there, when the captain decided the waves were a bit lumpy so he dropped out of warp and we chugged along with the entire hull in the water. If you're not familiar with these old vessels think of a giant, round-ended, flat-bottomed glasses case, now imagine that being thrown around in the sea: luckily we made it with our breakfast intact, but several other passengers weren't so fortunate.

Arriving at Skala we were met by Paula who took us to Grikos and Hotel Joanna where we had a traditional design ground floor studio backing onto a field. In the evening a flock of six or seven unusual-looking, yellow and black birds perched along the length of a power cable running high above the field. When we got back I looked them up and I think they were golden orioles. A few days into the Patmos holiday a group of Scandinavians arrived at the hotel (they were on the island to visit the famous monastery) and as dusk fell we discovered they were a choral society as their wonderful voices filled the early evening air for an hour or so.

Grikos is set by a bay resembling a lake with a lovely sandy beach and numerous well-kempt tamarisks for shade. The little harbour had some splendid caïques and wooden sailing ships, with tables and chairs from the adjacent tavernas spread out on the nearby sandy beach. The walloping great Kalikatsou rock at the southern end had what looked to be rooms and steps carved into it, possibly once a hermitage or a temple to Aphrodite. I spent many hours under a tamarisk writing and watched a team fixing electrical cables back on to one of the tall wooden poles: no mean feat as the cable was tremendously thick and wound on to a huge wooden drum, it must have weighed a ton. The high winds that had kept us on Samos for an extra day had brought the cable down, which gave some indication as to their strength and, unfortunately, they had started to pick up again.

One evening as we sat having our dinner by the entrance to the interior of Stamatis taverna, two guys arrived – resembling the *Men in Black*, equipped with walkie talkies and earpieces. They started looking intently around at the boats moored at the harbour front, beaming powerful flashlights around their hulls and about the decks. They continued their mysterious assessment around the outer edges of the taverna and checked carefully under parked cars, before scuttling off into the night. Sue turned to the two Greek guys sitting at the table just across from us.

'What was that all about?' she asked.

'The King of Belgium is coming,' came the reply.

'Oh really? In that case, I'm the Queen of Sheba!' she retorted.

'No,' he insisted, 'he is here on the Belgian Royal yacht and the bad weather stops him from moving on to the next destination. So, they are coming here for dinner.'

While still not entirely convinced by this peculiar turn of events, we carried on with our meal keeping an eye on proceedings. About twenty minutes later a group of eight smartly-dressed people sauntered in, taking their seats at a table to the left of the outside area. Of course, we didn't know what the King (or the Queen) of Belgium looked like, but the middle-aged couple sitting at the centre of the group were certainly immaculately turned out and there was a fair bit of bling in evidence on some of the other ladies. The two security guys reappeared and sat at the front of the taverna, keeping an eye on things with a large, sinister-looking briefcase prominently placed on the table. We detected from the manner of the taverna manager and the other staff that these people were indeed something special. When their drinks arrived we were pretty much the only other people there, so we caught their eye. The guy we assumed was the King raised a glass in our direction and we did likewise, smiling and saying 'yammas'. I was tempted to go over and ask if they had any weather updates, as we were hoping to get the ferry back to Samos, but having glanced at the bodyguards I thought better of it: looked like they could probably have wrestled me to the ground quicker than you could say 'Belgian chocolates'.

The monastery on top of the island is grimly beautiful in a rather reproachful way, and it crowns perfectly the small oatcake of the island: Lawrence Durrell

On arrival in Skala by bus from Grikos, the monastery dominated the skyline, like a colossal gothic, grey sandcastle, in which is a cave where St John the Theologian was said to have written The Book of Revelation. This is why Patmos attracts many pilgrims and religious visitors to this sacred place.

Skala is no longer the centre of trade for local pirates, but more a welcoming conduit for those seeking relaxation, or spiritual enlightenment, as well as retail therapy. It did, however, have a lovely little Periptero – one of the kiosks we'd often seen in Greece selling cigarettes, magazines, newspapers, phone cards (back then people still used payphones), ice creams, sweets, drinks, lotto tickets, you name it. I heard that a new law had come in around 2015, which stipulated that when a Periptero's license terminated it had to close and could not be handed on to the owner's children to run and thus be kept in the family. If so, it sounds like another crazy initiative similar to that effecting the caïques.

Another other thing we'd noticed on our travels in Greece was the phenomena we came to call "the truck of many things". The first time we heard one of them approaching us from afar we thought there might be a local election going on, with one of the candidates driving round canvassing for votes through a loudspeaker (as we didn't understand the shouted dialogue). However, an over-laden truck would then roll into view, with useful items such as plastic chairs and tables piled high, wobbling precariously. Some trucks would be stacked with fruit and veg, some would have livestock such as chickens and ducks, yet others offered a random array of handy items like a mobile emporium. The one in Skala was selling all manner of terracotta pots and storage vessels: goodness only knows how the truck's suspension coped with the extreme weight.

Later, walking along the harbour, sure enough there was an enormous, lavish-looking yacht moored up. Later the *Patmos Observer* reported that the King of Belgium had to prolong his presence on the island due to the wind (8-9 Beaufort) and their attempts to take his photograph had been thwarted by the bodyguards. They also mentioned that the Royal party had dinner one evening at Stamatis Taverna. So there we are: from time to time Sue and I have been known to make the bold claim that we had dinner with the King of Belgium...

After the wind died down a bit we caught the Nisos Kalymnos ferry back to Samos. We called in at a couple of small islands en-route. The first was Agathonisi – declared a Valuable Shelter of Rare Bird Species by the European Network of Natura in 2000, primarily for migratory birds from Africa – a tiny island that would make an excellent place to escape to. Next was Arki. From memory, I think the wind picked up again as we approached and there was a shuddering thump-cum-clang as the ferry clonked hard against the stone quay. Embarking cars and people hurled themselves onto the pitching ramp and into the hold with a respectable amount of shouting and general encouragement.

Arriving back on Samos the next part of the plan was our bravest yet, having left booking our accommodation to chance due to the weather. We quite liked the look of Votsalakia as a resort so we hopped in a taxi and off we went over the mountainous centre of the island. On arrival, we tried to find a room at a couple of places with no luck, but walking along the main road we saw a sign for Aspres studios, situated above a souvenir shop. The owner spotted us and took us up to see the studio. It was more a very small bedsit than a studio, but it was clean, with a nice view and we only wanted to stay for a week ... plus it was only 15 euros a night!

The next morning the meltemi wind returned in force, clearly refreshed from the previous day's rest. It howled and whirled impressively around the outside of the room as I held on tightly to the door and poked my head out to investigate a loud banging sound. The scene that met my gaze was of an elderly Greek gentleman balancing-precariously on the far edge of the flat, concrete roof adjacent to our upstairs room, hastily hammering and lashing down an air conditioning unit that had been making a bid to escape from the roof in the high winds.

'Kalimera,' I called out.

'Kalimera, sas,' he shouted back above the gale, 'koíta ti thálassa.' He pointed over the roof towards the sea and I could see what he was getting at. As the waves tried to break on the shore, the wind was blowing them back flat against the surface of the water, driving a mist-like spray back out to sea.

I ducked back inside so that we could consider our options. According to the guidebook there was another beach about three kilometres away that might provide a bit more shelter from the Northerly wind. The walk there afforded some spectacular views out to sea and a good look at the colossal form of Mount Kerkis, second highest peak in the East Aegean. We walked on past an enormous stack of lengthy logs, presumably destined for making charcoal or to keep the winter fires burning and several wonderful, giant prickly pears. Arriving at Psili Ammos we could see it seemed to be divided into two sections and dropping down to beach level the protection from the wind was evident. The gently shelving shoreline made for perfect swimming and the setting was wonderfully picturesque, so much so that it pretty much became our daily commute with an excellent taverna overlooking the beach to dally in over lunch. Our route home took us past a telegraph pole displaying a rather unusual poster: "Miss Mirea's Crazy Cobra Show", the mind boggles.

There were several great restaurants to check out in the evenings: at the Votsalakia taverna we sat out on the edge of the raised platform overlooking the sea, sampled some of the excellent local wines and met some of the lovely local cats.

The days passed by pleasantly and soon the day came to head back across the island to the airport for our return flight. So we hefted our bags down to the seafront road and stood by the little blue taxi hut to call or hail a cab. Taxis had been prolific throughout our stay and we'd assumed there would be no problem in flagging one down to take us back to the airport that morning. However, it seemed strangely quiet everywhere with no taxis in evidence at the rank, but we waited for a while next to the blue hut. I'd picked up the taxi company's business card on our way there, so called the number on my mobile. At that moment the phone started to ring in the empty taxi hut next to me. I stopped phoning the number ... the hut phone stopped, too. A couple more attempts confirmed that my little contingency plan was doomed, as a bit of dry bush blew past us like tumbleweed in a spaghetti western. A large coach drove by on its way to pick up some package holiday-makers and we entertained the idea of asking if we could hitch a lift back to the airport, but then it disappeared up a nearby road. Fortunately, we'd left a fair bit of time to get back, but the clock was now ticking and check-in time loomed. There were definitely no taxis, so there was only one thing for it: we dashed a little further up the road and into a Hertz car rental office. Explaining our predicament and need to reach the airport pronto, the young lady seemed relatively unphased by our request to hire a car simply to drive across the island to the airport. Having said that, she did seem unjustifiably amused when I produced my old pink paper UK driving license, despite also having a card. Luckily they had a car we could rent and we were told we could drop the keys off with their rep' back at the airport, so with the time racing past, we threw our bags into the back and off we went. The Hertz lady had recommended that we took the coastal route all around the island to the airport, but the tourist map suggested it would be far quicker to drive over the middle through the mountains (this was the same route the taxi driver had taken when bringing us to Votsalakia). However, on the way in we hadn't taken much notice of the exact route taken by the taxi and the mountain roads were scattered with debris from rock falls. We took a wrong turning at the beginning and drove along a narrow road through a small village. Several old men sat watching us – twirling their komboloi beads – as we squeezed the car past their tables on the pavement, showing little response other than drawing their feet in a bit closer to the wall. We soon realised our mistake and managed to turn around, repeating the process to their evident amusement. Having finally found our way back onto the correct road, we climbed up the ever-narrowing and pothole-littered route shown on the map, before we eventually came to a junction somewhere up around Myli. The road ahead was barely passable due to a large, flatbed truck surrounded by men stroking their chins and throwing ropes around something big. As we inched by we could see what they were up to. An enormous, dead wild boar was tethered to the truck, presumably the result of a hunting trip, poor thing.

Sue kept saying to me, 'just don't get a puncture!'

We raced into the airport car park with barely minutes to spare until the flight check-in closed. I dashed off to find the Hertz desk located at arrivals. Naturally there was no one there, so I left the car keys and a note with the very obliging lady occupying the adjacent bureau de change and just managed to run back to the check-in desk in time to show my passport seconds before they closed. We leapt through passport control with just enough time to buy a couple of bottles of ouzo as the flight was called. Phew! We had learned a valuable lesson: always book a taxi to take you to the airport on the day of departure – don't leave it to chance! Oh, and ideally try to be on the same island as the airport on your day of departure, in case the wind had any other ideas about your ferry connection.

Patmos: Grikos beach

Kalikatsou rock

Patmos: Grikos beach caïque Chora, Periptero Chora heavily-laden pot truck

Samos: Crazy Cobra Show poster and Psili Ammos beach

Sue and Kitty in Votsalakia taverna and Mount Kerkis

Chapter 22

Kefalonia
(2005)

The flapping of the sail against the mast,
The ripple of the water on the side,
The ripple of girls' laughter at the stern,
The only sounds when 'gan the West to burn,
And a red sun upon the seas to ride,
I stood upon the soil of Greece at last!
Oscar Wilde

Imbued with a tranquil majesty, Kefalonia boasts beautiful scenery ranging from lush fertility to epic mountains, amazing caves, excellent beaches (one of which – Myrtos – is one of the most photographed in Greece), picturesque villages and harbours, superb food and a splendid range of local wines. The island's natural verdancy is seen in the form of countless olive trees, Italian cypress popping up like exclamation marks, orchids in spring, crocus and cyclamen in autumn, as well as the National Park and the wonderful endemic *Abies cephalonia* – the fir trees that sit atop the mountain peaks. This is echoed by the locals' love of gardening and the apparent profusion of garden centres on the island creating a glorious abundance of oleander, bougainvillea, palms, roses, lavender, pelargoniums and cacti, to name but a few, not to mention the passion for home grown produce.

We flew from Gatwick to Kefalonia with Excel Air (a great charter airline, sadly long defunct) and it was a short hop on arrival to our studio at the newly-opened Avithos Resort in Svoronata, which we'd pre-booked with

Kokolis Travel. The accommodation was some of the best we've ever had on our travels in Greece, being spacious, brand new, and with the resort complex built in traditional Kefalonian/Cycladic style, which was well-spaced so we didn't feel crowded. There was even a gorgeous little garden in front of the patio area. Like a lot of Greek small-holdings and large gardens, they are watered on a drip-feed/"leaky hose" system. Around dusk on the first evening we were intrigued by, what seemed to be, the garden briefly humming to us like a happy little gnome as the water feeds got going. Later that evening we heard a rustling in the undergrowth: knowing that the island had a few snakes (sacred or otherwise) we kept a wary eye, but were delighted when a tortoise shambled out, set off across the patio and into the night. Our stay was further enhanced by a couple of friendly local cats; we called the ginger boy Jerry and the black and white one Tom. The view of Mount Ainos from the back of the studio was stunning, especially from the shower, looking out of the small head-height window in the bathroom. Late one afternoon there was an epic thunderstorm, which reverberated around us, the sound of thunder bouncing back off the mountain and reflected by the sea. At around 7am one morning we were woken up with the bed gently rocking from side to side and the crockery tinkling excitedly in the kitchenette. A sound like a hundred bowling balls, clacking together in sequence, shot underneath us and off into the distance. It was all over in a few seconds, but we'd just experienced our first earthquake. I felt a mixture of shock and thrill, bearing in mind the utter devastation that the 1953 quake had wrought on Kefalonia, but we later learned these small quakes are common and sort of essential, like the Earth wriggling a bit to get comfortable. The locals said it happens all the time...

We did our usual pottering for the first few days, just chilling out, and took a stroll from Svoronata up the winding road to the charming little villages of Domata, Kaligata and Kourkomelata. Tranquil, sleepy, quite well-to-do places, they had some superb gardens – we dallied a while to watch a huge butterfly uncoiling its watchspring proboscis into a type of drinking straw to access the nectar of a large flower. The church tower of Theotokos Koimisis in Kaligata poked up through the sea of green like a white and blue fairytale turret. Metaxata is nearby, where Byron stayed to finish writing *Don Juan*.

Ammes beach was not very far from where we were staying so we walked the short distance and settled on the sand and swam in the inviting waters. This beach would certainly suit holidaymaking aircraft enthusiasts, as the airport runway is right next door and the planes take off and land directly overhead, although not so frequently as to be a major nuisance.

Avithos beach was a couple of miles saunter away. A long, narrow sandy beach, gradually shelving into the sea, but quite pebbly and stony along the shoreline. From the beach you can see Zakynthos on a clear day and also the nearby tiny islet of Dias – named after another little island near Crete; it used to have an altar to Zeus and sacrifices on Mount Ainos were carried out at the same time via smoke signal communication. We went to To Enetiko taverna one evening and had a splendid fish plate. After dinner we got chatting to an older Greek couple on the table next to us. They were slightly downhearted about the beach and explained that it had been totally covered in sand, but a recent big storm in May had pulled a lot of that off, revealing the stone pebbles underneath. However, it had happened before, many years ago and the sand had gradually returned by the action of the sea, so they remained hopeful for the longer term. They asked where we were from and they knew Brighton. The wife had visited several times over the years and said she regularly went swimming in the English Channel. I said it was very cold and a bit murky compared to the wonderful Greek sea. The gentleman nodded in agreement and reminisced:

'Polý krýo. I went to swim in your English Channel, but only once. I went in a man and came out a woman!'

Before booking the holiday we had a look around on the internet to see what various car hire places were offering. We were attracted to one called Greekstones, partly due to the obvious sense of fun and the pun on the Flintstones. We went into the office at Svoronata and were made to feel really welcome by the very charming Melis. We established during the paperwork-filling that Melis and I were born in the same year and concluded that we were an excellent vintage! We booked a car for a few days and Melis gave us one of Greekstones' maps, kindly spending over twenty minutes suggesting an itinerary for the five days, pointing out things to look out for along the way. When we went to get the car he carefully showed us all of the controls and features, as well as highlighting the most important control when driving in Greece ... yep, the horn! The general signage and road conditions are very good on Kefalonia, although it can be useful to familiarise yourself with some of the place names in Greek, in case you come to a vital junction and the English translation isn't present. Many of the blind corners around the towns and villages have obligingly placed mirrors, but it's customary to give a bit of a hoot as you approach. It gets a bit bumpy here and there where the road has been recently dug up and resurfaced. The roads twist and turn their way up and down the steep hills and mountains, and there are some splendid hairpins on the roads down to beaches/villages. The locals will overtake at every opportunity, but that's fine, just keep an eye in your rear view mirror and give them a bit of room if you can. Every once in a while you'll come across novelties, such as goats/pigs/dogs/cats/people in the road, but just be patient. Watch out for recent rock falls or pot holes and stay on the surfaced roads, as apart from being really bumpy, the insurance may be invalidated if you drive on unsurfaced roads unless driving an all-terrain vehicle.

We came across a huge sow on the road back from the Lixouri peninsula so we stopped at a safe distance. A young couple on a motorbike had been approaching in the other direction, but they'd thought better of trying to squeeze by and were standing watching. I got out of the car and waved over to them; they waved back and shrugged their shoulders giving the "What can you do?" sign with their hands, laughing. After 10 minutes or so the huge animal dragged herself to her feet and toddled off down the side of the hill.

Kefalonia's capital, Argostoli, is tucked in the shelter of a large bay across from the Paliki peninsula. The promenade is laid with a lovely, undulating, black and white pebble walkway – reminiscent of waves on the sea – lined with palms and we loitered to watch fishermen unloading their catch. We came across an enormous vertebra from a Fin whale found near Ammes beach in 1997. As we were having lunch in Kalafatis taverna a loggerhead turtle bobbed up in the water next to us, followed by a visit from a lovely little cat. Wandering around we came across the impressive main square, the Drapanos bridge (linking the town with the mainland), the obelisk-like monument to Bosset who built it, the busy thoroughfare of Lithostroto, a great fruit and veg market, the striking Kefalos theatre and the Korgialenios museum. The museum is beautifully laid out and labelled, giving the visitor an excellent insight into the island's history, with lacework, ecclesiastical displays, folklore and a fascinating collection of photographs of the island before the earthquake, just after and during the rebuilding phase. From time to time we would hear Helena Paparizou on the radio singing *My Number One*: which indeed it was, as she'd won the Eurovision Song Contest in May watched by almost the entire population of Greece.

As we drove up the road from the town on the Lassi peninsula we found the Ag. Theodori lighthouse. It's a doric rotunda built in 1829 by British High

Commissioner Charles Napier and then reconstructed to its original plans after the 1875 earthquake. In 1986 Sue and I met in a Brighton pub called the Sir Charles Napier, so it was nice to see the name here.

Of the Greeks, Napier said: '*...Now I am once more amongst the merry Greeks, who are worth all other nations put together. I like to hear them: I like their fun, their good humour, for they are like Irishmen. All their bad habits are Venetian: their wit, their eloquence, their good nature are their own...*' How true.

Along from there we found Katavothres, swallow holes with a reconstructed watermill (the originals used to produce electricity, but were destroyed in the 1953 great earthquake) and a lovely taverna to watch the sunset from. The swallow holes thing is incredible. Saltwater runs down into conduits at Argostoli that were carved out of the rocks by freshwater in the ice age, these run right under the mountains which feed into the flow with their own runoff, sucking the water in from the Argostoli end. Then it bubbles up into the Melissani lake (more of which later) and out into the Gulf of Sami. This was all figured out by some Austrian geologists in 1963 when they bunged loads of green dye into the water at the Katavothres end and a couple of days later it appeared at Melissani and then in the sea near Sami. Quite amazing.

We visited many of the beaches: Antisamos with its bleached-white pebbles enveloped by densely-forested hills; the pebbly Petani with a great-value fish taverna (and a playful kitten); busy Skala with very tame sparrows panting in the heat of the midday sun and a shepherd who brought his goats down to the beach in the early evening for a snack; the gorgeous fishing village of Katelios around the bay from the loggerhead turtles' prime nesting site; the legendary Myrtos beach and Xi on the Paliki peninsula with its fine red sand like brown sugar and cliffs made of Glina which can be made into a natural "mudpack" to rejuvenate the skin.

In the north of the island we wound our way down dozens of hairpin bends to reach the peninsula that is home to the village of Assos. Rebuilt by the French after the 1953 earthquake, it exudes a gentle, sleepy charm with some of the buildings seeming to grow out of the rocks. It is set around a beautiful bay of crystal-clear water where time just slips away. I strode up the road to the Venetian fortress in the afternoon heat (rather than in the evening to watch the sunset, as more sensible people would do) taking about 40 minutes to reach the top. The curving brickwork through the arched entrance gate was fabulous and I spent a happy hour or so exploring the ruins before taking just 20 minutes to return to the beach and cooling off in the wonderful lagoon-like bay. We had lunch in the Plateia Paris next to an ancient olive tree where an 18th century missionary was said to have had his sermon drowned out by cicadas.

We travelled on along the vertiginous road to the northern tip and Fiskardo. Something in the local geology meant that Fiskardo was spared the ravages of the terrible earthquake so its brightly-painted 18th century Venetian houses remain intact. The car park is on the edge as the town is a car-free zone ... not so with yachts and there were some very luxurious examples jostling with the local fishing boats in the harbour. The dense collection of upmarket tavernas and bars gave a clue to their average clientele. We also found out that the King of Belgium had arrived in Kefalonia on the same day as us and had naturally gravitated towards Fiskardo (he seemed to be following us about, like the trend-setters we clearly are). So, that was quite a day-trip and sunset had been and gone by the time we returned to Svoronata.

We had a day of contrast and fascination as we set off across the middle of the island. Travelling through the fertile plane of Omalos we paused to take a picture of the monastery of Agios Gerasimos: named after Kefalonia's patron saint, his remains are kept there and he is said to be able to exorcise demons/mental health problems via processions on 20th October (there are quite a few Kelalonian's with his surname).

Next we went to the hamlet of Chaliotata to find the 2 million-year-old Drogarati Cave. We figured things were getting a bit unusual as we began our descent and the temperature rapidly dropped, accompanied by moss growing on the rocks, in Greece! Sensible footwear was a good idea and the variety of weird rock forms and colours were remarkable, unearthly shapes and "melting stones" mingling with stalactites and stalagmites, overhangs and fins. 60 metres down, the acoustics at the bottom were great and there have been classical concerts held down there with a story that Maria Callas once came to sing.

Next stop, Karavomilos and Melissani Lake: this was absolutely magical. We made our way down a cool passageway and waited for one of the row boats to return. Our very own *Captain Jack* welcomed us aboard the *Black Pearl* (!) and rowed us out into the most extraordinary and iridescent lake, lit by the sun shining through a hole in the roof collapsed from past earthquakes. It's 39 metres at its greatest depth and so translucent you can clearly see the bottom; deep orange colours dress the walls of the still-enclosed area with an island composed of the old roof as you emerge. All of this is fed by the amazing brackish conduits, which start at Katavothres. This place is a must-see if you're visiting Kefalonia. The name is said to come from the immense bee hives that used to hang down in great fins around the stalactites until the roof caved in. Excavations in 1963 found oil lamps, a sculpture of Pan and a relief featuring nymphs dancing to Pan's flute (now to be found in the Archaeological museum at Argostoli). One school of thought is that Homer's Ithaca included Kefalonia and that Melissani was the cave of the Nymphs where the Phaecians left Odysseus.

We made the short hop to Sami, still in the shadow of the filming of *Captain Corelli's Mandolin* (Matt Barrett in his Greek Travel website jokes that a few waiters were possibly hired on the basis of their resemblance to Nicholas Cage). It had unusually spacious streets and a very modern feel to it, as well as a host of beautiful caïques. We spent a few hours on Antisamos beach before heading back to Svoronata.

We took the Agios Gerasimos ferry across from Argostoli over to Lixouri on the Paliki peninsula and the Ainos ferry on the way back: these two ferries chugg to and fro every hour. Lixouri is the second largest town on the island, but despite being a thriving port it retained a traditional Greek feel. There's a statue to Andreas Laskaratos on the seafront. He was a poet and satirist who took regular literary 'pops' at the church until they eventually decided to excommunicate him (that was a kind of curse in those days, as the belief was that your body would never break down after death). So, he dashed home, grabbed his children's tattered shoes and headed straight back to the church to see if they would excommunicate them, too! Although it has little in the way of night-life, other than the excellent tavernas, the locals are said to be a musical lot and the town has the second oldest philharmonic orchestra in Greece. As we returned to Argostoli we were treated to a lovely sunset from the ferry.

Ionian Jewel

Twisting roads and alpine views,
Scenes steeped in epic wonder,
Hidden lake blue crystal hues,
Ancient caves to ponder.

Church bells peal across the fields,
In tones of conversation,
Tending gardens, striking deals,
They call their congregation.

The twins ply their daily trade,
Twixt Argostóli and Lixoúri,
Delivering cars and new friends made,
Past Laskarátos and his story.

Cicadas samba sparking static,
In the olive's laden boughs,
'Neath twilit avians' acrobatics,
Far from Lassi's crowds.

Omalós tends the vines,
Hillsides crop fresh horta,
An alluring breeze plays the pines,
As wine flows like water.

With the kiss of fortune she deserves,
From Mother nature's givers,
Ainos guards her verdant curves,
As the dreaming feline quivers.

(Dave Burnham 2005)

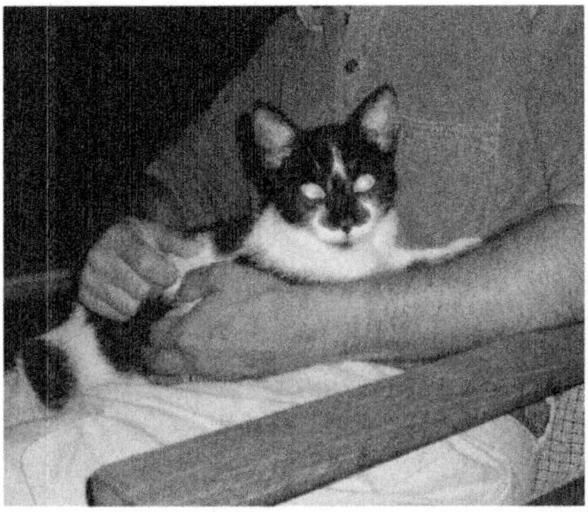

Kefalonia: Avithos Resort in Svoronata with Tom and Jerry

Petani cat and Kalafatis taverna cat

Greekstones and Katovathes

Argostoli Promenade and Drogarati Cave

Melissani Lake

Lixouri Ferry

Chapter 23

Crete

(2006)

There is so much of Greece you can't know even if you're Greek. It's sprinkled out all around the edge of the Aegean, all over the place. It's already a secret place wherever you go, even if it's somewhere huge like Athens or Corinth. The place enchanted me:
Joanna Lumley

We flew to Chania and then spent another couple of hours on the bus as it drove right over the twisty-turny mountain roads, which brought us down to the resort of Paleochora in the South-western corner of Crete. Trundling our bags down a quiet little side alley near the main beach to our studio, we entered via a beautiful garden and found our room on the first floor. Lying on the bed you could open the balcony doors and look straight out over some trees to the hills beyond. Looking out of the bathroom window, we were welcomed by a black and white cat happily sitting on the steps outside. At the back of the studios was a rather non-descript car park, but enlivened by the incongruous sight of a Disneyesque "Happy Train" parked up. We later discovered it plied its trade around town in the evenings, much to the delight of the children.

The village is on a small peninsula jutting out into the Libyan sea (also known as the "Libyan Bride") with the long, sandy Pachia Ammos ("thick sand") beach to the west and Chalikia pebble beach and harbour to the east. A line of impressive rocks/boulders create sea defences: and it was quite handy to have a choice of two beaches, depending on which direction the wind was blowing from. By the sandy beach there was a silhouette statue of two gentlemen wearing pith helmets called "The Traveller": bearing a slight resemblance to Oliver and Hardy. The impressive Evangelistria church had a remarkably ornate freestanding bell tower, which, from the castle of Selinos (*celery*) near the end of the peninsula, you can get a good view of. One of the stories tells that the infamous pirate, Barbarossa, forced the fort's garrison to hide in its water tank. It's well worth having a potter around the ruins and look back at the view over the village. Paleochora is a delightful resort with tree-lined roads, lots of cats, lovely plants and private gardens to be discovered. A walk along Kontekaki Street, linking the two beaches, revealed the clothes, jewellery and local produce shops; it was rather appealing to have a sign to a choice of beaches in two opposite directions, as well as a very "happy" pedestrian crossing sign. There was a lengthy power cut one evening while we were having dinner and as we strolled past, the taverna staff were scuttling about with candles. Walking past a sizeable ice cream parlour the owner seemed quite keen to invite us in to try some, presumably worried about how long his freezers were going to last. Sitting under the stars by candle light eating mastic ice cream with gentle laughter and chatter all around was quite magical. (Mastic is a kind of sweet, minty/aniseedy resin from the island of Chios.)

One Saturday evening we had a meal in a restaurant featuring Cretan dancing. In traditional dress, the young men wore wide, grey breeches – Vraka – tucked into long, black leather boots with rough-woven black shirts, red silk sashes tied around their waists and black, fringed kerchiefs wrapped around their heads. Their high leaps and kicks were positively gymnastic. The women's dress was more elaborate with embroidered blouses, aprons, jackets, white head kerchiefs and decorative jewellery. It struck me that just as the different regions and islands have their own identities and cultural idiosyncrasies, there are subtle differences in the format of Greek dance. We've seen a ring of twenty school children dancing on a stage in the main square in Paros, carefully carrying out quite formal, matching steps. During evening social gatherings, where all age groups form rings and stick to a basic principle, one person will often break off and enter the middle to put their own stamp on the dance – be it the more energised hops and jumps of the younger participants, or the gentle, complex, foot-waving signatures of some of the older generation. Whatever form it takes it's always a joy to watch the Greeks dancing.

Our happiest discovery in the village was an eatery called the Third Eye Restaurant. It was definitely our kind of place, with vegetarian dishes from around the world and a menu that changed each night and when the food had sold out that was it. You could walk into the kitchen area and choose what you wanted, with tables either at the front of the restaurant under the trees or at the back under a canopy of thick grape vines. We chatted to the owner and he told us that much of the food came from their own farm and the whole caboodle was run on a kind of cooperative community basis. He also told us that he was an ex-Greek Army tank driver turned Buddhist – quite a volte-face! After dinner, he would come round each table with a bottle and miniature glasses shaped like beer mugs to offer us refills of complimentary tsikoudia/tsipouro. Quite often he would clamber up on a chair with a pair of grape scissors and drop a fresh bunch onto the table. On a couple of occasions when we went there was live music, a Rembetika band and one night a splendid range of Indian dishes were on the menu with two guys playing brilliant sitar and tabla: it was a great little place.

We walked the 4 kilometres from Paleochora along a dirt track to reach Gialiskari beach with big pebbles and crystal clear water. After a bit I wandered over to the nearby taverna/café to buy a couple of frappes. The lady serving at the takeout section was helped by her daughter (probably about 12-13 years old) who suddenly called out, 'Delfini!' Sure enough, a few hundred yards out to sea a pod of about six dolphins were arcing by. I happened to have my binoculars with me so I watched them for a moment and then handed them over to the girl, much to her delight. I was about to walk back with the frappes when something way out on the horizon caught my eye. I placed the frappes on a nearby table and looked through the binoculars again … just in time to see the unmistakable black flukes of a whale tail majestically slip back into the water: it was quite breath-taking. On the walk home we passed a slope covered in fine shingle with the odd rock scattered in its midst. I took a photo of it and used that in the artwork on the cover of my first collection of short stories *Test Drive* to represent the surface of Mars.

We decided to go on a dolphin-watching boat trip from Paleochora, but unfortunately weren't lucky enough to see anything that time, however it provided a great vantage point to admire the coastline and see an epic sunset. Some years later I made a pastel painting of how I imagined a dolphin would look leaping from the water against that sunset, turning its body into a silhouetted window onto the full moon-illuminated sea.

To the east along the coast from Paleochora is Sougia and we took a ferry there. The view from the beach wouldn't have been out of place in Southeast Asia. During a leisurely lunch at a seafront taverna in the peaceful little village, we were joined by a pair of handsome cats and then after a brief mooch about, spent a very pleasant afternoon on the beach. As we prepared to catch the ferry back to Paleochora we watched as a group of about 30 walkers arrived, having just descended the Agia Irini Gorge (itself part of the National Park of Samaria). It had clearly been quite a challenging hike with various downhill scrambles, loose scree and rockfalls on the path. Indeed, some of the walkers who were heading to the ferry looked like they'd just returned from a first aid convention specialising in multiple-bandaging demonstrations. I've no doubt it is blessed with wonderful scenery and wildlife; but fitness, good solid walking boots and hiking poles would seem to be a good idea.

At the end of the holiday we took one last boat trip, this time going west to the utterly magical islet of Elafonisi. Greeted by a loggerhead turtle as the boat moored against the rocks, we made our way across the first huge sweep of amazingly fine pink sand (circumnavigating the beach beds and brollies). We carried on walking along the sandbar, wading through gently-lapping shallow water to access the smaller beaches to get away from the bulk of the visitors. Pink and red shells had been ground into tiny particles by the sea, giving the white sandy coves an exquisite pink blush as well as the stunning aquamarine sea. The beach is a Natura 2000 protected area and over 100 bird species have been registered with a plethora of fauna (such as the charming sea daffodil) adorning the windswept sand dunes in the quieter areas. It was absolutely beautiful and hopefully fully-protected from over-development.

Crete is a large and substantial island and there are so many more beautiful places to see. Hopefully we'll get the chance to explore a few more of them at some point.

Crete, Paleochora: Cats

Paleochora: Beach both ways sign

Happy pedestrian crossing sign

Cretan dancing

The Third Eye Restaurant

Dolphin pastel painting

Sougia cat

Sougia beach

Elafonisi sea daffodil

Chapter 24

Astypalaia

(2008)

Among all peoples, the Greeks have dreamt life's dream most beautifully:
Wolfgang Goethe

Everything was lined up to fly into Athens and transfer onto an internal Olympic Air flight to the island the same day, but a few weeks before we were due to travel, Olympic changed the departure time of their flight. As a consequence, we had to rebook the internal flight for the next day and stay an extra night in Athens, which was no great hardship. It gave us the opportunity to have our first 'mini' Athens experience. We caught the bus from the airport to Syntagma Square and wheeled our cases along Ermou to the Hotel Electra. We then had the afternoon to explore the area (Ermou, Monastiraki, the Roman Agora, Hadrian's Arch and the environs) and spend an evening at a taverna just below the Acropolis. It whetted our appetites to see more, but that would have to wait.

Next day we caught the metro back to the airport from Syntagma and then the Olympic flight to Astypalaia. The Olympic Dash-8 aircraft were a fabulous way to see the islands from the air and a great way to fly. Prop-driven, they removed the chocks from under the tyres and you were away. Carrying a maximum of 36 passengers it felt like the closest we were ever likely to come to flying on a private plane. The stewardess had a narrow little trolley so it would fit between the rows of two seats either side of the gangway; we had a couple of soft drinks and some nuts and settled back to enjoy the trip. You get a great view of the islands en-route, as well as all the boats and ferries plying to and fro across the Aegean sea. The flight took about 30 minutes: a really great experience.

As we approached the island of Astypalaia it became clear why some people had likened its form to that of a butterfly, divided into Exo Nisi and Mesa Nisi, connected by an incredibly thin isthmus called Steno. Also known as *The Mistress of Poseidon* it is the westernmost island of the Dodecanese, but has Cycladic hints. Kostas picked us up at the airport and drove us to Oneiro studios high up in the Chora. (Kostas and his brother Michael ran the studios and a car hire business on the island.) A large studio room led out onto a huge balcony, which gave us the most epic views we'd ever had anywhere in Greece (the price for this view would be the steep daily descent/ascent to reach our room if we ate down by the port). Pera Yalos sat far below and we looked out towards Mesa Nisi and a scattering of smaller islands. The fabulous Chora, sprinkled with white Cubist houses, had a line of red-topped windmills and the magnificent Kastro at the summit, topped off by the light blue dome of Panaghia Kastriani. We never tired of that view during our stay, although our lofty eyrie did suffer from the strong winds, causing the solidly-built, glass-sided, wooden-covered outer pergola to creak and groan rather ominously. Some mornings the tops of the white balcony walls would be covered with dew and the local sparrows would drop by to have a drink. Over the fortnight of our stay we watched the comings and goings of the various yachts and gin palaces in and out of the port, as well as the Nissos Kalymnos ferry and a naval frigate. Late one afternoon we saw a huge, two-masted, shiny black sailing ship had docked and, watching through binoculars, it seemed the crew had a quite unusual dress code as they scurried about the decks: wearing what looked like black robes and with their acrobatic movements we nicknamed them the 'Ninja Monks'.

The row of restored windmills led us to the base of the Chora and as we made our way up the narrow streets the Cycladic-style buildings had wooden balustrades, some external wooden staircases and lovely wooden balconies, most of which were brightly painted. Continuing upwards, we came across nine white, barrel-vaulted chapels – or ossuaries – said to contain the bones of some of the Chora's oldest families. We carried on further uphill, finding a sign here and there for the Kastro, until we eventually found a narrow doorway leading into a vaulted entrance passage with a cobbled floor. That in turn led to one of Greece's best preserved castles, laid out on a plateau overlooking the island with some fabulous views (it was built, as is usually the case, to defend against pirates) and there were also a couple of lovely churches.

A steep descent led us back down to the port and Pera Yalos (the climb back up the hill was quite hard going after a meal and several glasses of wine) – Pera Yalos is also known as Skala, which is Greek for stairs: rather apt. Around the bay was the Akti restaurant where we had an excellent evening meal at a table perched on a balcony, at the foot of many sets of steps, jutting out above the rocks. The taverna appeared to be hanging over the water with views of the bay and the Chora above. The waiters certainly had their work cut out as they belted up and down all the steps with trays laden with food and drink, but they seemed to cope admirably. We thought they must be part man, part mountain goat. Right on the beach was a family-run taverna called Akrogiali offering perfect home cooking and a great view, with local children playing happily on the sand and a huge tamarisk around which they'd built a shady pergola. The tree was covered in flower when we were there and it was alive with contented bees happily feasting on the nectar. We also explored the Archaeological Museum with a range of Minoan pottery, chamber tombs and a coat of arms of the Quirini family who built the Kastro.

A bus from Chora took us to the nearby beach of Livadi set in a lush, fertile valley with a splendid view of the Chora and some great caïques in the bay. We made numerous trips to this beach, tending to settle for the same spot where drinks and snacks were brought out to you. The young lady got to know us after a few days so I engaged her with my fledgling Greek.

Dave: 'Kaliméra.'

Young lady: 'Kaliméra, ti káneis;'

Dave: 'Polý kalá kai eseís;'

Young lady: 'Kalá. Thes éna potó;'

Dave: 'Nai, dýo frapé, métria me gala, parakaló.'

Young lady: 'Entáxei.'

Sue asked me what I'd said to her, so I said I'd arranged to meet her behind the bike shed in 10 minutes – Sue chuckled and went back to her book while waiting for the frappes to arrive. Walking back in the late afternoon one day we came across ten young cats, all huddled together fast asleep in a car port. Shortly afterwards we saw one of those extraordinary Makanakis – agricultural mechanised tricycles – that we'd first encountered on Alonnisos about ten years previously and in an adjacent garden a Greek wheelbarrow painted bright pink with a flower motif running around the top. How does a Greek wheelbarrow differ? You might well ask. Well, it has a much deeper tray and longer handles than the British barrow so I suppose it can carry heavier loads. Some people say the Greeks invented the wheelbarrow: possibly true for that design, but I think the Chinese were first with wooden ones. Anyway, this particular specimen was unusually ornate.

We caught the bus across the narrow steno and just into Mesa Nisi to reach Analipsi and Maltezana Bay (possibly named after the Maltese pirates who used to anchor there – those pesky pirates again!). The fabulous sandy beach, clear waters and a sheltered bay became a regular haunt for us. With the tiny islands of Ligno and Hondro on the horizon, it had rows of tamarisks with their white, asvesti-painted trunks and the shoreline, forming a curved, scalloped margin along the breakwater. (The photo on the back of the book is Maltezana Bay.) We found a sign to Loutra Tallaras (Roman baths) so naturally followed it. They were quite well-preserved remains, but the mosaics had all been covered by soil and sand to keep them from being damaged by the sun and general weathering. Had they been visible, we would have seen a central figure with a surrounding wheel featuring the 12 signs of the zodiac in blue, white and terracotta. Run by a local family, Taverna o Astakos was just on the other side of the road by the beach. It was charming and served wonderful food, which we tried both at lunchtime and one evening when we stayed to try their fish. My Greek was still pretty rudimentary – and still is, to be honest (I think it's like learning an instrument, new doors to higher levels of complexity continually open). I wandered round the back of the taverna one quiet, balmy afternoon and found the owner busily prepping vegetables for the kitchen. He spoke very little English, but as he was peeling some potatoes we had a go at talking about them and I told him that I grew them back home. Sign language and laughter filled the multiple gaps in our conversation and when we parted with a cheery wave I had a feeling of tremendous, friendly warmth. On the way back, the bus needed to turn around on the narrow road to make its return trip, so it went past the place we'd got on, then stopped and reversed onto what looked like a small projecting outcrop of flattened rock above a sheer drop. Stopping just short of recreating the final scene from the film *The Italian Job*, the driver swung back onto the narrow road having executed a precise 3-point turn to face the right direction. Along with another (rarely-sighted) English couple, we burst into spontaneous applause, although this didn't exactly meet with the driver's approval. He had probably done this manoeuvre many hundreds of times and didn't appreciate the endorsement of his skill from a bunch of tourists.

We were also fortunate enough to spend two wonderful days on board the Thalassopouli, or Seabird, with Captain Ioannis and his charming wife, Betina. One Sunday we left Pera Gialos from Astypalaia at 11am and visited Kounoupa Island for a couple of hours (passing several islets on the way). A short sail later and we anchored at another bay between Koutsomytis and Tigani, returning back to harbour around 6pm. The next day we set off again at 11am and sailed along the south coast with its fabulous rock formations to spend some time at Ag. Ioannis bay, then sailed back to Kaminakia bay and Ioannis took us right into a sea cave. After a couple of hours swimming and dozing on the beach we headed back with a brief stop at a deep-water bay rich in mineral salts, before returning home. You can see a little video I made on YouTube:

https://youtu.be/aTgJo1rN_i4

Astypalaia: Pera Yalos

Chora and Kastro

Chora Windmills

Kastro

Livadi kittens

Maltezana shoreline

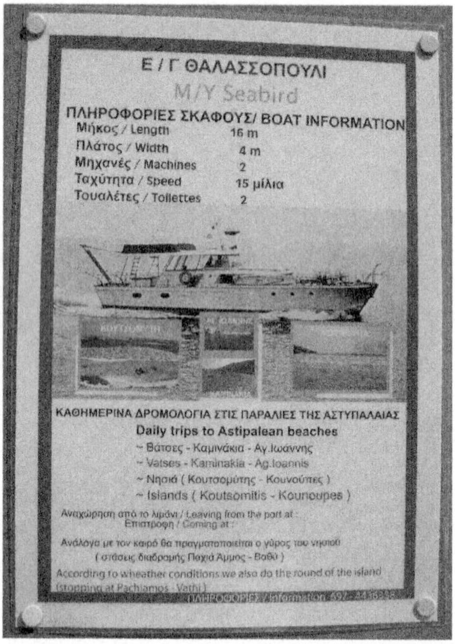

Poster for the Seabird Boat

Chapter 25

Paros

(2010 – 2015)

Greece is a good place to look at the moon, isn't it.
Kari Hesthamar

In 2000 Sue and I had been sitting at a table on the beach in Naxos, under the stars and tamarisks, at the Paradiso taverna on the outskirts of Agia Anna. As we looked out across the sea to the twinkly lights of Paros, it seemed like fairyland. Now, in 2010, we were actually going to visit the island itself. Traveling with some friends (Jon, Sue and Sarah) we took an overnight flight from Heathrow, arriving in Athens at 'Silly o'Clock' in the morning. Knowing that the X95 bus from the airport to Piraeus ran regularly throughout the night, we bought tickets and had a fast, mad, bumpy and somewhat dangerous journey to the port (the bus collided with a car at one point which was a bit alarming). Luckily still in one piece, we arrived super-early and waited in the pre-dawn darkness until we were allowed to board the Blue Star ferry to Paros. We soon located our pre-booked aircraft-style seats and gratefully nodded off for a few hours' rest and recuperation.

Our dear friend, Wendy, had gone to live on Paros a year or two previously. A few years earlier, she'd been visiting one summer, helping a friend to run a beach café. One of the regulars at the café was an English ex-pat and they'd struck up a relationship. She used to regularly visit him on Paros when she could. She told us that one wet, cold and windy November morning, as she was stuck in the usual traffic on her way to work, she reflected that she could make a permanent move to Paros and set up her jewellery making business there. As the traffic crawled along and the wipers struggled to clear the rain beating down heavily on the windscreen, she made up her mind.

We had known Wendy for over twenty years at this point. We'd met her through a music connection – many of our friends have arrived that way – her sister Sue is married to Jon, who was (at the time) the lead guitarist and songwriter with the Brighton-based folk-rock band Altogether Elsewhere (who were contemporaries of The Levellers). We liked their music and started going to their live gigs in the late 1980s. Wendy had always showed remarkable strength and resourcefulness whilst providing for her daughters as a single parent, seizing opportunities to work, but still making time to enjoy herself along the way. She was always laughing, dancing, keeping up with friends and being the life and soul of many a party.

Arriving at the port of Parikia, Wendy met us from the ferry and we walked along the seafront in pouring rain to the house we had booked for a week. She apologised for the unseasonal rainfall for June, which we found highly amusing as it was still wonderfully warm. In the evening we strolled to Selini Bar at the far end of the seafront by Kato Gialos beach. A favourite with the island's ex-pats with a very friendly vibe, it was a superb place to watch the sunset and the fishing boats moored at the small marina under a windmill. We met quite a few of her friends that first evening – rather like the opening scene from a film – some of whom were introduced quite cryptically by Wendy's other half, Rick, such as the marvellous Ian who he insisted was the original Milky Bar Kid: although that seemed pretty unlikely as the suggestion was met with a long-suffering glance from Ian. Other stories included that of a local who got so drunk he couldn't walk and decided it would be better if he drove home in his JCB, by taking a direct route and driving straight through someone's garden wall, demolishing it in the process: that one turned out to be true. It was quite a night, compounded by multiple bottles of Mythos and travel fatigue, blended with the joy of seeing Wendy and the excitement of making new friends.

After a refreshing and sobering swim in the morning we headed just out of town to the Magaya Beach Bar and spent a great afternoon watching an Athenian reggae band and reacquainting ourselves with some of the people we'd met the previous night, plus meeting some more new folks. After dinner there was a blues singer in the Pirate Bar in town.

The medieval capital of Lefkes was interesting to explore with its peaceful paved alleyways, narrow streets and a mix of Cycladic and neoclassical buildings, many with beautifully-kept courtyards and gardens. Looking down on some of the rooves, the walls of the cuboidal houses looked like they were coated with cake icing and some had chimneys resembling dome-covered dovecotes. It was easy to see why the serene atmosphere and enchanting scenes around every corner attracted many creatives to this mountain village, complete with its 'House of Literature', where writers and translators could stay and work. Having taken far too many photos – of the village and its cats – we reached a point where we could look out at the views from the vantage of the mountain. Agia Triada with its ornate marble bell tower and a small church nestling in the pines below; with windmills on the hilltops and views out towards Antiparos and Naxos.

Wendy drove us round the coast to the south, then up a winding road into the hills to visit the place she now called her home. It was an old farmer's cottage bought many years previously by her partner and was a mix of traditional Greek charm and his eccentric English adornment. The tranquillity was unsurpassable, interrupted only by the occasional, wind chime-like tinkle of bells as goats wandered along the track at the bottom of their drive. There was the odd 'moo' from the neighbouring farmer's cattle in the adjacent field and the clucks of their hens, as well as the songs from a procession of wonderful birds and the intermittent clicking buzz of the cicadas. They'd recently built an extension to the cottage, creating a workroom for jewellery-making, with a single bed for guests to stay over. It was a nicely-designed, breeze block (aeraki) construction, perfectly-rendered with the top of the adjacent loo/shower room finished to resemble a Greek dovecote. As most of the jewellery work was commissioned, I thought she could use an internet presence so on our return home I set up a website for 'Pica Designs', showing examples of her work past and present. I was more than happy to help our old friend.

The garden was their pride and joy with a cool bamboo-covered seated area, a built in barbeque and a superb 'picture window' seat in the wall with views looking across the adjacent fields and out to sea, framing the island of Sifnos in the distance. An outbuilding – which Wendy called "Chicken Mansion" – housed their hens, one of whom (Mavis) developed an immediate fascination with her sister Sue's red toenail polish, pecking hungrily at her toes. Next to that was a storage room that had once been a smoking house for preserving food, set behind an elevated area that would, in time, become a stage. We sat in the lunchtime shade of the porch at the side of the cottage, giving their rescue cat plenty of space: DJ was a 15-year-old tabby who lived life very much on her own terms. Meanwhile, *Pépé* the dog curled up under the table as we enjoyed the wonderful meal prepared by Wendy.

Another day Wendy drove us to Pounda to take the car across to Antiparos on the ferry. About 8km from the Chora she pointed out various landmarks and features and told us that, apparently, Tom Hanks had a place there and Madonna was also said to have visited. Our first stop was the Cave of Antiparos (also known as the cave of Agios Ioannis church). It's an extraordinary natural museum, descending vertically some 85 metres with the most breath-taking display of stalactites and stalagmites (the one near the entrance is reckoned to be over 40 million years old). The cave was once thought to have been used to worship the Goddess Artemis. At the lower end of the cave, what at first appeared to be graffiti turned out to be more of a historical Who's Who of visitors' autographs, such as Otto (the First King of Greece), Alexander the Great, the Marquis de Nointe (a French ambassador), Alexander Dumas and – for me – the greatest thrill of all, Lord Byron himself. We were lucky because the staircase and handrail comprising 411 steps had been upgraded the previous year. Divided into chambers with various features resembling pipe organs, dragon's teeth, melted candles, icicles and alien cauliflowers: it was the most remarkable place ... and also delightfully cool. When we made it to the very bottom we clustered around for a group photograph before ascending the 411 steps to emerge blinking into the Greek sunlight and heat. We spent the afternoon at Still Waters, a beachside taverna on Apandima beach; swimming, chatting, eating and drinking, before heading back to the Chora to stroll along the quay admiring the many fishing boats, spotting jellyfish on the sea bed and finally catching the ferry back to Pounda.

Parikia is Paros' lovely Chora, with charming narrow backstreets strewn with bougainvillea petals here and there, white Cycladic architecture (some in a modern adobe style) – including some splendid balconies with carved stone supports and ornate metal balustrades. There are tucked away churches, tavernas and cafes along the seafront and a good-sized main square, where we watched 30 or so local school children doing some traditional Greek dancing on a stage as part of a local festival. The streets take on a charm of their own at night with subtle shadows cast around their contours. There's an incongruous former windmill at the entrance to the port that acts as a kind of roundabout (I heard that the owner charges the port authority rent for it). The Panagia Ekatontapyliani is a very impressive Orthodox church, said to be one of the best preserved in Greece. Also known as the "Church of a Hundred Doors" the story goes that there are in fact 99, but the 100th is a secret door which will only open when Agia Sofia in Istanbul (Constantinople if you're talking to a Greek) becomes Orthodox again. The Venetian Kastro's wall was constructed from the "repurposed" blocks and columns of the ancient temples of Apollo and Demeter, giving it an unusual 'collage' appearance. As in most of Greece the mortar between the paving slabs on the pavements is painted with asvesti (a form of limewash), just like many of the houses and the trunks of some of the trees. I've often wondered why this is done. I can understand the fabulous white gleam of the houses (just as they used to paint castles in the UK in medieval times) and the tree trunks would be given both an antiseptic/insect repellent effect with asvesti, as well as preventing the powerful sunlight from causing cracks in the bark that could allow ingress of pests and diseases. But why paint the mortar between the cracks in the paving slabs? Maybe it reduces weathering and the need to repoint, but I have also seen it done on solid concrete pathways creating a 'crazy-paving' visual effect. So, it must be some kind of tradition and it's a beautiful feature: in my more philosophical moments (usually involving ouzo!), I've conjectured that the pattern resembles that of a sandy seabed as the sun reflects on the gentle waves from above. Many cats roam the streets of Parikia, so we filled a fair bit of camera space with their images. One day Jon and I walked along the seafront and came across a caricature artist and as we'd never had one done before we sat for a few minutes, intrigued as to how it would turn out. The finished results were not necessarily flattering, but the artist definitely caught some of our more "defining" features!

Wendy and Rick organised a barbeque and many of the folks we'd met previously came along. We were also introduced to several more ex-pats, plus a group of American art students. We found ourselves sitting next to a lovely couple, Mick and Gina, who it transpired were originally from near our neck of the woods – Telscombe Cliffs, a small place just along the coast. About ten years previously, the rock band Hawkwind had played an impromptu outdoor gig for former band member's birthday. This free event was held in the middle of a group of New Age Travellers who'd pitched up on a large patch of ground called Telscombe Tye. Mentioning this during our conversation with Mick and Gina to our amazement they not only remembered it but had also been there! Mikrós kósmos (small world).

As night fell, the music began. The American students had several talented young singer-songwriter-guitarists in their ranks; Adam Zierten and Carrie Cooley stand out in my memory. We were also treated to a rousing rendition of Dr Hook and the Medicine Show's *Cover of the Rolling Stone,* performed by our host and his chums. Later, as people started to drift away, we realised we were halfway up a mountain in the middle of nowhere and would need someone to give us a lift back. Luckily, a young man – who'd just got out of hospital having ridden his motorbike all the way from Germany (only to crash it when he reached Paros) – was heading back into town in his small hire car. So we and several other revellers sat on others' laps, squished against the inside of the roof of the car as we bumped down the dirt track off the mountainside and drove back to Parikia. I have no idea how/if the suspension survived. Back at Selini's Bar for a nightcap, I found myself between an ever-effervescent Scotsman, Harry, and a Viking colossus (and gentle giant) Leon. Earlier, during the more sober part of the evening I couldn't always manage to understand their strong accents, but by this stage of the proceedings I seemed to understand every word! I really don't remember very much about that part of the evening ... other than Sue smiling at me as an inflatable alligator bobbed behind her.

After a week or so, Sue and I relocated to the village of Alyki to a room above the wonderful AquaMarine restaurant run by the irrepressible Denis. Wendy and Rick were regulars at his place and had got to know Denis very well, so they'd arranged for us to stay there. Wendy knew we loved a sea view and particularly one of a bay in an active fishing village with a beach within easy walking distance, so it was a perfect location. There were dozens of beautiful fishing boats (caïques) in Alyki, their gorgeous shapes and colours reflected in the blue-silver mirror of the calm bay on hot, still afternoons. I took multiple photos (and painted a pastel picture of one of them a few years later) and we watched them chugging to and fro, unloading their small catches. Sometimes in the early evenings, cormorants would perch on the rocks near to AquaMarine, stretching out their wings and preening their feathers as we watched from the balcony sipping an ouzo, waiting for the sun to set like liquid gold behind the opposite hills. Our last few lazy days were spent relaxing under the tamarisks on the local beach, in between writing, dozing and swimming.

By now we were getting to know Denis pretty well and, a few times, I had been up quite late chatting with him and a couple of the other guests. Like me, he shared an appreciation of ouzo and claimed it gave him extra energy, or as he put it: 'Ouzo Power!' My birthday fell on the day before we were due to travel home, so we decided to have dinner with our friends at Aquamarine. We had a lovely evening and the drinks flowed, at one point Denis leapt onto another table and started singing *I'm Too Sexy for my Shirt*. His performance was rounded off with a surprise nightcap, which I think involved 'Souma' (Greek fire-water), but I suspect his secret recipe might have been based on something that escaped from NASA's propulsion laboratories. This, it turned out, was not the greatest thing to be drinking before a lengthy ferry journey back to Piraeus, then a four-hour flight from Athens to Gatwick, but I wouldn't have changed it for the world...

*

In 2011 our early morning flight from Gatwick to Athens was quite delayed and by the time we picked up our bags it was looking really tight time-wise. We needed to make it from the airport to Piraeus on the bus in time to catch the late afternoon (5pm) Blue Star ferry to Paros. I sent a text message to Wendy to let her know we might not make it that day, as she'd booked us a night in a hotel in Parikia. Luckily, when visiting us in the UK a few months previously, she'd bought our ferry tickets in advance so we didn't have to faff about at the Piraeus Port ticket office. The bus journey was spent anxiously checking our watches and hoping the traffic wouldn't delay us any further. The bus arrived with only a few minutes to spare before the ferry left and we ran across the port to where the Blue Star ferry was about to depart. I arrived first at the ramp, planted one foot firmly on it with the other on the quay as the jangly departure music played and officials waved their arms about urging me to board. Sue was following close behind, but I didn't want her to be left behind at Piraeus! Ignoring the loud protests and shouts from the boarding crew, we just managed to run on with seconds to spare before the ramp was raised. We stowed our bags and arrived on deck with a Mythos in hand as the ferry sailed out of Piraeus – a 'fashionably-late' Greek-style boarding if ever there was one! I let Wendy know that we'd made it by the skin of our teeth and were on our way to Paros. We found out later that no one else there thought we'd make the boat, but knowing us better, Wendy had taken bets on us making it and had cleaned up.

Arriving about 10pm we dropped our bags into the hotel room and headed for the nearest taverna for something to eat: it had been a long day. Much to my delight, they had stuffed squid on the menu (it's been a quest of mine to try to match the one I had on Santorini several years previously) and it wasn't half bad, as well as being the size of a small planet.

Next morning we headed for Piso Livadi in the middle of the east coast of Paros. Driving down a long road under a eucalyptus tree-lined archway we arrived at the small, picturesque fishing village. It had a curved, sandy beach with shallow water, perfect for swimming and floating about, as well a great collection of caïques to admire.

I think someone told me that the famous Parian marble was shipped out from Piso Livadi back in the mists of time (although the main marble mine was meant to be around Marathi, which would be closer to Parikia). It is very special stuff, the Parian marble: its light-catching properties made it much sought after in ancient times and some 70% of the sculptures excavated in the Aegean region are reckoned to be made from it, including the Venus de Milo, the Acropolis and many of the famous Greek temples.

Logaras beach was a short walk away with a longer curve of sand and glorious sea and was not as busy as expected, possibly due to the draw of Chrysi Akti *Golden Beach* for the younger crowd. We stayed at Elena's studios with its Cycladic architecture, lovely rooms and gardens, many artistic touches with pots, painted chairs, tables and decorations, plus a great view of Agios Antonios high up on the nearby hill. There was even a bamboo-covered shady car port to keep the hire car cool and having it for the whole fortnight would give us the chance for much greater exploration of the island than previously. Almost instantly we had a little, furry, ginger visitor to our studio room whom we christened "Timmy Minchios", having recently seen the wonderful Tim Minchin in concert. He was a delightfully playful, bold and very friendly little boy who made our first week extra special. Evenings in Piso Livadi were serene and lovely with some excellent tavernas and bars; Halaris Ouzery (*Seahorse*) was a particularly good seafood place. Captain Yannis' bar was wonderfully chilled out with great views of the lights of Naxos in the distance and the moon's sublime reflection shimmering on the sea. We were finally on the other side of the mirror from when we were on Plaka Beach on Naxos ten years earlier, from where we'd watched the fairyland lights of Paros twinkling across the water.

We drove up to Naoussa, parked the car and mooched down the main road, past a black stone, three-arched bridge and down to the seafront.

White geese plodded along the shoreline adjacent to the harbour – with another caïques fix for me. Gouna was both hung up and spread out on wooden fish crates: gouna is a speciality of the island, mackerel opened up like a butterfly, sprinkled with herbs and left out in the sun to dry for several days. They were laid out near a mound of purple, red and yellow fishing nets, topped off with round floats like giant grapes under an old twin-lamped street light. We found a seafront café and ordered a couple of frappes – they were a bit pricey and we got the impression that Naoussa was quite a chic, cosmopolitan, touristy village. Taking a wander through the backstreets under archways and through painted alleys, we came across some beautiful gardens and pot plants as well a collection of quite 'chi chi' establishments, one with a little kitten sitting expectantly at a table. Wendy told us about a tradition in Naoussa: on 23rd August 100 torch-lit boats storm the harbour to re-enact their battle against the pirate Barbarossa (and the crumbling Venetian castle at the far end of the harbour must make quite a backdrop). There's a Greek restaurant in Brighton called Archipelagos and it used to be managed by a friendly guy from Olympia called Theo. He left a few years ago and we heard recently that he has opened a new restaurant – also called Archipelagos – in Naoussa, so if we're ever back that way we'll have to look him up.

We drove the short distance from Naoussa to Kolimbithres, set in a bay looking back across the water to Naoussa. A series of small, fine-sand coves edged the shallow water, surrounded by the most extraordinary natural features. The grey granite rocks had been weathered over the centuries to create the most mysterious-looking shapes and forms. Some resembled rows of alien skulls, others were smooth elephantine bulges, or the prows of ghostly ships, with successive honeycomb-like hollows worn by pebbles in their midst, with outcrops and fins all jostling for attention. An occasional lizard skittered across them and vanished into one of the holes. We settled down on a pair of sunbeds for a few hours and I pottered off to examine the rocks more closely. As I emerged into another nearby cove and ambled across the sand to take some pictures another tourist waved some money at me. It took me a few moments to realise that I resembled the guy who collected the sunbed fees ... with my black bum bag slung jauntily about my waist. Resisting the urge to take the fellow's euros, I explained that I wasn't the right guy and continued to the rocks – this wouldn't be the last time I got mistaken for a sunbed hirer; maybe I should get some raffle tickets for another year.

With the car we tried to visit a new beach more or less each day. (A few Greek island road signs, by the way, can be more of a birthright than convention, such as an old broom or mop handle hammered into the ground with an upturned bucket on top at dangerous junctions being recognised as a Give Way sign.)

At Ambelas on the northeast coast, we had a leisurely lunch in a taverna by the harbour watching the fishing boats come and go with a view of the Naxos Chora in the background – we could see the Portara and the Kastro through the binoculars (the photo of the table, chairs and harbour on the cover of this book was taken there ... I added the cats). After lunch we spent a few hours on the sandy beach. An elderly local couple trundled up in their equally elderly car and steadily made their way along to what we reckoned was their regular spot on the beach. The old boy set up his chair and we watched with interest as he tied one end of a long coil of rope to the chair leg, attaching the other end to a large inflated tyre inner tube. His wife, meanwhile, was standing watching him in her bathing suit. Having satisfied himself that everything was secure he popped the ring over her upstretched arms to fit around her waist, she then meandered into the sea, adjusting her broad-brimmed, white hat as she went. Once she was happily bobbing about he followed until the water reached his shorts, grasped the ring and gave her a good strong shove. She happily floated off further into the sea and he sat and read his newspaper until about forty minutes later, when she called for him to haul her back in. Fabulous.

Tzanes, Chrysi Akti, or Golden Beach, is a favourite with the windsurfers and is the location of an annual World Cup event for that sport. The sand has a subtle sparkle to it and it's certainly a very impressive spot, although I'd guess it gets pretty busy at the height of the season. Turning and looking back inland we had a fabulous view of the Agios Pantes mountain.

Krios beach, just around the corner from Livadia (effectively the Chora beach and very pleasant with it) is right next to Parikia and is another lovely, long, sandy stretch. It also benefits from shelter from the prevailing wind and has a steady, shallow slope into the water, such that people would stand up to their waists some way out with fishing rods. We sat below the biggest, droopiest reed umbrella, which we had to duck down underneath to reach the sunbeds and affectionately nicknamed it the "Rasta" brolly.

Parasporos is just south of Parikia town, so it can get busy, but is yet another delightful spot. To the left of the bay the rocky hill sloped into the water and resembled Tolkien's *Smaug*, like a dragon on its holidays cooling off in the water with its chin in the sea.

We visited Agia Irini beach with Wendy and had lunch at the taverna at the end of the charming little bay under a collection of magnificent palm trees. She told us about the threat to Greece's palms from an invading species of beetle that was already causing devastation in some parts.

Wendy and Rick obviously had to carry on with their day jobs while we were on holiday there, but we spent the second week in Alyki at AquaMarine with Denis, so we arranged to drive up the mountain one evening to have a barbeque with them.

Sue and I went into Parikia to visit the fishmonger and bought some excellent sea bream, but we also wanted to make some vegetable kebabs for the BBQ. As we walked towards the supermarket along the seafront we noticed, behind the church near the ferry port, a group of old men selling vegetables from their gardens/small holdings. It looked great and they seemed pleased by my admiration for their produce and camaraderie as a fellow gardener (despite my limited Greek). We left with two carrier bags loaded with fresh vegetables at an incredibly reasonable price, along with a chorus of "Yassas" and hands waving goodbye. A much nicer way to shop than visiting the supermarket.

As we prepared the veggie kebabs up at Wendy's place, we looked out of the window to see an unusual little bird perched on the wall outside. She was steadily getting to recognise her feathered visitors and identified it as a Sardinian Warbler. Later that afternoon she took us further up the mountain track to a little patch of land that one of the local farmers had kindly allowed her to use as her own veg patch/allotment. Somehow, she had aubergines, tomatoes, sweet peppers and courgettes growing in what looked to us like the most unpromising dry, stony soil. Luckily the farmer let her take a little spur off his water supply; but she explained that here you had to treat the plants tough, sparing the water to force them to drive their roots deep into the soil, otherwise the relentless summer sun could actually burn the roots if they were too close to the surface. We heard a little meow and turned to see a small white cat with a ginger head and tail emerging from the bamboo hedge surrounding the veg patch. Sue picked him up as he was desperate for attention, and we'd have loved to have taken him back with us, but our Simba would never have tolerated another cat in 'his' house. The little kitten called plaintively as we drove away and it almost broke our hearts to leave him there. It seems that many cats were abandoned when their owners left the island at the end of the summer holidays to return to the mainland. Fortunately for some of them, Mick (who we'd met the previous year) went up there to feed them regularly and the Paros Animal Welfare Society (PAWS) also did what they could to help the stray animals.

Living half way up the mountain they were miles from the usual utilities, but they managed brilliantly ... what Wendy described as "Posh camping". When a 'suited and booted' Greek official conducting a census trudged up the track to find them he was quite mystified by their answers on the census form:

'So, you don't have running mains water, you use gas cylinders and wood fires for cooking, and you have batteries to store the power from your solar panels ... but you have the internet?'

He traipsed off down the hill, muttering under his breath incredulously, apparently unfamiliar with the modern sorcery of an internet dongle.

At sunset we had our photo taken sitting in the picture window seat of their garden and Wendy told us how one early evening she had been standing by the sink when a string of butterflies flew past outside, gradually increasing in numbers until hundreds were streaming past. She went outside to watch them for ages; they were on their way to Petaloudes, the "Butterfly Valley", two or three miles to the north of them around the mountain. Eating out under the stars in the stillness of the hills that evening was paradise and it was clear why Wendy was so content to be living there. I only drank a single beer and drove very carefully back down the mountain side. Just as we were going past the airport a cat suddenly ran out across the road right in front of us, but thankfully I managed to avoid it. One of its nine lives...

The quayside road at Alyki was cordoned off to traffic in the evening, unless you were actually staying there, so I had to get out and move the barrier, drive through and put it back again before we could slowly creep past the other tavernas and park up at AquaMarine. There was a Periptero just by that barrier and the old guy running it had got to know Wendy and Rick quite well, so every time they drove past he would lean across the newspapers and magazines and call out, 'Viva Las Vegas!'

Wendy had told us about Scorpios Museum near the airport road, describing it as a collection of "big miniatures", so we went to investigate. Using traditional techniques and natural materials Benetos Skiadas had taken years to create an amazing open air display of Cycladic Civilisation. The exhibits included a watermill, dovecote, the Parakian Venetian castle, the Blessed Virgin of Folegrandos, a superb Greek windmill, the Lions of Delos, the Antiparos cave, and Fira at Santorini to name a few. Benetos' wife, Popi, also proudly showed us his exhibition of hand-crafted model Greek boats, with their incredible detail and complexity. Also known as the "Museum of Cycladic Folklore" I highly recommend a visit if you're in Paros. I think the miniature lighthouse by the bay in Alyki might by him, too.

The party up in the hills had grown from an impromptu gathering into a mini-festival. Wendy's years of festival experience was evident in the bunting, wall-hangings and LED lights swinging in the breeze as friends started to gather. First up on the new stage was the mild-mannered *Viking,* Leon – from Denmark: Leon was proud of his Viking heritage and sung some suitably rousing songs in his own tongue. Then came Jim and Harry who were only just getting to grips with the guitar, but made a splendidly spirited attempt at playing as the wind blew their sheet music away. Incongruously, as dusk fell, a big group of burly guys took to the centre of the garden and went into a full-on Māori Haka: that got everyone going. The evening continued with Brian performing songs such as *Fisherman's Blues*, *Bankrobber* and *Gloria* with Rick on bass, Mike on lead guitar, Jim on spoons and Wendy herself on tambourine and maracas. Various performers drifted on and off stage until things steadily devolved into glorious, semi-melodic chaos. We stayed overnight and lent a hand to help clear the debris in the morning, before slinking back to Alyki for a couple of gigantic, reparative chocolate waffles. We drank loads of fruit juice and had a lazy day on the local beach as the obliging tamarisks sheltered us from the sun, creaking and groaning like Ents from Tolkien's *Lord of the Rings*.

Back in Alyki I tried my smattering of Greek in a beachside taverna one evening to request a Greek salad: I pronounced it "Horiatiki salata" with the emphasis on the "tiki". The guy taking our order was an older gentleman and he looked puzzled by my attempt, so he went off to find a younger chap. When I tried again, a smile spread across the younger chap's face and he said: 'Ah, you mean Hori-A-tiki!' Just that tiny adjustment made all the difference and I realised I was going to have to pay a lot more attention to where I put the emphasis accents on Greek words: Χωριάτικη Σαλάτα. I don't know how true this is, but I have heard that the Greek language has very few – if any – dialects. Possibly a slight difference between Athens, Crete and Thrace, but overall pretty similar. Our English ear is used to all manner of accents so we can usually discern what someone from another country is saying in English (even with a strong accent), but maybe this is not so with Greek.

We flew back to Athens from the tiny Paros airport (referred to by Rick as "Paros International"), recognising the young lady at the check-in desk from her other job at the main post office in Parikia – great multi-taskers, the Greeks.

Alyki

Goats still their bells in afternoon shade,
Sleepy siesta in climbing centigrade,
We do the same and bless the gentle breeze,
Under the whispering, rustling tamarisk canopies.

Traversing shoreline stones into the Aegean,
An any-day match for the Caribbean,
Immersed in a sandy-bedded blood-cooling bath,
We swim,
We float,
Then we laugh.

Suspended in the water,
And in time,
Our friend waves to the beach,
To her valentine,
We applaud the move to her island home,
Grey-skied traffic jams left well alone.

Caïques chug by the harbour wall,
Nets filled,
Fruits of their trawl,
The quayside draws nearer,
Wakes ripple the mirror.

The setting sun spills liquid gold across the bay,
Roosting sparrows chatter about their day,
A gliding yacht chased by its faithful tender,
Farmhouse on a hilltop silhouetted in molten splendour.

The *filoxenia* of AquaMarine *c'est magnifique*,
Belgian twist on local cuisine delicious and unique,
Recharged with 'ouzo power' and postcard views,
The hour comes all too soon,
For reluctant *adieux*.

(Dave Burnham 2011)

In 2012 we dropped into Paros on our way to Syros. Wendy's daughters had found that flying to Mykonos and getting the boat to Paros from there was more convenient, so we gave that route a go. I recall sitting at a taverna at the end of a short road down to the old port waiting for the ferry and watching as a shepherd brought a flock of sheep up the road towards us: every now and again you'd still see that juxtaposition of old and new ways.

There were a couple of new residents at AquaMarine this year: Garfield and the Marquis de Sade. Garfield was a lovely ginger cat who looked very similar to our Simba and the Marquis de Sade was a characterful tabby who you had to watch out for in case you sat on a chair at one of the tables, without checking for feline occupation first.

We were only going to be there for a few days and our visit had been engineered to fit around the second of the parties/mini-festivals happening at our friends' place up in the hills. Taking a similar format to the previous year I set about filming it and later produced a DVD so that folks could remember it (some of our memories being somewhat hazy). Leon kicked off again with one of his Viking songs, joined for another by Liam on guitar and Tasos on congas. Jim had ditched the guitar for his instrument of choice – the accordion – and Ian sang *Your Cheating Heart* with him, backed by "The Jimettes", Gail and Sonja. Kirsty sang a few gutsy numbers from the likes of the Dead Kennedys (backed by Harry on guitar and John on bodhran), plus an acapella version of *Ace of Spades*. Brain did his thing again with various people drifting in and out of the band with Dan on guitar, Savas on keyboards and Kostas on congas; Rick somehow managing to play bass despite having his arm in plaster (having unfortunately broken it) with Wendy joining in on percussion. Mushy, Peter and Sol played guitar, and Ben sang and played. People took it in turns to perform (with Harry and Ian having a crack at it at some point, somewhat the worse for wear, but still highly entertaining) and the evening went on to become another legend in the ex-pat community. Later we had a lift back to Alyki with Terry and Sonja.

We'd planned to get the morning high speed ferry to Syros, but the meltemi winds had other ideas (sound familiar?). There was another boat due to depart around 7pm, a solid old vessel called the *AQUA SPIRIT,* that only the most severe weather would deter. With this new schedule, we changed our tickets and trundled our cases along the seafront to Tango Mar at the far end of Livadia beach. The manager very kindly allowed us to store our bags in the office for a few hours and, having swiftly changed into our beach gear, lying on a sunbed with a frappe certainly wasn't the worst way to kill a few extra hours. Wendy was employed to assist a charming local couple with some of their day-to-day chores, plus helping to organise their social events, etc., and she could see the port from their house. She'd noticed that the Syros ferry hadn't turned up that morning so she sent us a message to see what we were doing. With serendipitous coincidence she had planned to have lunch at Tango Mar to help to celebrate her daughter Sarah's birthday, as she was also on holiday in Paros. We were kindly invited to join them and we also got to meet her employers, Jean and John, who were a really lovely couple. John was a doctor and one of the pioneers in the development of the artificial hip, so, having a medical background I chatted with him about his time as a consultant and lecturer in the UK. His other passion was the city of Alexandria, where he had been born of Greek Macedonian parents, and he had written a book about it from its origins up to more recent times. He was a fascinating and erudite gentleman and I consider myself fortunate to have spent some time with him. Time flew past and the hour of departure came, so we bid farewell to Wendy for the second time that day and headed to catch the ferry to Syros.

*

2014 saw us on Paros for a few days at the start of our holiday and of course we returned to stay at AquaMarine. Wendy and Rick met up with us for dinner after a swim and Pépé their dog, came too. There were swallows nesting under the eaves of the restaurant's flat roof this year and we watched the parents flying in with insects to feed the chicks.

Following Wendy's story about the stream of butterflies she'd seen flying past her kitchen window, she took us to Petaloudes, the "Butterfly Valley", to see them for real. The valley is set out as a small park with pathways and steps running through it and from June to September, Panaxia Quadripunctaria (also known as the Jersey Tiger Moth) swarm to the area.

Having black and white markings on the upper side of their wings it is a delightful surprise when they take off and reveal a bright, vivid red colour beneath. It was a haven of tranquillity and dappled shade, not only affording the chance to see the moths in all their glory, but birds, dragonflies and lizards. From there we went back to Agia Irini beach for a cooling Mythos under the palm trees and then up the mountain back to Wendy's home.

There were two new members of the household this time: Bonnie and Clyde. A few months previously, Wendy had been driving from Parikia when a white kitten ran across the road directly in front of her car. She braked just in time to avoid it and something made her get out and follow it. Clyde (as she came to name him) ran to some rubbish bins next to the road where his sister was cowering. They had clearly both been abandoned and were in a terrible state due to starvation and a bad infestation of fleas. Wendy reckoned that Clyde had risked his life in an attempt to attract her attention and as a last ditch effort try to save themselves. Wendy was a cat lover like us and before she moved to Greece she had always owned cats. We used to send her postcards from our holidays with pictures of Greek cats, which she used to display on the kitchen wall in her house. So, naturally she couldn't just leave these poor defenceless cats to their fate, so she scooped them up and took them home with her. She nursed them both back to health and as their fur grew back she could see they were the most beautiful (possibly pedigree) cats.

A low-key barbeque with a few friends was followed by another day on Piso Alyki beach (when I think I first heard about the selling off and breaking up of the fishing boats – caïques – from Wendy) and then we set off for Andros via Tinos.

*

We were holidaying on Naxos in 2015 and we'd arranged to have a day trip by ferry over to Paros to visit Wendy and Rick. We spent most of the day at their place, chilling in the shade and enjoying one of Wendy's fabulous lunches. This time there was another addition in the form of Tigger, but very sadly their old cat DJ had passed away that very morning which made us feel rather sad. Their garden was looking magnificent: bougainvillea had grown over the top of the picture window seat, softening the edges and making it even more photogenic, the trees were looking lush in rich, green leaf with phormiums below, pelargoniums and hibiscus jostled for attention, an alstroemeria burst forth in peaches and yellows, the glossy rosettes of the aeoniums – nicknamed "aliens" by Wendy – jiggled in the light breeze and a hoopoe (crested lark) twittered on the fence. We went down to Piso Alyki beach to dip our toes in the sea and then to AquaMarine for a beer and a catch up with Denis, before catching the evening ferry back to Naxos. Up on deck in the cool air, we gazed up at a sickle moon reflecting on the sea with Venus and Jupiter forming an astronomical triangle, it was perfect.

In early December that same year, Wendy returned to the UK to do the rounds visiting family and friends, and she stayed with us for a night. It was a lovely evening of non-stop chat and laughter as usual (but she did mention in passing that she needed to have to have some medical tests in the New Year, but played it down in her typically up-beat way). I poured us a little Metaxa nightcap while we reminisced about a particularly late night at the Larmer Tree Festival in the early 1990s. We were at one of the cafes with a few of the musicians Wendy knew and she decided that a brandy was needed to conclude things. The guy serving at the tented café told her they only served brandy coffees, but – undeterred – Wendy replied with a twinkle in her eye, 'Okay, I'll have brandy coffees, but without the coffee, please'. He was so tickled by this that he actually obliged with coffee mugs about half full with brandy … it's still a phrase we use today.

Tragically, Wendy passed away just a couple of months later following a short illness. It was such a shock and just didn't seem possible that such a resourceful, generous-spirited, talented and wonderful woman was no longer with us. The warm recollections of our times with her in Paros are just a few of the many happy memories of her and we always smile when we think of those wonderful days. I have dedicated this book to her and I wrote a little poem that I read on the day she was laid to rest. RIP lovely lady.

Suddenly a thousand butterflies appear
Carrying her spirit every year
Past meadow valley flowers and orchid hills
With the scent of mountain herbs the air is filled
Kissed by the sun with the olives and the grapes
A legacy of laughter and Celtic shapes

Πολλά φιλάκια και καλό ταξίδι στα αστέρια

Paros: Wendy in front of her workshop extension up in the hills and DJ the cat

Parikia cats

Parikia: Backstreets, Jon and Dave caricatures, Kastro wall

Piso Livadi with "Timmy" and up in the hills with the allotment cat,

Kolimbithres

Scorpios "Big Miniatures" and the Antiparos Cave

Mini-festival up in the hills: set up and Haka

In Wendy's picture window and Denis dancing on the tables at Aquamarine

Garfield The Marquis de Sade Pépé

Alyki Fishing boat (caïque) in pastels by Dave

Tiger moths at Petaloudes

Bonnie and Clyde

2015 up in the hills with Rick and Wendy

Chapter 26

Syros
(2012)

We are all Greeks.
Our laws, our literature, our religion, our arts, have their root in Greece:
Percy Bysshe Shelley

The morning ferry from Paros was delayed by high winds so our tickets were transferred to the *AQUA SPIRIT* departing at 7pm to Syros. She weathered the swell remarkably well and we arrived in Ermoupolis around 8:30. *AQUA SPIRIT*'s story is quite interesting: built in 2001 and originally named the *AGIOS ANDREAS II* she remained in Greece through multiple transfers to different shipping lines until 2007 when she was converted into a floating supermarket in Sweden called *MR SHOPPY ONE*, returning to Greece in 2011 and becoming the *AQUA SPIRIT*, but NEL Lines went bust and she had a couple of years with Sea Jet before travelling to Canada and becoming the *NORTHERN SEA WOLF*.

The taxi from the port climbed high up into the hills and down the other side to Kini, but as it was dark we couldn't see the epic views. We were staying at the Captain's Apartments; Christiana had left the key in the door for us and we peered over the balcony at the lights of Kini village, which seemed to be very far below. It felt a bit like we were on the Mary Celeste as the wind whistled round the eaves, but in need of dinner we set off on foot down the main, twisty-turny road towards the twinkling lights. It took us a couple of days to discover there was a set of steps just over the road from our room that went straight down the hillside into the village! In most Greek towns and villages built on hills there will be considerably more direct routes to the centre than using the main road ... you just have to track them down. We arrived at the village, drawn by the lights and the smell of food, and rounded the corner at the bottom of the hill by the water. The first taverna we saw was called 'The Two Cicadas on the Tamarisk Tree'. That evening, as it was late and we were tired we ate inside, but on multiple return visits we sat on their lovely patio area right next to the sea. We don't eat meat (other than seafood) so can't comment on that side of things, but the menu was quite extensive and not limited to the standard Greek taverna fayre. During the course of several excellent meals we had: Spaghetti (pesto and mushroom), leek and mushroom tart with Portabello mushrooms, horta, courgette balls, fresh fish, superb skordalia ("garlic sauce"), a fabulous lentil salad (Puy lentils, tomatoes, red pepper, onion, carrot, rocket, spearmint and grated orange zest), a tabulae salad (with lovely, fresh, flat-leafed parsley), really nice spring rolls ("vegetables in pastry"), a huge flat mushroom with garlic and parmesan ("garlic mushroom"), melt-in-the-mouth briam, and freshly-baked bread rolls. The menu was all reasonably priced and their chefs really knew what they were doing: fish lovers and vegetarians were certainly very well-catered for (and I'd imagine meat options are equally excellent). The taverna had a lovely, warm welcoming atmosphere and was run by genuinely friendly people. As a bonus, there were several well-nourished, healthy-looking cats in attendance, mooching around the tables or just hanging out in the trees looking down at the diners below. We were told that the owners kept them fed over the winter months, out of tourist season: it is one of our favourite tavernas we've visited over the years.

In the bright sunlight of the next morning, the view from our room at the Captain's was stunning: looking out to the Stonichas hills with a scattering of white beehives on the slopes, Giaros Island, the fertile valley of Kini and the village spread out below us. We could see small fishing boats floating in the harbour and sandy beaches lining the bay, as well as the tight hairpins of the main road down which we'd walked the previous evening. Our high balcony was inaccessible to the local cats, but we were visited by a goat, who'd made its way up the adjacent marble steps after busily munching on some neighbouring vines. Once we'd discovered the nearby shortcut steps down to the village they made life considerably easier and much quicker and safer than trudging along the main road. Sometimes we had company as we descended the steps. There was a house at the corner of the road where the shortcut began, which had a wee dog who would trot out to greet everyone passing by and often follow us down the steps. Of course he then had to make the return journey all the way back up on his very short little legs – the silly boy – we nicknamed him "Sausage".

We spent several days lazing on Kini beach and the adjacent Lotos. On Kini beach, sea daffodils sprung up through the fine sand and mallard ducks patrolled the shoreline, with tamarisks for shade if we wanted to be distanced from the busier part with its sunbeds and umbrellas. The smaller Lotos beach was even quieter and perfect for an afternoon snooze and relaxing dip. A statuesque young woman appeared one late afternoon, divested most of her clothes and strode into the water with a bottle of shampoo to wash her hair, looking like a living *Timotei* advert, before sitting back on the beach to smoke a cigarette like a film star. On the seafront there was a superb bronze statue fountain by Giorgos Xenoulis of a mermaid cradling a sailor, the mermaid is Panagia Gorgona (Saint Mermaid/Virgin Mary the Mermaid) patron saint of fishermen. Dedicated to all of those who have lost their life at sea, the local legend is one of a local fisherman who fell overboard near the bay and was rescued by a mermaid: it's a lovely thing.

I got the chance to indulge my passion for admiring and photographing fishing boats (caïques) yet again in the harbour at Kini. The water was so clear the boats seemed to hover above the seabed, suspended in air. One had a pile of yellow nets where the fisherman had been removing what appeared to be knobbly lumps of lava, entangled and tearing at the mesh, where they had been dragged along the seabed. The village itself had several well-cared for gardens, one in particular with a remarkable array of potted succulents, as well as some spectacular hibiscus and bougainvillea around the place. Kini seafront is the place for mesmerising sunsets and we took full advantage of it on several evenings.

We came across a range of beautiful, healthy-looking cats as we explored the village. I've found out recently that there is a team of volunteers called "Syros Cats" local to Kini who help feed/neuter them, so that might be the reason: www.helpsyroscats.com.

In 2021, as I write this chapter, we watched a Netflix program about a couple who started a cat sanctuary in 2010 a little further north. The series is called "Cat People" and the episode featuring them is "God's Little People" which is also the name of their sanctuary and is an inspirational program: godslittlepeoplecatreascue.org.

We could see on the map that Delfini beach wasn't very far from Kini and there was a handy well-marked coastal path beginning at the far end of the harbour, so we decided to explore. The path started with a well-worn, narrow dirt track through low scrub, gradually giving way to the odd large rock to traverse here and there. As we continued along the path it started to climb higher up the side of the hill with correspondingly greater, vertiginous, drops down to the sea below and we started to realise we may have been inappropriately shod for the task (flip-flops are not ideal). The potential jeopardy was amplified as the path became composed of more large jagged lumps of rock than actual track, but we clambered on with tantalising glimpses of the beach just around the outcrop ahead. Eventually the rocks gave way to a much better path and we descended towards the lovely, sandy beach: that was one well-earned swim! We got a taxi back.

Sometime in the second week of our holiday we were having dinner at The Two Cicadas when we got chatting to a couple from Scandinavia. They had enjoyed a fabulous holiday and were due to fly home the following day. They weren't looking forward to exchanging 24°/25° for minus 3°. As we listened to a Greek gentleman playing guitar and singing traditional songs at a nearby table, they told us we should try a quirky restaurant along the way, located on one of the roads out of the village. They said we couldn't miss it, as it had very bright lights and would be full of people. So the next night we decided to go and, sure enough, set back a bit from the road was a building with very bright lights and quite a lot of people. We walked up the few steps to the entrance and waited to be seated. A woman came out and looked a bit puzzled when we asked for a table for two and went off to find someone to help us. A bit odd, we thought. A few moments later a very pleasant young woman came out to greet us and explained that today was her birthday and this was her private house, but we were welcome to come and join the party if we wanted to! Glowing with embarrassment we apologised profusely and explained the directions that had led us there. She smiled and pointed up the road, wished us a good evening and went back to her friends. As we swiftly retreated we could hear peals of laughter emanating from behind us: oh well, at least we'd given them something to talk about. (Some years ago Sue's parents had been on holiday somewhere in Greece when they came across a couple of tables outside with some empty coffee cups on them, so they plonked themselves down and when an elderly lady appeared they asked for two coffees. She went back inside and duly returned with their beverages. A while later they asked for the bill. She looked somewhat taken aback and said there was no payment required … she lived there…) No more than a hundred metres further up the road we found a really busy, brightly-lit restaurant with tourists sat cheek by jowl and it was obviously the place we'd been told about. Space was found for us and we were given a sheet of paper with a list of dishes and a sort of flow diagram of menu choices that we ticked and returned to the waitress. It was good value and certainly quirky, but I really can't remember what it was called: great fun though.

A large crowd gathered round a TV screen in one of the seafront tavernas one evening and we could see they were watching a basketball match: apparently Greece had been doing quite well and only narrowly lost the final of whichever series it was they were playing in with other countries.

We caught the bus into Ermoupolis (named after the god of Commerce, Hermes), the main town and the administrative capital of the Cyclades: divided into the original Catholic Ano Syros to the north and the Orthodox Vrondado to the south. We'd seen the Neorion shipyards from the ferry on our way to Paros a couple of times and glimpsed the town itself, but hadn't realised quite how grand it was. Ermoupolis had some very impressive buildings and more than its fair share of mansions and neoclassical influence, marble-paved roads and an unmistakeable elegance to it. Fabulously amphitheatrical, the multicoloured buildings clung to the two hills and its past commercial and cultural heyday were still in evidence. Chios Street had a great display of produce from both greengrocers and fishmongers as the marble paving led us to the immense central square, Plateia Miaoulis, with a magnificent statue of Andreas Miaoulis (chief admiral during the War of Independence) standing in front of a massive town hall. We walked to the right and came across the Apollo Theatre: apparently modelled on Milan's *La Scala* it was Greece's first opera house. As we made our way up towards Vaporia we had a closer look at Ag. Nikolaos with its spectacular blue and gold dome, in front of which was the first monument to the Unknown Soldier topped by a statue of a sleeping stone lion in a space surrounded by palms and pines. We turned to look down at the rocky waterfront below and thought the houses resembled Little Venice in Mykonos. Walking further up Babagiotou Street, admiring some of the old shipowners' mansions, we found a small square full of cats on the low walls, with plastic feeding stations wired onto the railings. I probably ought to be showing you our photographs of the architecture and statuary of Ermoupolis, but you can find that on the internet, so there are some photos of those lovely cats at the end of the chapter instead. We walked back down to the seafront and looked back up Eleftheriou Venizelou Street with the winged Victory statue in the foreground, the marble pavements, the balconies of the houses lining the street, the town hall and the multicoloured buildings covering Vrondado Hill crowned by the Anastasis church. It was all really quite breathtaking.

We passed a Loukoumia shop – it's a kind of sweet gel dusted with sugar, subtly-flavoured (sometimes with rosewater or mastika, rather like Turkish Delight) and Syros is said to have some of the best. We had lunch at Hotel Hermes (a favourite place of Matt Barrett's) enjoying a peaceful view across the water and then hired a car from Gaviotis Travel to start our exploration of Syros in earnest, having to give my driving head a factory reset to negotiate our first ever proper roundabout in Greece as we left Ermoupolis.

Here's a brief overview of our tour around the island.

Galissas: a crescent-shaped, sheltered, sandy beach – the most popular on Syros – and a little palm-lined promenade leading to a small harbour with a few pretty fishing boats.

Finikas: another popular resort and sandy beach (narrow in places) with a marina for yachts. We had a frappe in one of the seafront tavernas and got chatting to the owner who had spent a few years working at Tilbury docks (London's principal port).

Posidonia: verdant with pine trees and lovely gardens it had some impressive neoclassical mansions (some almost castle-like) built by the 19th century grandees of Ermoupolis and still well-maintained.

Agathopes: a very nice, sandy beach and clear water with a view of the Stroggylo islet next to it (monk seals have been known to arrive in Spring).

Megas Gialos: A family resort with a narrow sweep of sandy beach and tamarisks. We were approached by a very helpful older gentleman sporting just a pair of flip flops, a red cap and tight red speedos, who seemed quite insistent about something. I managed to pick out the salient parts of his Greek and realised he was suggesting we walked up a nearby road to see Ag. Antoniou church with its row of old bells and then carry on up to look back and get a better view of Megas Gialos in order to take a photograph. Very helpful.

Azolimnos: Another small, but lovely, sandy beach with good swimming and popular seafood tavernas. I strolled along the village coast road to reach a little church called Analipsi to look back at the view.

Vari was a particularly nice village with a deep, sandy beach protected from the wind by the hills around it. A small road led up the edge of Chontra hill adjacent to the bay to what looked like a miniature castle, privately-owned we assumed. We had lunch a couple of times at the Café Tropical, which was adjacent to an old house with a blue picket fence, datura spilling over it; pelargoniums, palms, oleanders, and aeoniums jostling for space in the beautiful garden. One busy lunchtime, the taverna had positioned some of the tables and chairs onto the compacted sand in front and had started seating people. At that moment the garage door of the adjacent house swung open and a dusty old car spluttered its way towards a gate in the garden wall. An elderly lady (who we reckoned had lived in the house for decades, probably well before the touristic invasion) walked round to the taverna and had a word. In moments they were moving the tables (and any surprised diners) so she could drive over the flat sand next to her gate and onto the concrete ramp leading off the beach. Once her path was clear, off she went with a few puffs of exhaust smoke and a good head of speed to negotiate the ramp, hoping for the best as she swung out onto the road at the top, so as not to lose momentum. Presumably the operation would be reversed on her return from shopping.

We drove ourselves to the airport at Manna just through Ermoupolis. The Dash-8 flight back to Athens was superb and once we'd picked up our bags we strolled out through the Domestic Arrivals to be met by film cameras and news reporters. A little surprised and initially feeling quite special to be made such a fuss of (Olympic Air's millionth passengers maybe?), we soon realised the media hacks were peering intently over our shoulders. We'd walked about 50 metres away when the reporters starting getting excited and the camera flashes went off ... it turned out they'd been waiting for the arrival of the Greek basketball team.

Kini: Two Cicadas taverna cat and a goat at Captain's

Kini: Mermaid Statue and Sunset margaritas

Ermoupolis cats

Chapter 27

Andros

(2013 and 2014)

Greece – The feeling of being lost in time and geography with months and years hazily sparkling ahead in a prospect of inconjecturable magic:
Patrick Leigh Fermor

In 2013 we travelled from Athens airport to the port of Rafina in the early hours of the morning and waited on the quiet quayside for things to get going. At 7am the Ekaterini P departed for the port of Gavrion on Andros and from there a taxi took us to Batsi and the Villa Galazio. As the ferry approached the island we got a good impression of how mountainous it is.

We were made very welcome by the Galazio's manager, George, and our room had a perfect view across the bay to the village climbing up the opposite hill and the mountains behind. We also had a good view of the attractive church of Metamórfosi with its terracotta roof and thin, arched windows picked out by brickwork with pink bell towers at the top. The Batsi village vista was to become one of our favourite holiday balcony views, both by day and night. With a lovely beach just a stone's throw away and a smaller one at Kolona just up the road, we lazed about for days. A lone swan would regularly glide across the bay from the small harbour, coming close in to the shoreline for bread and scraps. It had been there most of the summer and there was a theory that it had become separated from its 'Bevy' and was spending the season around Batsi as there was plenty of food to be had: we decided it was a female and called her Gloria Swanson after the famous American actress of the 1920s.

After a few days of lazing about, we did some local exploration and discovered a set of steps running up through the centre of the hillside part of the village. We'd wondered why there was a green belt of trees and shrubs demarcating the two halves of the village and all became clear. In the cool shade near the steps there was a stream running alongside the path in a stone gully (like a little rill) that would disappear under crossroads in lateral paths and pop out again below, gathering in pools along the way, with collections of moss and maidenhair ferns growing profusely – quite incongruous considering the heat just yards away from the pathway. The route was lined on each side by dry stone walls with overhanging trees and lovely plants in the adjacent gardens. We reported our discovery back to George later that day and he joked: 'Ah, you have found our mighty river!' There was a large storm drainage channel which doubled as a track from the beach to the main road behind Batsi, with an old stone-built bridge at the top, which proved a useful route for walking to the supermarket. To the north on the outskirts of Batsi we came across quite a few unusual dry stone walls, with larger standing stones interspersed between the normal horizontal stacks. These are known as 'Xerolithies' and this style of construction seems pretty much unique to the island. There was a lone olive tree standing close to the edge of the cliff, which became the starting point for another pastel painting. On the way back we passed by a little church with a row of stone-paved steps, on either side of which a pure white cloth had been draped like a waterfall, held in place with matching blue buckets filled with yellow, white and blue flowers, in preparation for a christening. Walking south towards Ypsili the rugged, rocky coastal cliffs fell sharply into the sea with tumbled boulders visible through the gloriously clear blue-green water.

A promenade around the harbour gave us a different view of the seafront and a closer look at the lovely fishing boats, one of which had an astonishingly colourful collection of nets spilling over the deck. Just near the main square with its cluster of tavernas, a chap was tipping a carrier bag full of rather smelly food scraps over the harbour wall. When we looked over the edge to see what he was feeding, some large fat ducks were having a field day. Indeed, one was sporting some swaying spaghetti on top of its beak like a white Greek moustache. I grinned at the man and he smiled back saying, 'Limáni pápia' (harbour ducks). I made some more appropriate 'Nom, nom, nom' sounds (hoping he realised I meant the ducks enjoying their meal, rather than me wanting to enjoy eating the ducks!). We paused to peruse the bus timetable pinned to a lamp post and it took a bit of head-scratching to decipher the various routes, but we photographed it for later puzzlement over a glass of wine. The important thing was that it looked as if you could catch a bus to the Chora and the main port from there, but you had to get off at a stop on the top road on the way back. We asked George where that particular stop was and he cheerfully replied: 'The whole of the island is a bus stop!'

We caught the bus to the main Chora of Andros a couple of times, but also hired a car for a few days. Following the west coast road, a little way along we parked off the road at Paleopoli and looked down to the sea below. We could make out the partly submerged ruins of walls and buildings, which had been the original Minoan capital of Andros (there are about 1,000 steps down the hill should you wish to explore). We then turned inland and off the main road towards Pitrofos and Melida, to have a look at the 12th century Byzantine Church of the Taxiarchis. With a square floor plan the main roof forms the shape of a cross, classically terracotta-tiled. The central octagonal structure has a tiled dome with a white cross on it. It's a striking building that looks remarkably fresh and clean for its age. Looking south we could see the start of the magnificent Messaria valley, the road follows one edge of it, with views down into the lush, fertile farmland below and the Melalos Potamos river, all leading towards the Chora. The valley is absolutely beautiful with a range of trees, farmland and a few scattered dovecotes – their striking designs like mini-castles – with house of cards style motifs associated with Andros and, particularly, Tinos.

Entering the town for the first time on the bus, the road wound down a long hill becoming fairly narrow in places, with buildings very close at either side – I made a mental note to check the bus times, so when we hired a car we could try to avoid meeting it coming the other way. The bus station was close to the centre of town, but when we drove we parked the car nearer to the coast (where there was another dovecote) and walked back up. The Chora sits on a long, narrow peninsula flanked by the bays of Neimporio and Paraporti. The long, marble-paved, pedestrianised main street led to a square of cafes and restaurants, shaded by plane trees with a steep row of steps down to Neimporio beach and the river. There was a family of swans on the river and we wondered if they might be the 'Bevy' from which our *Gloria Swanson* at Batsi had become separated. The view back up and along to Kato Kastro from Paraporti is well worth climbing the steps. There were some fabulous plants in the Chora: oleander, datura, passion flowers, canna, hibiscus, lilies, bougainvillea and flowering palms, as well as all manner of shrubs and trees: really enchanting.

I think it was down the steps on the other side, about halfway down, that we found the Museum of Modern Art. This is well worth a visit and houses works by Michalis Tombros bequeathed to his home town, works from the Goulandris private collection and a fascinating range of contemporary exhibits.

Panagia Theoskepasti church, with its twin towers, had a plaque that featured St. George killing the dragon and a marble water fountain. Continuing on to the actual peninsula we entered the Kato Kastro part of the town through a splendid archway with souvenir shops fronted by wood and glass cabinets. Kato Kastro had a maze of streets and highly-impressive mansions and gardens (apparently something like a fifth of the Greek merchant ships were owned by residents of Andros between the wars) with wonderful balconies and photogenic, original doors, some with fabulous door knockers. At the tip of the peninsula we emerged onto another paved square (Plateia Riva) with a striking bronze statue to the Unknown Sailor by Michalis Tombros. A stone arch linked the end of the peninsula with one more substantial rock on which was a Venetian Castle, Mesa Kastro. A little way out, marking the continuation of the peninsula under the water, was the Tourlitis Lighthouse balanced on a weather-worn rocky outcrop with stone steps winding up the rock to the entrance door. We also encountered numerous attractive cats in "Kato" Kastro who posed obligingly to have their pictures taken, several were curled up in the inviting gardens.

Continuing up the coast from the Chora we drove a short distance to the beautiful village of Stenies. Dotted with trees and greenery, many large stone-built houses and mansions sat majestically on the hill. We parked at Piso Gialia and spent a few hours on the beach there (the changing hut had a cartoon on the door that you could stick your head through). There had been a fall of "schist" at one end so it was fascinating to get a closer look at the layer cake-like rock with its sparkly mineral grains (the bedrock of Andros). I think we also caught sight of a Bonelli's eagle soaring aloft. Before leaving the area we explored some more and found a large pond filled by a river with ducks and terrapins, surrounded by clusters of bamboo, eucalyptus trees and bushes that wouldn't have looked out of place in the English countryside. A long set of steps eventually took us up to the little church of Agia Fotini from where we could admire the view and on the way back down there was a perky lizard basking on a rock.

Up the coast from Batsi was the very popular sandy beach of Psili Ammos and then on to the port of Gavrio, where the ferries came and went and I could indulge in my pastime of admiring the collection of caïques. There were some marvellously quirky driftwood sculptures dotted about the lawn on the seafront, making use of all sorts of flotsam to create intriguing shapes and forms. A beautifully-carved, obelisk-shaped memorial commemorated the Samina ferry disaster (I talked about that terrible incident in the Naxos chapter).

A little further on from Gavrio, was Felos beach, a peaceful, long curve of sand that provided us with a gentle day resting under a handy tamarisk.

Back at our room in Batsi we looked out one morning to see some large spider-shaped, nylon gazebos and *BIC* sponsorship flags fluttering on the beach. Later, a large group of young people had assembled all wearing bright orange, individually-numbered t-shirts, and we watched with fascination as the whistle was blown and they all grabbed their paddle boards and set off on what turned out to be the 3rd Hellenic Stand Up Paddle Surfboard Cup. Off they went, paddling at a furious pace for all they were worth, until the last one rounded Kolona headland and they disappeared from view. Peace and tranquillity returned and in no time the beach was ours again. As we walked along the beach road we saw something that was both fabulous and bewildering: a light blue, classic vintage Mini Austin Cooper originally from County Tyrone. That must have done some miles, unless someone had had it shipped over.

On my birthday in 2014 we went to the Marjo Café Pool Bar (a bar with a pool in the middle – does what it says on the tin) and had cocktails at sunset with a simply stunning view to the nearby group of small islands with Kea just visible in the distant haze. As the sun was about to go down a woman drifted in and sat down at the piano in the corner. She played very nicely for twenty minutes or so, before drifting off again. Another of those slightly incongruous, but highly memorable Greek moments ... *My Heart Will Go On* by Celine Dion sticks in my mind for some reason.

We spotted a poster advertising a production being staged by Batsi's ex-pat community entitled "Peter Potteraki and the Welsh Magic Dragon". Thinking it might be a fun way to spend the evening we bought a ticket. It's probably fair to say that the participating actors and local ex-pats had a lovely time, with quite a few in-jokes, the production sat somewhere between slapstick, Whitehall farce and am-dram. We did actually find it quite funny, especially after a few drinks.

On one of our last evenings we could hear a storm brewing somewhere to the north of Andros. Over the mountain some large cumulus bubbled up and every now and again there would be a flash and an ominous rumble. Fortunately, the rain never arrived, but we spent ten minutes or so fascinated by the effects of the lightning illuminating the clouds internally like something out of a Steven Spielberg movie.

There was a choice of many excellent tavernas in Batsi, but one in particular stood out for us, Giakoumis. The head waiter there had a fabulously gruff and dismissive attitude, although we reckoned it was an affectation for his own amusement. When we arrived he plonked the paper tablecloth down and theatrically twanged the elastic into place to prevent the wind from dislodging it. When he returned to take our order he snapped a curt, world-weary 'yes!' between each item we ordered, finishing with 'that it?' I think he got the measure of us when I chuckled and I caught the hint of a grin from him, but he gave it just the right level of sarcasm and mild irritation. It certainly wasn't at the level of pre-2014 Wong Kei in Chinatown in London's Wardour Street where visitors would go for the entertainment of being rudely shouted at by the staff, but it kept us amused. We watched one couple come in, sit down and wave to try to attract his attention. He ignored them and they became increasingly frustrated, calling out and clicking their fingers (despite having only been waiting a relatively short time), before standing up, loudly scraping their chairs and flouncing off into the night. It seemed that a degree of patience and good humour were the key. We returned regularly, partly for the amusement value and also because the food was excellent.

Over several evenings we had some good vlita (greens), a plate of magnificently garlicky skordalia, grilled mackerel, a prawn risotto (which had a lovely, tangy paprika flavour), lovely stuffed squid, excellent steamed mussels (moules), fresh fish and French fries. The house white wine was very good value. Complimentary slices of melon and glasses of fruit-flavoured 'souma' rounded off the evenings in style.

One night, as we were in no rush (not that we ever are in Greece, with the exception of catching planes and ferries) and as the taverna quietened down, he came over to sit and have a chat with us. He told us his name was Leo, as in Leonidas (he spelt it out phonetically: "Lee-on-eee-das" so that we pronounced it correctly), 'Ah, King of the Spartans', I said. That remark met with some approval, so he dropped the grumpy act and we got chatting. He told us about an incident from a few days previously.

Leo: 'This couple came and sat over there, at the front. The woman was waving her hand in front of her face. Not at me, but like she was too hot. So I went over to take their order. "Oh, it smells terrible here, there is such a stink of fish", she complained. "Madam," I replied, "this is a fish restaurant! What did you expect?" They left.'

He told us that he used to have his own taverna, but recent austerity had done for that. Now he was working as a waiter to try to put enough money away to retire. His wife was from Georgia and they planned to retire there, where property prices and the cost of living were affordable and the Black Sea was as lovely as the Aegean (or so he told us). A few other late customers had drifted in while we were talking and Leo judged that he'd left them long enough, so made his excuses and went over to see to them. We hope he got to realise his plans and can now put his feet up.

George's charming wife, Gella, came over to Andros at the weekends (she worked in Athens during the week) and they very kindly invited us to dine with them on a couple of occasions. Sitting around their large table, laden with wonderful food prepared by Gella, we met some of their other guests, their daughter and assorted friends: they were wonderful evenings. As they had been so kind and hospitable to us during our visits we stayed in touch, and we met up again for a meal when we were visiting Athens in March 2015.

Our balcony at Villa Galazio was a splendid vantage point and gave us a good view of events in Batsi. One evening a loud metallic thud echoed across the bay and we could see a group of people gathered at the far end of the harbour by the vehicle slope. The harbour road widened slightly by the slope and cars would often park there. There was no fence or barrier at the edge of the road and it appeared that on this occasion someone had misjudged the width and a car had fallen over the edge, landing on its roof. I'm not sure what make of vehicle it was, but it was a great advert for its roll bars, as the passenger had clambered out, apparently unscathed. The upturned vehicle was soon surrounded by locals and fishermen scratching their heads ... the solution eventually involved a crane.

One evening our pre-dinner balcony drink was interrupted by the sound of approaching traffic. The main road into Batsi was just below us and cars would slide by every now and then, but this was a veritable cacophonous procession making its presence known to everyone by hooting their horns as they drove by. The cavalcade carried on past us, along the seafront behind the beach, round by the tavernas at the main square, past the harbour and round the hairpin bend where the road rose up behind the village. Of course it was a wedding party and they were headed for the Metamórfosi Sotíros church. That evening at dusk we watched as a professional photographer captured romantic photos of the bride and groom together on the beach nearby.

It was quite late in the September season, so we were leaving Andros at the same time that George was closing the studios for winter and returning to Athens. He suggested we travel back to Rafina together on the Ekaterini P and we chatted for much of the journey. He told me about his time in the Greek navy (in a very prestigious role) and as we journeyed from Andros via Evia's Kava Doro, about the infamous Kafireas Strait. We talked about many topics, including Greek culture, Rembetika and Athens, as well as a lengthy discussion about the terrible effects of the recent austerity measures on the people of Greece. From Rafina, George very kindly offered to drive us to the Eleftherios Venizelos Airport to save us having to catch a bus, such was the generosity and calibre of the man.

Andros

Life flows from the mountains,
Tumbles from lion mouth fountains,
Hydroussa's streams babble and chatter,
Worldly cares no longer matter,
With time suspended,
The picture is bigger,
Priorities upended,
Sigά-Sigά.

By Chrysí Ammó: "golden sand",
Conductor cicada strikes up the band,
Horizon ferries make their Taxídi,
While bronzing recliners take things easy,
Beach bar chillout beats to the heart,
Micrá psária weave and dart,
Oleander flutter and wave in time,
The rhythm of the beach kissed with brine.

Skílos siestas in the shade,
Limáni pápia has got it made,
Majestic swan swims alone,
Bonelli's eagle in his throne,
Swallows skim and duck and dive,
Cats drift in to hypnotise,
Lizards twitch and scuttle away,
At night the bats have their day.

Celíni lays her silver over the swell,
Aegean whispers as though from a shell,
Candlelit village in flickering light,
Across the bay, Batsi at night,
Eavesdrop as a blend of tongues,
Ebb on the breeze with the giggling young,
Diners pronounce "Polí oraío",
We all have a role,
Each one a player.

(Dave Burnham 2014)

Batsi: Sue and George, Batsi harbour and village, Paddle Surfboard Cup

Chora: The Unknown Sailor and Tourlitis Lighthouse

Taxiarchis Church

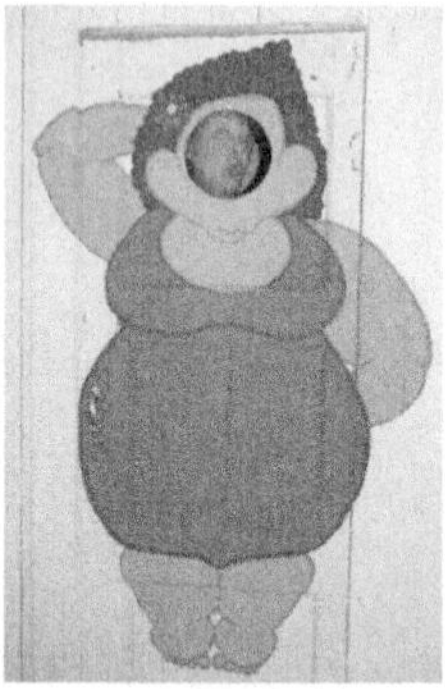

Kato Kastro Cats

Piso Gialia Changing Hut

Olive Tree in pastels by Dave

Meal with the lovely Gella and George

Chapter 28

Athens

(2015)

Athens, the eye of Greece, mother of arts and eloquence:
John Milton

Our old friends and fellow Grecophiles, Karen and Andy, have visited Athens many times over the years and they asked if we'd like to accompany them on another trip. It was too good a chance to miss, having never properly explored the City, so in early March 2015 we flew into Eleftherios Venizelos Airport and arrived in the District of Psyrri. We picked up the keys to the apartment that Andy and Karen had booked with *Live in Athens* and made our way through the front door and up the stairs. The apartment had a 50s/60s Deco-like vibe to it with some traditional fixtures and fittings and a balcony overlooking Iroon Square. After a quick potter around in the vicinity we found what looked like a good place for our evening meal and settled on Voliotiko Tsipouradiko, housed in what is said to be one of the oldest buildings in Athens (from around 1862). The interior was a mix of stone and brick built walls, with myriad alcoves, nooks and crannies, fantastic floor tiles, ornate old wooden doors, window frames and ceilings and all manner of fascinating adornments, photographs, paintings and curios. As we tucked into our food a trio of local musicians entertained us with two guys on guitar and bouzouki, and a young woman on vocals – just the best way begin our long weekend in Athens.

Next morning, walking via Monastiraki, we paused to look at the Roman Agora and started our ascent to the Acropolis. As we walked we passed some

ancient walls, several local cats, a tortoise and a spray canned graffiti message on a wall recommending "Make Moussaka, Not War!" The scale of the Acropolis soon became apparent as we approached the Propylia entrance and turned to look at the Temple of Athena, before setting foot on the Panathenaic Way. This gave us a true impression of the scale of the flat-topped rock on which the complex was built and our first up close look at the Parthenon itself. The biggest Doric temple is constructed largely of white Pantelic marble, and is extraordinary in that the subtle doming of the floor, fractional inwards leaning of the columns and their marginally swollen waists, all act together to fool the eye into perceiving it as following perfect linear form throughout. Like the temple of Karnak in Egypt or the Taj Mahal in India, you really need to experience these buildings in person to appreciate what all the fuss is about. And then there's the Erechtheion, with the story of Athena's olive just adjacent and replicated by a tree, said to have been planted by Queen Victoria's granddaughter. Also the Caryatids, where my thoughts turned to Elgin and the 'Parthenon Scupltures' or 'Elgin Marbles' and the debate therein. I have no doubt whatsoever that these objects should be returned to Greece and one of the most balanced and thorough reviews of the subject that I've read is to be found on Matt Barrett's website:
www.athensguide.com/elginmarbles/index.html

Andy kindly took a great photograph of Sue and I sitting on a rock in front of the iconic structure and he even managed to get the shot without the usual hordes of tourists milling about.

The scene across Athens from the viewing point is fantastic, although I did wonder what it might be like from the top of Lycabettus Hill. From the Acropolis it looked like a great rock balanced on a bed of horta with the dark green tops of the trees below – one day we hope to return to Athens and we'll go and find out. The epic panorama includes the Athenian hills in one direction and the Aegean in the other, with the Port of Piraeus and Salamis in the background and even, on a clear day, the distant Peloponnese across the Saronic Gulf. You can also enjoy great aerial views to the south of the Theatre of Dionysus and the Odeon of Herodes Atticus. This has the amphitheatrical seating and arched entrance structure to be expected of a Roman Theatre including niches for statues; it is very well-preserved – following a bit of restoration work on the stage and seating in the 1950s and is still in regular use. Over the years it has hosted performances from artists such as Maria Callas, Frank Sinatra, Elton John, Patti Smith and Jethro Tull to name but a few (Sting played two nights there to celebrate his 70th Birthday around the time of writing this chapter). The Theatre of Dionysus is a more accessible archaeological site, but no less interesting. The original wooden construction staged productions by the likes of Sophocles and was later rebuilt in stone. The front seats are pretty impressive, especially the rather nicely contoured seat of honour with its lion's paw and griffin designs. For me, the best part was the marble platform at the edge of the stage depicting the life of Dionysus. From there we walked down Dionysiou Areopagitou Street, with its grandiose buildings and some proper old front doors.

Returning to Monastiraki we paused at a fruit seller so Sue and Karen could make a purchase and then mooched around the shops. We found 120 Adrianou Street run by Angelo and referred to in Matt Barrett's Athens guide – *Angelo The Ouzo King of Plaka* – so, with my predilection for ouzo, a visit there was a must. I've never seen such a remarkable range and collection of ouzo and Angelo was a charming man who seemed quite chuffed that we'd made the effort to find him. I left with several small bottles to try and one in particular struck a chord with me: coming from Nea Aghialos, Thessaloniki it was called Babatzim or *Respected Father*, and I think Tzim would be pronounced Jim … my late Dad's name was Jim.

In the evening we met up with George and Gella at Diodos restaurant. Karen and Andy had also stayed with them at Villa Galazio on Andros, so it was a joy to see them again and catch up. Although the evening was cool, we had a table outside and it was the perfect setting, as the occasional graffiti-painted metro slid by below, we sat in front of the Ancient Agora just along from the Stoa of Attalos with the illuminated Acropolis above. We had a bit more "illumination" at one point as a fire breather paused to demonstrate his art next to our table: that warmed us up nicely.

On Sunday morning we got up in good time so we could reach Syntagma Square by 11am. We had a quick breakfast at the Boulatsadiko in Iroon Square, watching their baker buttering the dough then stretching, twirling and working it with incredible skill to make filo pastry (φύλλο being the Greek for 'leaf'). Fuelled up on fresh pastries and frappes we scampered off to get a good spot in front of the Hellenic Parliament. Right on time the Evzones assembled for their weekly parade. They are the most striking of soldiers, members of the Presidential Guard, and it is a great honour to be selected to serve. They change guard at the grave of the Unknown Soldier on the hour, but on a Sunday morning they undertake the full parade. Their uniform is remarkable, the white, kilt-like skirt – the Foustanella – has 400 pleats to represent the years Greece was under Turkish occupation (each Foustanella taking up to 80 days to make from some 30 metres of material), the red Farion cap has a long, black silk tassel, and the Greek coat of arms plus rank, which they point to when saluting. The Fermeli is like a winged-waistcoat made of wool with thousands of embroidered stitches, the white shirt (Ypodetes) flares massively on the arms to accentuate movement, the heavy Tsarouchia shoes have a horseshoe-like metal base under the heel and nails under the soles so when marching – or stamping their feet down – it simulates the sound of battle. The toe of the shoe curls up to be covered with a black pompom. Do not let any aspect of the uniform fool you and be under no illusion: these guys are seriously tough. As we watched they marched with tremendous power, dignity and accuracy of movement. Unfortunately while performing a powerful turn, one man did slip over (which isn't surprising when you consider the interface of metal nails on smooth marble), but he rapidly recovered his equilibrium and continued with barely a pause. The whole parade was undertaken with great precision and timing with some highly characteristic movements and it was a privilege to observe at first hand.

Continuing our explorations we took in the Lysicrates Monument. Apparently he had won first prize for a performance, so commemorated it with the monument and mounted the prize on a bronze tripod at the top of an acanthus ornament at its summit. We came across the Theatro Skion, home to the Athanassiou troupe shadow theatre – they give performances in schools and carry out workshops of traditional Karagiozis (a fictional character of Greek folklore). Reaching the Temple of Zeus we looked back at Hadrian's Arch with the Acropolis above. The Temple of Zeus still has some of its gigantic columns remaining (a large amount of those that collapsed were taken to be re-used for other projects in the city) but the original must have been incredible and apparently housed a large gold and ivory cult statue of Zeus. One of the fallen columns revealed how the discs slotted together for stability, resembling a colossal, sliced *Swiss roll*.

Our next stop was at an art exhibition on the adjacent Amalias Avenue. Karen had been following the watercolour artist, James Foot, on Facebook for some time as she was a fan of his work. Fortuitously, James was having an exhibition in Athens while we were there. Karen spotted him talking to another visitor, but afterwards she went over and introduced herself, having messaged him earlier to say she'd hoped to make it along. He showed us

round part of the exhibition before breaking off to welcome another visitor. We were really impressed with James' work, its distinct style, lightness of touch and gentle precision are absolutely delightful. His use and representation of light is captivating ... I wonder if, having lived in Greece for so many years, the "Phos" has entered his consciousness and is given expression in the paintings. The movement and reflection of his images depicting the sea, be they swimmers, fishing boats or harbours are fabulous. As is his subtle mirroring of décor, structures and decoration in the highly-polished floors of buildings' interiors. I became a fan instantly and we are now friends on Facebook, exchanging the odd message, and have discovered a mutual love of all things Greek, cat-related and gardening. James has developed a magnificent garden at his home in the Peloponnese and I've greatly enjoyed seeing photographs of his plants and garden design, sometimes sending pictures from my allotment (or my own humble attempts at capturing Greece in pastels). I can highly recommend having a look at James' website and artwork online:
www.jamesfootwatercolours.com

We had a walk around the Ancient Agora, which gives a feel of what Dorian architecture was all about, particularly the Temple of Hephaestus, still virtually intact in structure (although earthquakes and invasions have taken their toll on the decorative features). Another fascinating structure was a stone water clock, this is basically a tank that was thought to have been filled in the morning and a plug removed so the passage of time could be noted accurately. The water pressure would mean that it fell more quickly at the start of the day, so compensation would have been made to accommodate that. It could have been used to time Senate speeches, as a precise six-minute speech was considered to be an artform. The planting in the Agora is very attractive with a great range of trees, shrubs and perennials such as laurels, pines, olives, holm oaks, oleanders, cyclamen, mallow and myrtle. The Stoa of Attalos was a clonking great structure, with a splendid colonnade and an excellent collection of items excavated in the area.

Our last evening meal was at Krasopoulio tou Kokora in Psyrri, a delightfully quirky taverna, beautifully decorated with old antiques and various brick-a-brack found in the flea market at Monastiraki over the years. We enjoyed lovely homemade food in a very welcoming atmosphere and this is a restaurant we'd be very happy to return to on a future visit to Athens.

Andy and Karen took us back up the Acropolis Hill on a slightly different route, to Anafiotika. Like an enchanting little village hidden within the city, it originated from people such as masons and carpenters from Anafi in the Cyclades who arrived in the mid-19th century to transform the capital. They somehow managed to build their own homes almost overnight to comply with an Ottoman law. Whitewashed Cycladic-style houses, narrow alleys and attractive gardens – often with a friendly cat or two – made the area feel as if a little bit of the island had been uprooted and delivered to the foot of the Acropolis.

Another enjoyable discovery was the fabulous variety of graffiti artworks in Athens. Tagging is one (not particularly attractive) thing, but high-quality street art is something else and there was plenty of it on display. There was a work by Alexandros Vasmoulakis right outside our apartment in Psyrri and as we walked around we came across a fascinating mix of styles and statements. Loaf's work near Anafiotika was particularly striking. Another friend, Tiffany – who we met on Ios – has a video blog on YouTube and has uploaded a video in which she explores some of the Street Art in Athens. You can find out all sorts of helpful and interesting information about Athens and the islands at "A Girl and Her Passport" both on her website and her YouTube channel:

www.youtube.com/channel/UCfLCRgtcVwUKBecqDTJEvng

Another thing that struck me as we explored more of Athens is that shops selling specific items seem to be clustered together. So, you seem to get a district that specialises in car parts, another that does electrical stuff, an area for hardware or baskets, a parade of shops selling leather goods, etc.

I can highly recommend staying in an apartment and getting an immersive experience if you can visit Athens for a few days or more. It's a city that warrants a longer stay and it's very rewarding to do so. Thanks to Karen and Andy for organising our visit and for giving us a book of lovely photographs to remember it by.

Nine Lives Greece: by Karen French

When we first visited Athens many years ago, we couldn't fail to notice the cats everywhere we went, and this sparked an interest in finding out if there were any organisations caring for the street cats. After some searching I found the website for Nine Lives Greece and became a supporter, making a monthly donation to help with feeding and spaying the many colonies of cats around the city. We fell in love with Athens and the cats, and make regular trips there. There are many colonies around the city, and one we always visit is close to the Acropolis, where we have got to know the cats over the years. There is a photo from our trip with Dave and Sue which shows me stroking Beba, one of the adorable gang who later found a wonderful home in the UK.

Through becoming a supporter of Nine Lives Greece we were lucky enough to meet with one of its founders, Cordelia. I can still picture the first time we met, Cordelia followed by a large number of cats all anticipating the food to come! When our schedules allow it, we meet up in Athens and accompany Cordelia on feeding rounds in the city. As well as spaying and neutering, Nine Lives Greece also regularly check the health of the cats under their care and provide any necessary vet treatment. One of the cats from our favourite colony, Knut, had some skin damage to the tips of his ears – later confirmed to be cancer, which is a particular risk for white cats in hot countries – and we all piled into Cordelia's jeep to take him to the vets (Knut singing all the way!). I am happy to say that treatment for his cancer was successful, though he had to lose part of his ears in the process, and we always look forward to seeing Knut each time we visit.
www.ninelivesgreece.com

Karen with Beba

Knut

Cordelia with cats

Knut at the vets

View over Athens from the Acropolis

Dave and Sue in front of the Parthenon

Odean of Herodes Atticus

Theatre of Dionysus (depicting his life)

Temple of Zeus

James Foot setting up his exhibition

Evzones Parade

Loaf's work near Anafiotika

Dinner with Gella, George, Karen and Andy

Krasopoulio tou Kokora in Psyrri with Karen and Andy

Chapter 29

Milos

(2007 and 2016)

Milos is magical,
with its volcanic rock formations and stunning village vistas:
Laura Brooks

We have been to Milos twice, in 2007 and again in 2016. The first time we stayed with Ioannis at Villa Notos in a beautiful room with a veranda and traditional local furniture. On our second visit we stayed at Ageri studios. We flew with Olympic to and from Athens, staying overnight in Athens on the 2007 outbound trip as Olympic had moved the flight time. This meant that we had to change our flight to the following morning as the connections no longer worked: but it was no hardship to spend a night in the great city. Milos is one of our favourite islands as it has so much character and individuality. The island is shaped rather like a neck pillow, with its bubbling springs from volcanic heat, fabulous beaches and a variety of mineral deposits, you can expect to see all manner of colours in its rocky coastline.

In 2007, while waiting at Athens airport for the flight to appear on the information display we heard our names being called out on the tannoy. It seemed that the plane was ready to depart and our bags were on board. According to our tickets there was still some time before the scheduled departure and there was no sign of the flight on the display. However, it seemed the plane was waiting for us so we rushed through security to get on board; having moved the previous day's flight time, and with this 'earlier than advertised' departure, Olympic seemed to have a very relaxed attitude to the Milos flight.

On our second, 2016, trip all went smoothly with the Olympic flight timings so we arrived at Milos Airport and were met by Niko from Ageri Studios. We had just started unpacking when Niko suggested that he drive us to the nearby Papakinos beach, where we could chill, swim and use the nearby taverna's sunbeds. So we took up his offer, caught up on some sleep after a very early start and had a relaxing afternoon there. When we decided to walk back to the studios we realised that we couldn't actually remember exactly where they were! We wandered about for a bit along various narrow side-roads searching for a landmark to help find our way back. Eventually we recognised a small road with a family-run taverna that we'd had dinner at during our previous visit nine years earlier. Having found our bearings, we realised that this road would lead us back to Niko's studios.

Later that evening we returned to the family taverna for dinner, partly because it was nearby (and we were very tired by now) and also to re-live our previous dining experience there. After the waitress had taken our order, her mother appeared from the kitchen, leant across the low outer wall and blew a long blast on a football whistle with some gusto. Within moments her many grandchildren appeared from wherever it was they'd been playing in the adjacent streets or fields, summoned to come back and eat their dinner.

Our room at Niko place was large, in a bespoke semi-traditional design. There was a fully-equipped kitchen, plenty of shelves and storage space, a large bathroom and a sizeable double bed (with neon-edged underlighting!) created from curved, painted and polished hard material, as if it were sculpted from rock or marble. The room had a little patio outside at the front bordered by a small garden and this was the place for the many cats who came to visit and hang out on the surrounding wall. Niko's cat was called Bruno and he ruled over the others as it was his place. He was known as "King Bruno" and there was also an old blind ginger tom who Bruno would look out for, making sure he got his fair share of cat crunchies at feeding time. A young ginger and white boy came to see us regularly and our neighbours had named him "Rossini" after the Italian composer. We became very fond of him over the couple of weeks we were there.

When he discovered that I was partial to an ouzo, Niko presented me with a carton of chilled Lemoni (like orange or apple juice, but pure lemon) and suggested I try them together, as it was what he liked to mix with his ouzo. Niko also claimed it had the added benefit of preventing hangovers: I have to say it was a brilliant combination. Most days he also presented us with various little food gifts provided by his mother, such as homemade cakes and sweets. He was great at giving us tips and recommendations on what to do and where to go. As we hadn't yet hired one, he even kindly took us to several of his favourite places in his car. A little while afterwards another couple arrived in the neighbouring room and we had a quick chat before we headed out for the day. They were called Ty and Gina (who had come all the way from San Francisco) and we got to know them quite well over the next few days.

Niko took us to one of his favourite secluded beaches (Patrikia). He parked his car at the top of the cliff above the cove and proudly pointed down a steep bank with a narrow uneven pathway leading to the tiny beach below. He said he'd be back in about five hours to pick us up and sped off in a cloud of dust and loud techno music. We poked our heads over the edge of the cliff and decided to go for it. We could see there was a sort of path where others had scrambled down the embankment to the cove, but as usual were wearing unsuitable footwear and were encumbered by a beach brolly and other paraphernalia. We cautiously made our way down the steep pathway, slipping and sliding on loose soil and stones until we reached a tiny little sandy beach, probably no more than twenty feet across. We put up the brolly Niko had lent us, spread out our towels and spent the day relaxing on our own, perfectly-formed 'private' beach, swimming in the crystal-clear water and gazing across "our" cove. It had a view over the bay to Plaka and we watched as the occasional ferry arrived and departed from Adamas. It was a perfect, idyllic, chilled out day. Trying to scramble back up the path when Niko arrived to pick us up was a different matter ... luckily our 'mountain goat' genes kicked in and we survived the climb back up to the top.

Adamas (Adamantas) town was a splendid place to base ourselves with a wide choice of excellent tavernas, some stylish bars and shops, with nearby beaches and plenty of character. Palms sprouted flowers, vibrant lilies and colourful bougainvillaea adorned homes and hotels, and we walked past an outstanding display of aeoniums in a private garden on our route into town. There was a friendly traditional bakery and one zacharoplasteio had some stunning cakes and pastries displayed in their window. The most incredible were a group of enormous cream horns (like the *Doomsday Machine* from the original Star Trek series)!

A stroll along the harbour jetty gave us a closer look at the many fishing boats and yachts, as well as a great view of the town itself. One of the fishing boats had amassed a huge collection of multicoloured fenders, being almost eclipsed by them like a giant bunch of grapes. Further along was a pile of orange nets and green and brown floats that resembled a mound of saffron, sprinkled with huge olives.

Exploring up the steps and alleyways of the town above the seafront we saw some marvellous pebble mosaics ("Votsaloto") in the courtyards of the various churches. There was an amazingly elaborate design at the Holy Trinity Church featuring good and evil as a battle between a white and black centaur, and another huge, white bird at Ag. Charalampos. The views across the bay from up there were magnificent with many a lovely cat lazing around in the shade.

There was a photography exhibition (a panorama of Melian history) in one of the buildings near the port and it became part of the inspiration for a story set in Greece called *Snapshot*, which I've written, but have yet to publish. I also took some photos of the splendid Panagia Korfiatissa church in Plaka that features in the artwork for the story, as does a square near the harbour in Adamas with a memorial at its centre.

The Mining Museum is definitely worth visiting. Milos has such a wealth of mineral deposits and the samples on display explained a great deal about the colours in the rocks and the life of the miners with interactive and multimedia displays.

Langada beach is right next to Villa Notos, so was handy for us the year we stayed there. A nice little town beach with a calm bay in which we swam between the fishing boats. We were even joined by a cormorant and a little further along we saw an egret on the rocks. In 2016 we spent an afternoon there again, accompanied by four white geese and a pair of ducks. The hotel behind the beach had put a sign up to try to get people to put their cigarette butts in the bin provided: "Please don't put your cigarettes in the sand. The ones you placed last year didn't sprout!" On the main road back from Langada towards the town along the seafront there's an old cave with three "bathrooms" forming the municipal spa baths, which utilise the warm mineral waters – but we didn't give it a try, maybe another time.

If you carry on past Langada beach around the bay towards Bombarda there's a small monument commemorating the French soldiers who died in the Crimean War. There's a peaceful little beach with a few tamarisk trees for shade offering a great view back across the bay to the Chora. We also found some old reed beds with bubbles appearing in the water from the mud, a clear sign of volcanic activity below.

One morning we were waiting at the bus stop (next to pots of basil and chillies) for the bus up to Plaka, when Niko drove by and spotted us. He screeched to a halt, music playing as usual and insisted that he should give us a lift up the hill, so we clambered in. He seemed a little quieter than his normal ebullient self and confessed to having a dreadful hangover.

'What were you drinking?' I asked.

'Ouzo with orange juice,' he replied.

'Well, there's your problem,' I joked, 'If you'd drunk it with Lemoni as recommended, you'd be feeling fine!'

In Plaka, the Cycaldic white cubes of the houses led us up through the alleyways to admire the flowers, the shops and the cats. One shop had a craftsman busy at work creating plates, window-hangings, light fittings and delightful ornaments all handmade from glass. Another had a window display featuring two cats in period costume and the tiny streets were festooned with triangular Greek flag bunting.

We found a fascinating Folklore Museum near the Panagia Korfiatissa church, which had a beautiful pebble mosaic in front. There were numerous, wonderful old doors and many lovely gardens. We came across another splendid, small, round pebble mosaic of the dove of peace with an olive branch in its beak. We had lunch at Archontoula: a charming and traditional taverna that had some splendid features (even an old juke box) and fascinating Escher-like tiles on the floor outside. We had a Greek salad, toasted bread with oil and herbs, and a very nice plate of filleted fish in olive oil and dill, with skordalia and spring onions – plus a happy little tabby who enjoyed a spot of fish.

One early evening in Plaka we climbed up to the church of Panagia Thalassitra on the way up to Kastro (the 13th century Venetian castle ruins) and looked out at the view across to the western half of the island. Down below were the rooftops of Plaka, then across to the windmills of Trypiti and Triovassalos/Pera Triovassalos (we were told that they used to have macho dynamite-throwing contests on Easter Sunday!). There were a few clouds in the sky so we were treated to the most spectacular sunset, followed by the slow appearance of twinkling lights in the town below.

The steps, tavernas and alleyways took on a special charm at night with gentle lighting and the happy sound of diners at their tables (we came across a sign for "Goldfish Garlic Salad" on one corner ... something was probably lost in translation there, I hope).

Down the hill from Trypiti, we found the remains of a Roman Theatre, with several rows of seating intact. It offered a great view from above of Klima (the theatre itself is said to have had a capacity of 7,000 in its prime). Nearby we located a sign directing us to the site where the Venus de Milo was found by a farmer in 1820, while he was ploughing his field. We soon found a stone plaque on a dry stone wall next to an olive tree that showed the exact place the iconic statue had been unearthed. It had been sculpted from the famous marble of Paros and once it had been discovered, there was a bit of bargaining and arguing between the French and the Ottoman army officers about ownership, but she now stands in the Louvre. Not far from these sites were the early Christian catacombs of Milos, with a maze of corridors and niches cut into the soft volcanic rock, which were later used as an underground necropolis. When first discovered they contained a large quantity of bones, possibly running to many thousands of bodies. In 1840 the catacombs were initially discovered by illegal antique dealers who apparently stole much of what was worth having.

Niko also drove us to one of his other favourite beaches called Tourkothallasa, with thankfully an easier slope to negotiate than Patrikia – although there was a small rickety wooden ladder to negotiate. This time he had kindly loaded us up with sunbeds as well as a brolly, so we were well set up for the day. It was a small shingle beach with crystal clear water of the most glorious blues and greens. We had the place to ourselves again, so we made use of a weathered old wooden table that had been built under a tamarisk with a view of Mandrakia across the bay. Niko had also given us a couple of bottles of water from his freezer so we could sip ice cool water all day. The condensation from the bottles attracted a gorgeous lizard who scuttled about the table for ages and I spent a happy hour or so watching him and taking pictures. In the early afternoon we heard the sound of a quad bike up on the road above and a couple of people clambered down to the beach – we realised it was Gina and Ty who had also been tipped off by Niko to check out the beach. (On the subject of quad bikes, I heard somewhere that the Greek nickname for a quad bike is "gourouna" meaning a sow/pig.)

We were delighted to see our new friends of course, and we spent ages floating around in the sea together chatting about life, the universe and everything. It's a funny thing, but once in while you can be lucky enough to randomly meet people and it's like you've known them all your life. That was how it was with us and the charming, intelligent, hilarious couple we'd just met. Gina is a librarian and Ty a commercial director, but they also have several other creative sidelines, one of which is being writers for *Killing My Lobster*, San Francisco's biggest, baddest, live sketch comedy show. We decided to meet up later and go somewhere for a meal together. A day or two earlier we'd seen a menu board outside a takeaway gyros place called Ta Pitsounakia; not normally our kind of place, but there were some tables tucked down by the side and behind the take-away place in a small covered courtyard. Apart from the gyros at the front, the family-run taverna at the back was a real joy, very friendly with good, honest, Greek home cooking to tickle the tastebuds.

Paleochori beach is a natural wonder. The course sand has small, multi-coloured pebbles mixed in with it and when we turned to look at the rocks of the cliff it immediately became clear where they'd come from. The rocks look like the aftermath of the Hindu festival of Holi, when powdered paint of all colours is wildly thrown around. The mix of volcanic, sulphuric and iron mineral pigments, which are frozen in time in the cliff face and adjacent rocks are fabulous.

When we swim in the Aegean we're used to some changes in water temperature from one spot to another, but here we came across discernibly warmer patches than anywhere else, occasionally accompanied by trails of sulphurous bubbles. Just along the beach is the famous Sirocco restaurant. When we first saw the pale blue sign claiming "Volcanic Food" we suspected a gimmick, that was until we saw a gentleman appear with a long-handled spade, lift a cover off the square-bordered area on the beach next to the sign and start digging. We watched with interest and a short while later he had exposed a large parcel wrapped in tin foil. He carefully manoeuvred it up out of the sand on his shovel, teased the foil off the top to reveal the lid of a big cooking pot, which he carried to the restaurant with thick cloths to protect his hands. It was around lunchtime, so we followed him onto a veranda and sat down at a table next to an old red and white boat rudder. Sure enough, the menu had a section offering "volcanic" food, so we ordered the vegetable briam which was absolutely delicious (*nóstimo*). It must save them a bit on their cooking fuel bills! We also heard that the sea sometimes lapped up to the base of the restaurant, which sounded a bit odd as the Aegean isn't particularly tidal, but some research suggested that if the winds were blowing hard in that direction they could actually push and hold the water into Paleochori Bay to the extent of being able to raise the water level by as much as a metre. What an extraordinary place.

Ty had created a slow motion video of Gina dancing on some steps in town (twirling her dress like an American film actress) – suitably inspired I got carried away and Sue filmed me performing a little comedic sand dance on Paleochori beach:

https://youtu.be/4J1N-L6X278.

Both times we visited we did a "Round the Island" boat trip as it's such a brilliant way to see the incredible coastline of Milos. Starting from Adamas at about 9:30 in the morning we passed Klima, with Plaka and Trypiti above, and came to Vani where there used to be a manganese mine. The place still has the old rusty piers and buildings where they loaded the boats with the ore; its red, yellow and grey rocks resembling bacon slices. Journeying down the West coast we saw the monastery of Ag. Nikolaos above Triades and then on to Sykia, with its fabulous white rocks looking almost foam-like with preserved and eroded volcanic bubbles. Here the captain reversed the boat up close so we could look into a sea cave and were surprised to see sunlight where the roof had collapsed. Next we came to Psalidi cave and its striated rocks and oddly-weathered stone formations, looking like poppadoms stuck onto the ridge. Around the Southwest corner we stopped at Kleftiko bay, where pirates were said to have hidden their boats back in the day. It has some immense rock formations with sea-eroded tunnels and caves running beneath the dramatic columns jutting out of the sea. We continued along the South coast to Provatas (a nice sandy beach that we'd also reached one day by bus) and then Firaplaka with its red and white rocks, resembling a kind of tiramisu with an old clay mine above.

The remarkable beach of Tsigrado looked as if it would be quite challenging to reach with a large wooden ladder running down the cliff face to the beach. Then on to Kalamos with rocks which looked like they'd melted and run down the steep hill with sand running down from above in a mini, static avalanche, forming mounds on the narrow beach. Next was our old friend Paleochori beach with its psychedelic rocks and then to Paliorema and the old Sulphur Mines, with yet more colourful rocks and eerie abandoned buildings. Ty and Gina had managed to get down to them on their quad bike and described the scene as 'verging on apocalyptic'. Crossing the sea over to the island of Kimolos we stopped for lunch at the port of Psathi. Resuming the trip, we had a good view of Pollonia and then Kalogiros (*Monk*), a cone-shaped lava rock composed of a fan of columns like the bones in a fish tail. We ventured further off the North coast to Glaronissia with large rock columns like organ pipes. The first time we took the trip it was pretty choppy so we didn't stay there too long, but in 2016 it was a nice calm day and we were able to get up quite close. We then saw Sarakinikos from the sea, which looked other-worldly, but it was when we actually visited that the beauty and uniqueness of the landscape/"moonscape" really hit home. We were also able to figure out how a snack van had managed to park on what appeared, when viewed from the boat at sea, to be an inaccessible cliff top. We had a good look at Mandrakia and Firopotamos with their Syrmata boat houses and little chapels, before going around the headland down into Platiena Bay and past Arkoudes – bear-like rocks whose jaws welcome people into the Gulf of Milos – then Fourkovouni with a small group of syrmata. Admiring Klima one more time as we passed, we arrived back in Adamas at around 18:30 after what had been a long, fascinating and enjoyable voyage.

During the last boat trip we got chatting to another passenger who introduced herself as Linda Bentley. Later on we went on another day out together and she stayed with us for a few days during a trip to the UK a few years ago. Linda is an Australian travel writer and photographer and you can find out more about her travels at: www.thepackedbag.com.

The small village of Klima is another of Milos' little jewels. The first time we visited the island we only saw Klima from the sea (on the aforementioned boat trip), but in 2016 we hired a car and made a point of visiting properly. We drove via Trypiti, parked near a taverna and paused for a frappe before exploring the unique seafront of the village. Syrmatas are fishermen's houses which can also be found at a couple of other small fishing villages on Milos, but in Klima they are most resplendent. What makes them special are the "boat garages" down below at sea level, with the accommodation up above. As the winter storms approached, the fishing boats would be manoeuvred into the space at sea level and the heavy wooden doors closed, so as to protect them with an equally heavy wooden board set in place at the base of the doors. In the spring, once the weather improved, the fishermen would climb through the small hatches set in the doors to clear any debris washed up against the base during the winter, preventing them from opening. These days the garages are used as part of the overall accommodation – some might even be available to rent – and others are shops selling some charming local artistic artefacts to tourists. Each syrmata is painted a different colour while their individual designs vary with steps, balconies, balustrades, awnings and pergolas and I was so taken with them that I made a pastel painting based on several photographs. I'd definitely recommend a visit to Kilma, it's the most colourful and unique village, with the sea lapping at the very thresholds of the shops and homes.

After Klima we drove a little way North to Firopotamos, for a swim and to admire the little collection of syrmatas that we'd seen from the boat trip. We also took a look at the ruins of a building at the tip of the headland, which I think might have been the kaolin processing plant in the 1960s.

One day we came across a large, solitary old abandoned mansion: there was something strange about it, so we parked nearby and went to explore. The two empty windows on the first floor seemed to stare out across the Gulf of Milos like dark, soulless eyes. Around the exterior we came across yellow crosses spray-painted onto the cracked render – they were probably just to serve as a warning that the building was unsafe, but we fancied it might also be a warning of evil spirits. The garden seemed oddly devoid of wildlife and strangely silent apart from the sound of the steady swish of a large wind turbine on the hill in the distance. The interior of the place was in a state of advanced decay and we only briefly peeped inside as the depth and severity of the cracks in the masonry suggested that substantial lumps could drop off at any moment. It wasn't only us, Karen and Andy had found it when they visited Milos and thought the place was spooky, as did Ty and Gina who were creeped out by an old rotten bed frame and springs they found while exploring the ruin (much braver than us!). Several years later on, Ty's embellished memory is of a Victorian child's doll that suddenly opened its eyes when they picked it up – nothing like a bit of artistic license! Some while later I found a music video on the internet featuring a young Greek band who'd used the mansion as the backdrop, as they leapt around and cavorted about in the dark with appropriately spooky lighting. Hopefully the building might be restored to its former glory one of these days.

We decided to have a day trip to Kimolos so we took the Panagia Faneromeni ferry from Pollonia (a small car and foot passenger ferry similar to those that ran from Pounda on Paros to Antiparos and Argostoli to Xi on Kefalonia). Just a kilometre to cross, it was once connected to Milos by a narrow isthmus. We docked at Psathi and caught the bus up to Chorio. It was a fabulous town to wander about in, with paved streets winding all over giving quite an odd perspective to some of the asvesti-white buildings and we found ourselves popping out into various small squares from time to time. Balconies, archways and flowers beckoned us on with glimpses of Panagia Odigitria and Evangelistra churches. The presence of a donkey was a good indication of the traditional pace of life and it would certainly make a perfect destination for anyone wanting total peace and quiet.

Several days were spent at Pollonia with its long, sandy beach, tamarisk shade and calm bay for swimming. We explored the village itself and came across some lovely adobe-style, Cycladic buildings, gardens with lovely features and the sweet little church of Agios Nicholas (with its checkerboard courtyard and pebble anchor mosaic). Along the beach front was a line of tamarisks with asvesti-painted trunks, looking like a row of sailors in white trousers. There were several wonderful caïques gently bobbing in the harbour – near the Kimolos ferry departure point – just along from a row of excellent seafront tavernas.

On their last night before flying back to the States we went with Ty and Gina to Ammos taverna, along with Niko and Marco (a charming Italian friend of Niko who was a regular visitor to the island). It was a truly fabulous evening and one that we often think of – with constant laughter, excellent food, a little too much to drink and fabulous company. Marco very kindly drove us all back home to Ageri. We woke the next morning to find a bottle of ouzo and a box of eggs on the little table outside our room with a postcard of Santorini and a note from Ty and Gina saying: "So long and thanks for all the fish" ... a perfect Greek breakfast. (The quote from Douglas Adams' *Hitchhikers' Guide to the Galaxy* echoing our shared love of Sci-Fi.) I can't imagine what their long journey back to San Francisco must have been like, but as we didn't have to travel many thousands of miles we had a slow day. We were already missing our new friends, but have happy memories of that fabulous evening. Thanks to social media we've stayed in touch ever since and they kindly did some voice acting for Episodes 31 and 32 of my Ad Astral Podcast: *ICS Indulgence*, recording their parts at home and sending them to me. It was a joy to hear their voices again and one of these days we really hope to meet up in person, such a fabulous couple.

We drove to the North coast and found Agios Konstantinos, a tiny fishing hamlet with a few syrmata in a sheltered bay. Most interestingly, at the land end of the bay a cave was dug into the rock and a tiny underground chapel had been built, partially standing in the seawater in the cave. Adjacent to that was Alogomandra beach set in a cove with a tall rock face to the right with little marine caves eroded at the base. We stopped for a swim as the rocks also provided some handy shade in the morning and then walked the dirt road along the coast to see if we could get the car along to the next part of Alogomandra beach (possibly Agia Irini beach). After an afternoon on that beach we drove back up the dirt track and came across Galini Restaurant so we decided to have a late lunch/early dinner. The views from their wooden veranda were fabulous and the chef/owner Ms. Anna was so kind and accommodating. The size of her food portions were super generous and when we thought it couldn't get any better a tortoise pottered by in the garden and a cat joined it to just sit and watch its progress.

We heard about a cat colony somewhere near Embourios where they were safe and someone kept them fed, also labelling some food containers for dry food when people came to visit them. We located Agia Marina church near Embourios – dating back to 1616, it was a monastery until mid-19th Century, but no one lives there now. There's a great view across to the islet of Mikra Akradia and to Plaka, Typiti and Klima. The ornate door surround created a shallow porchway to an old wooden door with a silver plaque bearing the image of Saint Marina. In the courtyard a wall held back the soil in which olive trees and scrub grew, and there were the many cats and kittens. They were absolutely beautiful and happy to receive our donation of some cat crunchies. In an adjacent field two rows of about 50 blue and white bee hives stood like buzzing chests of drawers, some single and some double-layered. Later on, Niko invited us out for dinner to one of his favourites: Taverna Embourios. I'm glad he was driving. We passed the turning to Agia Marina and turned down a steep, uneven dirt track full of ruts and troughs with few signs to follow. It seemed to us like an epic journey, but well worth it when we arrived at the taverna set on the very edge of the sea, looking out across the Gulf of Milos to Plaka, Trypiti and Klima. It was a fabulous location to eat dinner, immersed in the tranquillity of an idyllic spot at sunset, and the food was great.

Niko was so generous with is time during our visit, driving us to little beaches, up to Plaka, Embourios and Pollonia, as well as the occasional surprise from his mother's kitchen. A splendid host.

One evening Niko insisted that we had to go to Sarakinikos that night, as the best time to see it was under a full moon. Naturally, we accepted his kind offer and after he dropped us off, watched as the lights of his car disappeared from view. We turned, hand in hand, and made our way along the track towards the unique lunar landscape. Illuminated by the full moon, the surreal shapes of the bleached white weathered rocks felt straight out of a Star Trek scene of a distant planetary surface, with just the sound of the sea echoing around reminding us that we were still on planet Earth. We carefully explored the magical scenery for an hour or so, before returning to the pick-up spot where Niko reappeared to drive us back.

Sarakinikos was a place we just had to see again in the daylight. The extraordinary landscape of bare, eroded, white rock looked just like a polished lunar surface where outcrops and boulders had been the subjects of alien sculptors. Folds in the rock gave clues as to its volcanic origins: weathered cliff faces resembled an extra-terrestrial Mount Rushmore, creases underfoot like the buried backbones of dragons, striations in the mounds resembling three-dimensional representations of map contours, curved projections like bandaged thumbs and jutting figures like Gaudi's sentinels. Near the small, sandy beach cove there were cave entrances carved into the grey/white, bone-like rock, their cool tunnels leading you on ... but if you do venture in, watch out for any sudden drops. This is certainly one of the most extraordinary and beautiful natural features we've ever encountered.

Adamas: King Bruno

Cat feeding

Rossini

Milos

Sleeping dragons and a roaring bear
Volcanic legacies and meltemi wear
Helios dancing twixt breeze-blown tamerisk
Pollonia my sandy bed one afternoon
A morning spent at Sarakiniko
Hand in hand walking on the moon
Klima's coloured boat houses
Sea-sprayed paintbox in the bay
Patrikia like a desert island
Micra paradise for the day
Paleochori's breakwater path of jewels
Alogomandra's cave mouth pool
Tourkothallasa aqua-floating chat
Ageri's Bruno King of the cats

Konda limani Adamas boulevard
To sit and smile at the promenade
Tavernas, cafes, rooftop bars
No finer way to while the hours
Tap your ouzo and take a drink
For those no longer in the pink
Then raise your glass to new friends made
'Til those lingering farewells are bade.

(Dave Burnham 2016)

Plaka: Shop window model cats

Roman Theatre

Lizard at Tourkothallasa

Catacombs

Kimolos

Boat Trip at Kimolos

Linda, Sue and Dave on the boat

Adamas: Dave, Ty, Gina and Sue

Ammos Taverna Pollonia with Niko, Dave, Sue, Gina and Ty

The Ag. Marina Cat Colony

Chapter 30

Santorini and Ios

On a summer's night, I have sat on the balcony drinking Ouzo, watching the ghosts of Greek Heroes sailing past, listening to the rustle of their sail cloths and the gentle lapping of their oars...and lain alongside Pythagoras watching him study the myriad of triangles in the constellations twinkling above us. Whether it was Crete, the heat, the Ouzo, or a combination, it is unequalled anywhere other than Santorini, in my humble opinion:
Phil Simpkin

Santorini

(2002 and 2017)

We spent one night in Santorini in 2002 on our way to Naxos and again in 2017 when we travelled to and from Ios. I can't really justify a whole chapter on Santorini, as we have only stayed for three nights in total. Our visits were of short duration as we used it as a convenient jumping off point to fly to before taking a ferry to connect with the other islands, but there are some recollections of interest.

Obviously, the most enduring memory for us, and anyone visiting Santorini, is the awe-inspiring view from the Island's capital Thira, across the incredibly deep caldera of the volcano that reputedly saw off the Minoans. It's so deep that cruise ships have to secure onto chains strung in the bay. The odd puff of smoke or steam from the little island of Kameni in the middle of the caldera indicates its past volcanic history. With its brilliant white buildings clinging onto the side of the island like icing on an elaborate Christmas cake, it is rightly one of the "must see" places in the Cyclades.

It may be a trick of the memory, but on our first visit I recall seeing price tags on the displayed items in the upmarket jewellery shops being changed (i.e. increased) as the cruise ships' tenders approached, presumably in readiness for the 'fresh meat' of the newly disgorged, usually wealthy tourists. Certainly the 'ringside seats' in the bars and tavernas with the caldera views carried a premium, as we found out when we ordered a couple of small beers to accompany our first Santorini sunset. You can ascend to the town from the old port by cable car, or sit astride a donkey, or on foot. There continues to be considerable controversy over the poor treatment of the donkeys by their owners, so it might be wise to consider one of the other two methods. The old Karavolades stairs do take some doing, but are feasible if you're reasonably fit and take your time with some rest stops: we noticed numbers painted on each step; I think there are about 588.

The free-draining volcanic ash soil is said to have contributed to the prevention of the grape vines' nemesis, the Phylloxera insect: in combination with the Assyrtiko vine it makes Santorini a haven for excellent wines.

In 2002 it rained overnight and we had some time to kill before departure so took a little stroll out of town. We were amazed to see hundreds of pretty little striped snails mooching about everywhere; they had come out to make the most of the rare summer moisture. Santorini is extraordinarily photogenic in its vertiginous beauty, but a combination of its epic views and the never-ending parade of cruise ships does make it a busy, full-on and expensive place to visit, especially in the high season. The night before catching the plane back we took a bus up to Oia. There were quite a few hundred others assembled at the best vantage point, but we found a good spot and watched a magnificent sunset as it illuminated a tall-masted sailing ship gliding by far below. Just as the sun dipped below the horizon most of the crowd broke into spontaneous applause (which we'd never experienced before or since – a bit cheesy, but quite apt given the location). Afterwards we retraced our steps and found a small cliff top taverna where I ordered the stuffed squid (a dish I'd never had before) and it was absolutely superb. I thanked the chef, discovering that it had been slowly braised in white wine, stuffed with a mix of finely chopped vegetables and feta cheese. I've actually been searching for one as good as that ever since; I've come close on Paros and Astypalia, but they never quite matched the taste of that first dish.

The large bustling port of Athinios is the place to catch ferries to the other islands and the first time we were there I can remember seeing a small horse freely trotting around between the cars, lorries, buses and people swarming about the harbour front. Memories of the last time mainly focus on the bus journey from Thira, when just before arriving it became stuck in the ludicrous amount of traffic trying to wind its way down the narrow road towards the port. This delay made things quite stressful and we nearly jumped off the bus to walk the rest of the way, but luckily it arrived just in time for us to catch the ferry. On the return leg, we had to change buses at the main terminus in Thira, in order to get to the airport for our flight, but there were few, if any, clues as to which bus went where. We bought tickets and waited expectantly, looking out for any indication as to which vehicle among the throng of buses was going our way. With an ever-growing crowd milling around and with about five minutes before the bus was due to leave, suddenly a man appeared from nowhere and yelled out 'Airport'! We surged forwards and followed behind him towards a rather dilapidated stationery bus, as if he was the Pied Piper. We embarked and grabbed a couple of seats near the front, only to find mine was broken and swung backwards into an overly-jaunty semi-horizontal position, delivering me helplessly into the lap of the passenger behind. Otherwise the journey was uneventful, taking about 45 minutes, but the small airport was pushed to accommodate the number of passengers. About 30 minutes before boarding began, we were crammed into the departure lounge, like heavily-perspiring sardines, before finally being permitted to escape onto the plane. (I'd like to think Santorini airport has been considerably upgraded since then).

Santorini, Thira: Views

Thira

The Karavolades numbered steps

Ios

(2017)

There is a time for many words, and there is also a time for sleep:
Homer, The Odyssey

We arrived by ferry at Gialos on Ios and were met at the port by Bernice's husband who kindly drove us the short distance along the seafront to Galini pension. The property had a gorgeous shady garden at the front and although our room at the back was quite basic, it was very clean and tidy and only a few minutes on foot from the beach. Bernice was extremely helpful and gave us a map and some suggestions about places to visit. There was a sweet little tabby in attendance from time to time, mostly in the flower beds. This trip turned out to be quite a lazy holiday – not that we rush about at the best of times – and mostly beach-based, but Ios is just right for that. During the peak season Ios plays host to hordes of youngsters from all over Europe, the UK and elsewhere, who come seeking the nightlife at the many clubs and bars up in the Chora or over at Mylopotas. We had to laugh out loud when we saw a sign pinned on one of the nightclub doors saying they opened at 2am, but like most of the islands the month of September is much quieter. While we were there only a handful of frazzled-looking young party goers emerged blinking into the daylight. Gialos beach has to be one of the best 'port' beaches we've stayed at, with a long sweep of soft sand in a well-protected bay and calm waters for lengthy floating about and swimming, just the very thing.

We strolled along the neat promenade to get our bearings, coming across various promising-looking tavernas, a 'pirate ship' cocktail bar, a cluster of fishing boats and a statue of Homer at the junction near the marina (his tomb is in the North of Ios). There was also a handy supermarket as well as the main bus stop for destinations all over the island. The main square had some great-looking pebble mosaics and a cluster of tavernas. It appeared there'd be no problem finding a variety of places to eat (not that there ever really is in Greece). We walked around the bay and along to the church of Aghia Irini, up a path and through a little archway to reach it. There was a lovely view back across Gialos from there and the whitewashed church was charming with a sizeable bell tower. The dome had small projections set into it, presumably as handholds or footplates for whoever drew the short straw to paint it each year (they looked a bit like cloves stuck in an orange used to make mulled wine).

We certainly ate really well. The Allo Bar had a nice vibe going on and very generous portions with live music some nights and it seemed quite cat-friendly. The Aphrodite restaurant had some tables set out along the harbour side – so some surreptitious cat feeding was enabled – and had very nice fish on their menu. Also recommend is the Octopus Tree round by the marina, with lovely food and very relaxed atmosphere – plus a friendly cat. We were having dinner at one of the tavernas near the port when an elderly gentleman appeared among the tables, playing a clarinet and singing a well-known Greek song, *S'agaopo* (I love you) ... well, I say singing, it mostly involved a quick refrain on the clarinet and a lot of 'Po, po, po, po, po'. Whether other people appreciated his efforts, or just hoped he'd move on if they made a donation I'm not sure, but he seemed to be doing quite well for loose change – one of the taverna owners later told us they reckoned he made a small fortune over the summer months, just for a couple of hours' nightly 'Popopopo-ing'.

Our real 'find' was Marina Bar and restaurant located by the beach quite near to where we were staying. It was run by the very fabulous (and Einstein look-alike) Ioannis, with shady tables at the front under a long fringed veil of dried palm fronds, with others right on the beach just across the road. The bar played a fantastic selection of music – including a selection from a great reggae band we hadn't previously heard of called The Jolly Boys. The bar was named after his cat (or possibly vice versa). One afternoon we were on the beach making use of his sunbeds and after Ioannis had enjoyed his daily swim, I went in to get a couple of ice creams. There he was laying a napkin on the floor near the door to the kitchen. Marina the cat came wandering over, purring happily, and Ioannis placed a neat row of cooked sardines on the napkin for her: she was one lucky cat. The chef was Scottish and his menu was excellent, if a little 'meaty' for us, but we ate there a few times and the food was delicious.

Another day while relaxing at Marina a ferry, which was just leaving the port, suddenly produced several sustained blasts on its horn and we saw what appeared to be smoke pouring from the prow. It started spinning around on its axis, while still quite close to the harbour – not an easy thing to do with a big ferry. The smoke was red-tinged, at first suggesting a fire, but if it was on fire we wondered why they weren't immediately returning to the dock. It was quite a mystery, and we watched with many others on the beach as the ship continued to pirouette for several minutes whilst blasting its horn, before eventually heading off around the headland. What was all that about? A little later we discovered that it was the captain's last day of duty before his retirement, so as a farewell gesture the crew had let off a flare and the spinning was like the ferry equivalent of an aircraft's barrel roll in celebration! You've got to love the Greek sense of theatre!

We found a row of wide shallow stone steps that went from the port up to the Chora, so that made for a good bit of exercise and a chance to explore. As we made our way towards the steps we passed by a small church that seemed to have sunk into the ground. It was an enjoyable walk, with some good places to stop and enjoy the views, as well as a splendid mix of vegetation to enjoy. The pathway ended near the Post Office and there was a little road round the headland that had a great sunset view. Just above was a very posh looking bar at the view point, but it seemed to be closed for a private party the evening we went there. Undeterred we decided to hang around anyway to enjoy the sunset from the road and while waiting we got chatting to a few others who had the same idea. Among them was a girl with an excellent camera and we started up a conversation about photography in Greece, etc. We quickly discovered that she was delightful company and after a long chat we agreed to meet again one evening for a meal – that was how we met Tiffany, more of whom later.

There were some very impressive churches in the town so I made my way up the side of the hill via some glorious alleyways and arches. Gradually finding the route up to the three churches standing along the top of the hill that you can see from all around. The view from there is magnificent, including the Bronze Age settlement of Skarkos on layers of terracing, and you can see right across the bay of Gialos. While we were there it was hard to imagine the Chora during peak season as a nocturnal, ear-splitting, Hellenic Gomorrah of ravers.

We made our way to the Eastern outskirts of the Chora to the famous row of windmills. In varying states of disrepair they still stand as majestic reminders of the past and I was inspired to paint a pair of them in pastels. Carrying on over the crossroads I managed to track down the modern Odysseus Elytis Open Air Theatre and it was well worth the trek. It can hold up to 1100 people attending concerts and plays organised by the municipality. There was a great view over Mylopotas from there, too, and on the way back down I happened across the increasingly rare sight of a proper old Greek donkey.

A little stroll from Gialos took us to Koumbara beach with rows of chain-suspended double mattresses under palm leaf rooves at one end and standard beds and umbrellas at the other. Standing on the hill behind was a building with what looked like giant golf balls, or "Rovers" from the 1960s TV series *The Prisoner*: I assume they were some kind of satellite receivers, but they looked incongruous in that setting. The Koumbara seafood restaurant had great food so we ate lunch there a couple of times and I got talking to the owner. On the wall inside was a collection of his old family photos, one of which was of him as a little boy going fishing with his father. Another evening we took some wine and a couple of glasses and sat at the far end of the beach on the rocks to watch the sunset – soppy old romantics that we are.

We caught the bus to Mylopotas beach a few times and enjoyed its magnificent crescent of golden sand and clear water. There were some very groovy, funky, colourful beach bars/restaurants with soft seating, scatter cushions and hammocks; more than likely the epicentres of some legendary beach parties in season. Another bus took us to the Southeast of the island, giving the opportunity to see some more of the coastline and interior – as well as having to give way to a herd of goats on the road. We arrived at Manganari beach having left the bus by the end of the road behind Antonis Restaurant. It was a lovely series of sandy coves with shallow waters going some way out and made for a great day trip.

We arranged to meet up with Tiffany at the Marina Bar, starting with cocktails and moving on to their excellent dinner menu. Originally from the US state of Texas, Tiffany is a travel blogger who not only gives some great tips on her website (agirlandherpassport.com), but also posts some very informative travel videos on her YouTube channel. We met up again while we were eating a "Buddha Bowl" for breakfast at Thai Me Up (!) by the port on our last morning and we've kept in touch. Tiffany lived on Naxos for a while and has more recently moved to be in Athens. She's still exploring the Greek islands, Athens and mainland Greece and we really enjoy her videos,

both for their content and that much needed 'Greek fix' whilst having to stay at home in the UK.
youtube.com/c/Agirlandherpassport
Hopefully we'll be able to meet up again before too long.

Ios Cats: Galini Pension, Allo Bar Restaurant, Octopus Tree Restaurant

View from the very top church at Chora

Odysseus Elytis Open Air Theatre Donkey

Chora windmills in pastels by Dave

Dave and Sue at sunset, picture taken by Tiffany when we first met

Dave, Sue and Tiffany

Chapter 31

Tinos and Mykonos

(2002 and 2018)

The spirit of Greece, passing through and ascending above the world, hath so animated universal nature, that the very rocks and woods, the very torrents and wilds burst forth with it:
Walter Savage Landor

Tinos

(2018)

We had changed ferries at Tinos en-route to Andros from Paros a few years earlier. What struck us at the time was the enormous quayside with complex-looking painted blue sections for pedestrians and red for taxis, plus a large area for coaches and busses – clearly it must be a very busy port, although it was quiet that day.

We flew into Mykonos and caught the ferry to Tinos where Marina met us at the port and drove us to Kyklades studios. Positioned just above the seafront at the far end of Agios Ioannis Porto beach, our studio had a fabulous panoramic view over the bay and across the sea to Mykonos, Delos and Agia Irini. On a clear day in the distance we could see Naxos, Paros, Sifnos and the edge of Syros. The night sky was epic and mesmerising, sitting outside our room with a glass of wine. Marina was a kind and lovely lady who it was a pleasure to meet. The one thing that swiftly became apparent about Tinos was that it can be a tad breezy (Aeolus was appointed by Zeus as God of Winds and he made his home on Tinos – maybe that's the reason for it).

We had some regular feline visitors who we called Hermes, Ariadne and Purr-seus. They regularly kept us company on our balcony during breakfast and while watching the sunsets. Of the handful of tavernas nearby we had a good meal at Porto Raphael – with accompanying cat – but our favourite place was Anatoli tou Porto. This place had super-friendly hosts and such generous portions that we found ourselves with quite a few 'doggie' bags for next day's lunch. An added bonus was a group of four playful kittens to keep us amused.

After a few days we hired a car and set about exploring the island. There are many beaches on Tinos and accessing them gives some good Greek hairpin bend driving practice. Ormos Ysternion (with a view of the village high above) had a sweet little sandy beach and an equally sweet and lucky tabby, as we had our usual supply of cat biscuits to hand. There was a classy fish taverna called To Thalassaki, where we had an excellent lunch one day. The waiter directed us to a table on a level above those positioned nearest to the sea (which seemed to be relatively calm), but it soon became apparent why the lower deck was to be avoided. Another group of tourists arrived and insisted on a table located on the lower deck. As the waiter was bringing their food out, a large wave sloshed over the edge of the concrete floor and sea water shot straight under their table soaking their feet, legs and their bags which they had to grab whilst lifting their feet. Meanwhile, the waiter had leapt up onto a nearby chair so that his feet didn't get wet! We were grateful to have taken his advice – he clearly had a firm grasp of the timing of passing ferries and their attendant wake. In fairness, there was a prominent bright yellow sign on the lower deck which read: "Sitting at your own risk, high waves on your table"... top entertainment.

Aghios Romanos was a beautiful small beach, although there was a steep incline to drive up in the hire car (and there'd been an ominous clonk from underneath the car when we'd arrived, but I looked and couldn't find anything obviously wrong). We had to take a good run-up at it on the way back, hoping there wasn't anything coming in the opposite direction. The local beach nearest to our studio could get really windy so we went round the corner to Sostis (reminiscent of one of Naxos' West coast beaches) and chilled out there for a couple of days. Whilst relaxing there I had a great neck and shoulder massage from one of the young women who work on the beaches of Greece from time to time. As we were there later in the season the sun casts long shadows as it sets, so we played the long legged game along the beach on the way back.

The Chora has the usual harbourside promenade, with banks, shops and cafes along the other side; the locals draw up in their cars to randomly dash in on some important errand, using their car hazard warning lights as "shopping lights" in typical Greek fashion. There was a fine collection of fishing boats and various mounds of nets to give me my 'caïques fix' and some interesting statuary around the place. The huge quay soon made sense as we approached a busy intersection at the bottom of Evangelistra Street. The Panagia Evangelistra church at the top of the hill is a magnet to Greek pilgrims: rather like Patmos, Tinos is a Holy island. A narrow strip of metal-edged carpet runs right up the hill at the side of the street from the intersection to the church and the devout pilgrims crawl up it on their hands and knees. Apparently this is in penance for prayers that have been answered for their loved ones. Most of the shops and stalls lining the street sell all manner of votive offerings to the pilgrims and visitors, but most popular are the candles – not just the standard dining table size, some are up to five feet tall! There was a bronze statue near the top depicting a woman crawling to the church with one hand reaching out for salvation – it appears that it's usually women who seem to undertake the arduous task. At the summit outside the church, red carpets run up the grand and substantial marble steps towards a stunning black and white pebble mosaic laid out across the entire front of the building. We didn't go inside as it felt like a place for the truly devout only, but we have seen footage of the interior, like some kind of cave of artefacts dangling from the ceiling, representing requests made to the icon, such as glasses for eyesight, model boats for safety at sea and miniature limbs. The devotional act, deep belief and giant candles seemed like a stark contrast to the Brighton equivalent of pub crawls and huge sticks of rock candy.

There was a ring road around the Chora, presumably built to move all the 'pilgrim' coaches from the port, but it made getting about much easier, and we took it to get to Konia, just along the coast. A long, but slightly commercialised beach resort, it has the Sanctuary of Poseidon and his sea nymph wife Amphitrite: a pile of old ruins to the untrained eye, but the guide would explain more – despite being such a sea-faring civilisation, it's the only Cycladic island to dedicate an entire temple to the God of the Sea.

Two villages up in the hills were particularly worth a visit so we took the car to explore. Triandaros was perched on the hill with a fabulous view of the Chora far below. It was a joy to discover the archways, passages, alleyways and traditional buildings. We found a marble water fountain carved with a dove motif and a set of steps covered in fallen Bougainvillaea leaves that could have been dressed for the Chelsea Flower Show. Still further up was Dio Hora with more fabulous gardens, archways and passages as well as a series of natural springs feeding fountains and what looked like some ancient stone sinks that might have been used for laundry or even bathing. Two very charming villages. We passed the enormous rock of Exombourgo on our travels with the remains of the Venetian Fortress of Aghi Eleni at its summit.

On Andros we had seen a few traditional dovecotes, but Tinos is famous for them and there could be as many as a thousand still on the island. The white towers (peristeriones) are elaborately decorated with finials of mock doves along with triangular and circular slate patterns. The lower storey is meant for storage and the upper is for the doves, built to take the prevailing wind into consideration for the birds' take-off and landing. Originally kept for food and the manure from their droppings, the doves are now kept more for their aesthetic appeal. We'd read that Tarampados was the place to see dovecotes at their best and we weren't disappointed by the variety and beauty of the examples there.

A couple of days before we were due to return home, Marina advised us of a severe weather warning for our planned departure date and recommended that we try to get a boat over to Mykonos a day early, as the ferries might not operate in the bad weather (force 9 winds were forecast). Mykonos isn't our favourite island (a bit too 'Chi-Chi' for our liking), but heeding her words and checking the forecast, we quickly looked on the internet to see if there was any chance of getting a room there for the night before our flight home.

Ariadne

Purr-seus

Hermes

Porto Raphael cat

Sostis beach sunset shadows, Dio Hora Fountain

Tarampados Dovecote

Mykonos

(2000 and 2018)

Describing Naxos: *Where Zeus himself was said to live. Where his son Dionysus frolicked and presumably drank and threw orgies and dropped E and danced all night to the BC version of EDM.*
These days you have to go to Mykonos for that.
Anthony Bourdain

Unless you have seen the houses of Mykonos, you can't pretend to be an architect. Whatever architecture has to say, it is said here:
Le Corbusier

Why two quotes for Mykonos? Well, it divides opinion between its visitors and I think the truth probably lies somewhere between the two: Cycladic architecture isn't limited to Mykonos and it's not the only party island/town in Greece.

We've passed through Mykonos quite a few times over the years on our way to/back from other islands, but have only stayed overnight on two occasions. First in 2000 on our way back from Naxos and then in 2018 due to a bad weather forecast making it likely that the ferry from Tinos would be cancelled, thus leaving us stranded (not a disaster, but a little inconvenient).

So we booked a room at the Hotel Philipi in the heart of Mykonos town and caught the ferry across from Tinos a day earlier than originally planned. When we reached Mykonos we decided to take the sea bus from the new ferry port. This was a much nicer way to do it than by taxi (or Piaggio!) and a fair bit cheaper to boot. On arrival, we trundled our bags along the seafront until we found a shady spot where Sue stayed with the bags (with assistance from a friendly pelican) while I went to buy a pocket street map to help us find the hotel. Mykonos town is infamous for its complicated maze of backstreets and the resultant game of déjà vu so, being unfamiliar with the labyrinth, I did a quick recce. I made a mental note of shops and landmarks on the way back, which didn't take quite as long as I'd thought, so Sue didn't have to wait very long. Locating the hotel was actually quite easy and the contrast between the bustle of the streets and the beautiful garden and environment behind the hotel's facade was amazing; I imagine you might get a similar feeling on entering a riad from the bustling streets of Morocco.

We dropped our bags and headed back out into the jumble of alleyways to do some sightseeing. Firstly, a magnificent marble fish market area on the seafront with dolphin and seashell carvings. Then we walked back along the harbourside to Panagia Panaportiani church, past the souvenir shops with a yawning, stretching tabby cat and strolled in front of the many bars and restaurants of the area known as 'Little Venice'; pausing for the obligatory selfie. The windmills of Kato Mili are iconic and highly photogenic – if you can manage to get a shot without someone else in it. We carried on along Xenias, past a pizza restaurant which looked promising for dinner, and went in search of the bus station as we'd need to locate it the next day to catch a bus to the airport.

Afterwards we dropped back down a side road leading to a school when Sue spotted something that seemed too good to be true in Mykonos: a small bar offering a €5 happy hour! A few minutes later we were enjoying a pair of large Margaritas, served in half pint glasses!

Our flight didn't leave until the evening, so the next day we packed our bags and left them at the hotel while we spent the day pottering around the town. Across the street from the hotel was the Rarity Gallery, so that was our first stop. A contemporary art gallery with all manner of fascinating exhibits: we were kindly shown around by a very glamorous young lady who seemed genuinely happy that we were taking an interest in the various displays. There were a mind-boggling range of artworks; from spooky hyperrealist sculptures of people to kinetic curiosities and some large contemporary paintings. Although most were for sale, a large bank loan would have been necessary for us to purchase anything; a fascinating glimpse into the high-end art world nevertheless. Exiting the alleyways to find ourselves out on the seafront again, the weather forecast was living up to the predictions with large waves breaking over the harbour wall, as we were buffeted about by the high winds. We slipped back into the maze of backstreets and spent a delightful hour or so wandering around the shops marvelling at the Gucci, Armani and other designer labels, before heading along the Agia Ana beach to the Archaeological Museum. We had a snack and frappe at a local bakery, which had three wonderful little animatronic puppets inside.

Following a leisurely late lunch at the Marco Polo taverna, we collected our bags and made for the bus station, feeling quite like old hands as we negotiated the many twists and turns of the streets that we'd committed to memory. As usual it was fairly chaotic at the bus depot, but quite interesting to watch the comings and goings as we waited at the appointed place for the airport bus. We reflected that it must be quite trying for the local residents of Mykonos when the (mainly) younger tourists start to reappear at dusk (and we noticed that some start to flag a bit under the barrage of unruly hedonists). We observed one young woman wearing some shorts that were little more than a wide belt and a minute top covering something, but not her modesty, posing and pouting into her phone camera whilst standing right in the middle of the busy main road ... doubtlessly providing some fodder for her Instagram account. She was staggering around and laughing, seemingly oblivious to the cars, buses and mopeds trying to avoid her ridiculous antics.

For now at least, it was time for us to head home, but we hoped be back again to visit new islands, meet new people and delight once more in the many joys and wonders of Greece.

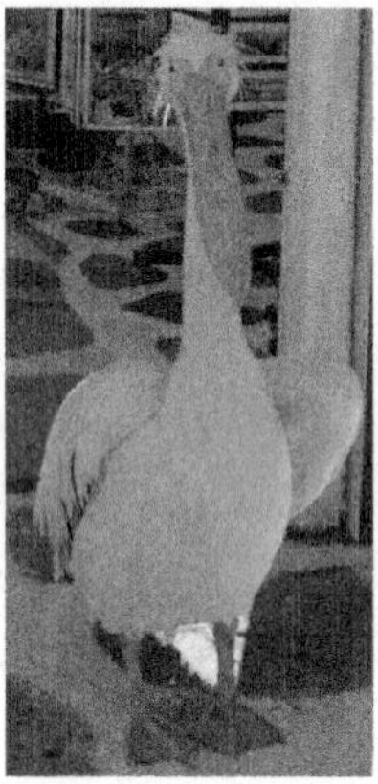

Mykonos: Pelican

Little Venice

Marble Fish Market

Kato Mili Windmills

Epilogue

Dogs come when they are called;
cats take a message and get back to you later: Mary Bly.

Thompson Pet Travel continue to do incredible work in bringing the "Greekies" to their new forever homes in the UK. They experience occasional difficulties en-route, but always manage to find ways to overcome them with remarkable initiative and lateral thinking. Although they do encounter some not-so-nice people out there on the road, so they have to have their wits about them. We love following their journeys on their Facebook page as well as the photographs of the cats and dogs (the "kids") settled happily in their new homes: it's so heart-warming and we continue keep up with their progress.

Trisha is still looking after about 60 street cats and another 25 in her own home. Rebecca managed to get back to Poros and help Trisha again in 2021.

Rebecca returning kitties after sterilising

Monty in a hammock

Monty came across Barry, another stray/street cat, and brought him home with him. Trisha tells his story:

'Well it was like this Dave. I was no longer a kitten so I wasn't wanted.

I packed myself off over the mountain.

On the way I bumped into a cool ex-bin cat called Monty. I put on my saddest face for effect, so to speak, and he said "hold that face Baz boy and you will have Gourmet tonight" so I did and here I am ... at Trisha's house.'

Barry putting his sad face on

Asprooli still living a life of luxury

Trisha is still taking in strays where she can: 'Two people want Tiger Lily Tiggy, but they are in the UK so time will tell.'

Tiger Lily Tiggy

Trisha, Rebecca and Alexandra went up to the forest to repair and renew the cat shelter for the colony of strays they look after there.

With the forest cats and the renewed shelter

Robert continues to do fabulous work, too.

Robert and Archie

Trisha tells Archie's story:

'My name is Archie and yes I may have royal lineage, too, but somehow I was born on the steps of a village house on the island of Poros. I liked to play with my siblings, however, I was different ... I couldn't run and jump like my brothers and sisters because I am paraplegic. One day we were all playing on the road down below the house late at night when two men on bikes scooped me up and took me with them. Michael and Peter took me to Nikos, the island vet, who said I was very lively and special. So, I moved in with Robert and Brenda and they have been so kind. They make me do exercises. They wash me and take me to the vet. I now have a new jacket to help me when I run on the floor. I have toys and cat beds. 🐱They spoil me. Except they keep bringing more rescues home 🙀... I am talking on their behalf now, because of them I am still here bright as a button. They need some help for my food and care. Every little helps thank you. Love Archie 👑'

Sid and Robert

Trisha with Sid's story:

'Now Sid. He is amazing ... Robert and I were looking for the kitty with the bad eye in the same area where we found the abandoned kittens in the unfinished building. Robert heard a tiny meowww and said there was a small kitten down in the foundations of a house, but when we looked he was down the sewer trench. But it was difficult to get down. Robert climbed down the first bit, but could not get into the sewer trench so tied a rope around a box. Then he dropped a rope into the trench. I said, "Robert you are not expecting that mini kitty to grab the rope?" But the kitty did. Unbelievable! 😳😻 Then Robert lifted the kitten up (like *Mission Impossible*) and dropped him into the box. He climbed out of the trench and handed me the box with the tiniest kitten in it. All this was in the dark. Robert wore a head torch. That night we had a huge storm. Divine intervention again? 👼🧚'

I remain ever-hopeful that we might be able to get a few more of the cats in Trisha's care adopted in the UK: Rachael is still waiting for several. Trisha has managed to get some of them to Holland in the past and has contacts there willing to help, but with the difficulties in acquiring all the necessary paperwork to get animals from Greece to the UK, more people are looking to rehome within the EU and it sounds like Holland is quite overrun as a result.

Archie and Sid

Trisha and Rebecca: the team that saved Teddy's life

Nikos and **Litsa** are working hard to care for the stray cats of Poros and to keep up with the neutering program, as well as caring for the island's other animals.

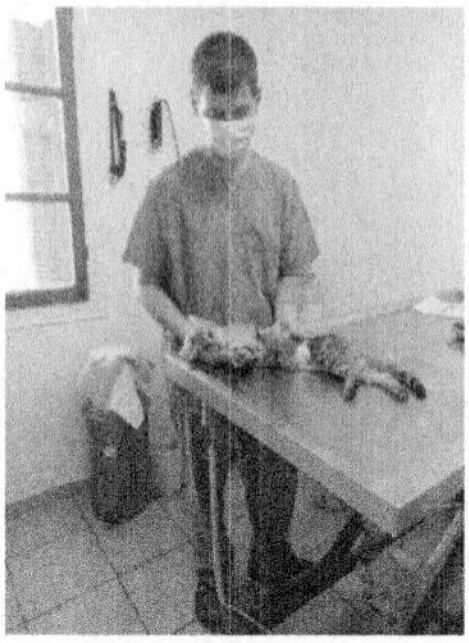

Litsa with Charlotte, Nikos sterilising another cat, Litsa and Princess

Smokey was left outside Nikos' clinic so he decided to adopt him

Vincent is having a lovely time now he is living with Martin and his other cats, Lara and Benjy. Martin loves him to bits and finds him excellent company.

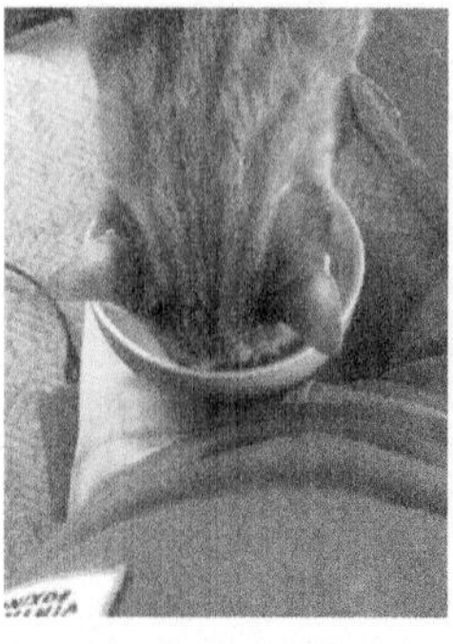

Vincent eating Martin's breakfast   Cat crunchies   with Lara and Benji

So, what's the future for cats and dogs still in Greece?

Of course, some are lucky and have loving homes and caring owners. Certainly there has been a big move in the right direction recently with regards to animal welfare, including new regulations for pet owners and sellers, as well as stricter penalties for animal abuse. I have heard stories in recent months of cats being found poisoned and the Greek police taking the matter very seriously indeed. Equally I have heard of instances where there seems that little can be done; with one suspected perpetrator trying to sue their accuser for (non-existent) defamation of character (having apparently publicly threatened to kill cats). However, we need to remember that these problems sadly exist all over the world. Only recently a man was arrested in Brighton and subsequently jailed for five years after being convicted of stabbing 16 cats, 9 of which died from their injuries.

There is a new bill in Greece which sets out to protect animals from harm and suffering, improve animal welfare education, and lay the foundations for the management of strays. There is also a move for a national neutering program, but it needs to be addressed with finesse or else there could be substantial resistance. The key wording from the point of rehoming and adoption is: "*... to establish a comprehensive program for the management of strays by the local Municipalities and participation of Animal Welfare Organisations in a supervisory framework ...*" I think this may be where solutions to the current predicament facing those wanting to adopt strays into the UK could be found.

We are aware of the dreadful time that many people in Greece have suffered during the recent period of austerity. One of the obvious consequences is one of fiscal priority; some pets must have become an unaffordable luxury to owners who were struggling to put food on the table for themselves and their families. It was a horrendous situation and we must be careful not to apportion blame in these extreme circumstances.

It was heart-warming to see that the Greek Prime Minister himself has adopted a rescue dog, hopefully this will be seen as leading by example rather than as political point scoring. However, I wonder if there is still, understandably, a degree of national pride at play in allowing their unwanted animals being adopted by non-Greeks? We need to give reassurance that this is being undertaken for the purest of reasons and win the country's trust to accept any help on offer, as this is a situation that is beyond the control of most.

However one might feel about Brexit, it has not only exposed the animal welfare charities to a raft of paperwork and regulations (which hitherto the UK was exempt from as they applied to non-EU member countries); but it has also highlighted the levels of animal adoptions to the Greek authorities, due to increased record-keeping. Prior to Brexit, a Pet Passport – and possibly TRACES in some circumstances – was all that was required, so most adoptions proceeded smoothly and quietly.

Clearly some form of regulation is necessary. If you're reading this book you are almost certainly an animal lover and you will be aware of the amount of pet thefts, trafficking and illegal breeding going on in the UK – especially during the Covid pandemic. This was also happening in the rest of Europe, with animals being smuggled into the UK and sold to the unsuspecting public.

So, I can quite understand why Greece would want to see some sort of legal provision for accountability, origin and destination for its adopted animals. An Animal Health Certificate is now a requirement to import a pet into the UK, but as I understand it these documents can be issued by the owner's private vet in most EU countries. The stumbling block appears to come with the pre-existing system for TRACES in Greece that has been superseded by the new Health Certificate. This means that the new forms are being processed in an inflexible and complex manner. In addition, there is the requirement that they have to be actioned by a "State vet", rather than a private vet (although I know that some of the UK's vets have found the administrative burden of processing Animal Health Certificates for travel from the UK to be too much to cope with). Not only does this take up the Greek Ministry Vets' time, but many also try to do battle with an on-line system that doesn't seem to be fit for purpose. While some appear to be happy to simply stamp and sign the pre-filled Health Certificate form (as long as it is presented and completed correctly along with the necessary accompanying documentation), others insist on battling with the on-line system. Simplification and unification of the system is required.

Returning to that statement earlier on: "*...and participation of Animal Welfare Organisations in a supervisory framework ...*", it would seem the time may have come for a meeting between the Greek government and the Greek Animal Welfare Charities, so that an amicable arrangement can be reached. There is nothing to be done about the foolishness of the UK's representatives who "negotiated" (and I use that term loosely) the Brexit deal and the subsequent bureaucratic fallout. However, I feel certain they could work within that framework to come up with a solution that would benefit the animals who could then have happier and safer lives if things were resolved. It could also be agreed that only registered animal charities would have the legal permission to engage in rehoming the strays. Personal ownership is and should be, a different matter.

An animal's origin would be quite simple to determine if the microchipping regulations were followed:

"Article 5
Liabilities home pet owners
1. The owner of home pet obliged:
"A) provide for marking and registration of the animal, as well as for issuing health card before leaving the animal in place of birth and in any case within two months of the birth of that or within a month from finding or acquisition ..."
(LAW 4235/2014 – Government Gazette 32 – 11/02/2014)

That covers both newborns and strays. So, if they are microchipped they should then be registered on the Panhellenic database. That way, if and when the animal is rehomed previous ownership, or responsibility, can easily be checked and hopefully the system would flag if an animal had been stolen. It should be a relatively simple task to use a scanner to confirm that the animal's identity matches the paperwork at the point of departure and arrival.

With regards to destination the new owner should undertake to immediately register the animal with a UK pet microchip registration database, which could be accessed by any UK vet. There was a suggestion that the UK pet registration databases do not all cross-reference effectively. I looked at the list of 16 approved databases on the UK government website and ran a search through each one using Teddy's microchip number. Only 3 returned a negative result, the others all directed me to the company that Teddy is registered with for further information. So I think the infrastructure is pretty sound (I asked the UK government to contact those databases who failed the test, but so far I haven't had a response).

Pets would need to be scanned at every visit to a vet and there are scanners (such as the *Scanner Angel®)* which will alert the operator if the microchip belongs to an animal reported lost or stolen. There would have to be a policy/protocol to follow which would enable the vet to employ a means of retaining the animal if it flags as stolen (possibly a difficult thing to achieve). However, there could be other strategies employed with some sort of Finder's Fee payable to the vet to encourage compliance. Perhaps there could also be an International Registration Database.

In an ideal world, the new owner should be required to obtain a licence that would be officially registered, with an undertaking to care for that animal for the duration of its life. That would mean anyone who was attempting to traffic animals would be immediately flagged when they were sold on, as the recipient would also have to register both the microchip number and a new license. A national pet licence registration database could be created to record recent registrations, or possibly combined with the microchip register to trigger alerts. Another reason for suggesting a licence is there are many reports of people taking on pets (especially dogs) during the Covid lockdowns, who hadn't thought through the consequences of what might happen when they returned to work, or the realities of the responsibility of pet ownership. Consequently, some animal rescue organisations have been inundated with unwanted pets. I would even go so far as including a fine if the previous owner didn't have a valid reason for effectively abandoning their pet. One further consideration might be making some provision for the animal's welfare were the owner to die. I have made provision in my will for Teddy to be cared for by named individuals, whom I trust, alongside a defined sum to be paid from my estate to those named individuals to cover his care.

I think these ideas would (as well as making the Greek end of the bureaucracy a little less arduous, along with getting the Greek people on side), go a long way to resolving some of the difficulties currently faced by the Greek Animal Welfare Charities who continue to do such amazing work.

Neo and Dorian continue to visit our allotment, popping in to say hello on their patrols, while keeping the mouse and rat population at bay. They are always up for a little bit of fuss and attention.

Dorian and Neo

Teddy

After his first 8 weeks of living with us and being entertained indoors with ping pong balls, bouncy balls up and down the stairs, milk bottle tops, a rechargeable flapping fish, a wind-up mouse, myriad catnip toys, learning "kitty parkour" and exploring every nook and cranny he could get his nose into ... it was becoming quite clear that Teddy's horizons needed extending. He was now ready for the great outdoors as his "right to roam" instincts took hold; even his favourite toy – feather on a stick – wasn't quite cutting the mustard.

Early one evening in August we popped a smart new, red collar and tag on him, bit the bullet and let him outside to explore. After a few perfunctory sniffs of our small patio, he trotted out through the gate, down the passageway behind our garden wall and straight through a gap in the neighbouring fence (caused by a loose board that we didn't know about). He then disappeared off into the neighbours' (somewhat overgrown) garden behind ours and then completely vanished! We managed to follow him into their garden via a gate at the far end and spent the next half-an-hour calling him, rattling the crunchie bag and trying all the tricks to entice him, but to no avail. Dry-mouthed, rather shaky and cursing myself for having lost him on his first outing, I briefly returned to the house to get a drink of water and use the loo. Whilst upstairs I happened to glance up at one of his favourite places to sit (on top of a wardrobe) and had to convince myself I wasn't hallucinating: there he was!! Sitting up there, cool as a cucumber and wondering what all the fuss was about. He must have slipped back through the gap in the fence and scampered back into the house and upstairs, just as we went around the longer route to look for him. A bit like a Whitehall farce, but much relief all round.

After that incident, I joined Pet Trackers Community Facebook group and asked what sort of thing the kind people there recommended. They gave me loads of help and advice, so we eventually settled on a Ubeequee tracker. If we were letting him outside, then it would really help if we had a rough idea of his whereabouts, at least until he became familiar with the surrounding area. Having set the tracker up, I asked Sue to take it on a secret walk so I could see where she'd been. It worked a treat, so we attached it to his collar and opened the back door. He was more cautious than his first outing, but gradually expanded his horizons, mapping the area as he explored. I had to wean myself off continuously pressing the update button on my phone, but at least I now had a reasonable idea of his whereabouts. Each time he returned home he was greeted with fuss and tickles, and the odd kitty treat especially if he'd been gone for some time. The feeling of letting him explore the world outside was like a combination of a child's first day at school/swimming lessons/solo bike ride, but Teddy was clearly enjoying his outdoor adventures.

One day the sound of a clearly dis-chuffed cat could be heard from a few gardens away. The noise went on for some time and then suddenly fell quiet. The chances of Teddy being involved were confirmed by his tracker location which I checked as we sat in the garden, having failed to get him back by calling him. The doorbell rang and it was Mark from down the road (owner of Daisy) and he had Teddy's collar and tracker in his hand.

Mark: 'Hi Dave, your cat was in our back garden. I think this might belong to him.'

Dave: 'Oh dear, I'm so sorry, we heard the noise. Is Daisy alright? So sorry if Teddy's being a nuisance.'

Mark: 'No, no, it's Daisy. She really doesn't like other cats. She took a swipe at him and then we found his collar in the garden. He left and was very polite, he wasn't the one making the noise. I hope he comes back soon.'

With that, Sue called: 'He's back, it's okay.'

Teddy and his collar/tracker were re-united once more. This was to become a theme…

The next afternoon another round of caterwauling erupted from nearby. Sue sent Mark a text telling him to sprinkle some water at Teddy if he was being a nuisance to them or Daisy. A short while later the doorbell went again. I was out on the allotment, so Sue sent me a message:

Sue: 'Ok, Mark and Ellie rang the doorbell on their way out for a walk. It was Teddy and Daisy squaring up to each other again (but mostly Daisy yowling – they think Teds just wants to be friends with her). It wasn't in their garden but next door. They've put Daisy indoors while they go out, so he's probably wandered off. I'll keep calling him in case he's nearby. They're cool with him visiting but apologised for Daisy's unwelcoming attitude! Poor little Tedster! They did say he was very handsome, though. Xxx'

Dave: 'Looks like he'll have to take his bunch of roses and box of chocolates elsewhere.'

After so much difficulty trying to get him into a carrier at the pick-up point when he arrived and his apparent fear of cat baskets, we were worried about how we were going to get Teddy to his first vet appointment. So we left his cat basket upstairs in the bedroom with its door open and each day randomly placed a cat treat inside: thankfully his fear of the carrier was overcome by his love of a treat. He was getting used to being inside it, but time would tell how he would react to being shut in it during a trip to the vet. Happily, when the fateful day came he went into his carrier as usual to claim the treat and there was just enough time to close the door and drape a towel over to reduce the light. Teddy made a right old racket in the car on the way to the vet, but luckily it's a very short journey and once we'd managed to get him back out of his carrier at the vets, he was as good as gold. The vet checked him over and he was quite keen to get back into the familiar environment of his carrier for the return journey, none the worse for his adventure.

Teddy arrived home one evening missing his collar and the GPS tracker app showed it was somewhere in one of our neighbours' back gardens towards the end of our street. I put a note through the letterboxes of all the likely neighbours with my mobile number. I asked politely if people could listen out at around six o'clock when I would set off the ringing chime on the tracker to see if we could locate it. I tried the ringer, but didn't get any responses, so thought that was probably that – the tracker was lost. However, the next morning I had a text from a chap whose house backs on to our row, about 6 houses away.

Russell: 'Hi Dave, this is Russell. Sorry, I've only just read you note re: cat GPS collar. I did hear a little tune playing when we were out in the garden last night. It sounded like it was coming from a couple of doors away, but we have a lot of foliage in our garden so it could be buried in there somewhere. You're welcome to come round and see if you can pinpoint it. Cheers.

PS – Is your cat the ginger one? He just appeared in my hallway as I type this!'

Dave: 'Hi Russell, thanks for letting me know. That would be great, if you don't mind. When would be good for you? Ooh, little monkey! Please feel free to chase him out if he's being a nuisance.'

Russell turned out to be a splendid fellow who I warmed to immediately and he showed me a photograph he'd taken of Teddy, sitting at the top of his stairs! It turned out he was quite a regular visitor and Russell's cat, Rocket, didn't seem to mind too much. We stood in his back garden and I used the phone app to set off the ringer on the tracker. We both burst out laughing as the chime erupted into life right next to us, beneath a nearby bush, as if a little pixie was playing an electronic tune somewhere in the undergrowth.

Rocket

A few weeks later I sent Russell another message.

Dave: 'Hi Russell, I noticed from his tracker that Teddy's been over your way quite a bit. Hope he's not being a bother and all's well with you.'

Russell: ' Hi Dave, Teddy has been visiting quite a bit! We have the doors open quite a lot, but he's discovered the cat flap, too! He's not a bother though, it's nice coming across him as he peers around a door. So far there hasn't been any trouble between him and Rocket and hopefully they'll become friends. Here's a photo of Teddy from just now.'

Russell sent me a picture of Teddy emerging from under Russell's desk in his office.

Dave: 'Aw, thanks so much Russell, that's really kind of you and very reassuring to know he's on his best behaviour and not being a bother to either you or Rocket. He's a friendly soul. I think he misses his feline companions from Greece so Rocket is probably a great comfort to him.'

Teddy didn't come back at his usual time one evening and it was quite dark. Alarmingly, his tracker was showing his location as outside the local back gardens and possibly across one of the nearby side roads. I immediately went out to see if I could find him using the location given on the tracker. There was no sign of him in anyone's front garden, so I began to peer under parked cars and then I saw a little shape over the road. It was Teddy, cowering under a large car. Luckily, there was a set of temporary traffic lights nearby where the road was being dug up, so traffic was either quite slow or avoiding that road altogether. I called out to him and he came out from under the car immediately. Although he hadn't been used to being picked up much in his younger life, I didn't really have a choice so I grabbed him and carried him back home, struggling in my arms. Sue answered my urgent banging on the front door to be met with the sight of me "covered in blood" as she put it, carrying a ginger blur... Luckily the scratches weren't as bad as they looked, but ... a small price to pay to get Teddy safely home again and thank goodness for the tracker. One of his nine lives used!

A few weeks later Teddy returned without his collar again and the GPS suggested it might again be near to Russell's house, so I sent him a text. It seemed that Rocket had popped out of his cat flap and had pretty much run straight into Teddy in the garden. They had both reared up on their hind legs for a boxing match without much harm done, but that explained the missing collar. Russell kindly returned it so all was well.

Shortly, Sue spotted Teddy approaching our cat flap with what looked like something stuck to his collar, but he was actually carrying it in his mouth and trying to push it through the flap. Closer inspection revealed that it was an open, but half-empty, pouch of cat food! So I sent Russell a photo.

Dave: 'Hiya, Umm ... Teddy just appeared through his flap with this. Sorry if he's pinched Rocket's food.'

Russell: 'It is Rocket's.' 😂😂😂😂

Dave: ' Oops, Sue's laughing hysterically having watched him try to get through the flap with it. 😂 Would you like it back?'

Russell: 'It's given us a great laugh, too. Happy for Teddy to eat after he's gone to so much trouble!'

Dave: 'Well, it certainly wasn't as troublesome as bringing a mouse home would've been. He does seem quite pleased with himself ... we think he's giving us hints for his menu the next time we go shopping. Thanks, you lovelies.'

Russell: 'Rocket hasn't brought a mouse home for a while – maybe Teddy's been getting all them all! Bless Teddy for his perseverance getting it out of our house, across all the gardens and into yours!'

Yet again Teddy came back minus his collar and I was just setting up an Apple Air Tag as a spare collar, when the doorbell rang. Amber from about 8 houses away stood at the door with his GPS tracker collar in her hands. Sue had met her a few weeks earlier when Teddy was late coming home and she went looking for him based on his tracker signal. Amber explained that their cat flap batteries were playing up so Teddy had got into the house and lost his collar there whilst paying a visit to their two cats. We apologised on his behalf, but Amber said he was a lovely cat and no bother. He lost the collar in their house again soon afterwards and, Zoe, Amber's Mum, called me to say she'd found it and popped it through our letterbox. We were certainly getting to meet lots of our neighbours through Teddy!

Losing his collar/tracker was becoming a habit and not long after that he came home for the seventh time minus his GPS collar. This time the signal showed it to be right at the far end of Zoe's garden. I sent her an apologetic text and we arranged to set the ringer off to see if we could locate it, but by the time Zoe got home from work it was dark, so we would have try it the next day.

The following morning I checked the tracker signal again and scratched my head, as it seemed to have moved from Zoe's garden to the space behind the pub at the far end of the road. That seemed a bit bizarre, but we wondered if one of the neighbourhood foxes might have picked up the collar overnight and moved it. Anyway, the pub opened at 3pm so off I went to ask the landlord if he would very kindly agree to give me access to the overgrown space at the back of the pub. This was a slightly bizzare request, but he agreed so long as he accompanied me and I set the alarm chime off. We could just hear it ringing somewhere in the tangled undergrowth, so we clambered over fallen trees and brambles and then he spotted it. The tracker was now completely separated and only the plastic ID tags remained – the rest of the red collar had been eaten and chewed to bits! We think this was probably done by a fox, or maybe a rat or mouse. After that, we decided to bite the bullet and trust him to roam with just a collar and ID tag (he is of course micro-chipped). No more anxious checking of my phone to look at his whereabouts!

Teddy has been a gorgeous boy ever since the first moment he arrived with us. He has a really gentle and loving nature and chats away with a considerable vocabulary of varied meows, squeaks and chirrups. To say he has a healthy appetite is an understatement, so we'll need to watch his food intake, or we'll end up with a "Teddy Tubby". He is endlessly entertaining and fills our hearts with joy and happiness. On recent colder nights we often drift off to sleep with our bodies vibrating to the contented purrs of a ginger pussycat snuggled up against us.

Sitting on the desk in my office as I write the closing words

As Teddy perched on the kitchen doorstep the other day I said to him:

'Aftó eínai to spíti sas, aftós eínai o kípos sas, aftí eínai i tavérna sas kai sas agapáme.'

(*This is your house, this is your garden, this is your taverna and we love you.*)

The photographs in the printed and Kindle book versions are in black and white, but you can see all of them in colour at: **www.adastralpodcast.com/herdingcats.html** where I may also post the occasional update.

You can also join the book's Facebook group to comment, share your own animal adoption stories and see updates at:

facebook.com/groups/1471681759877496

Thanks

Firstly, I would like to thank my wonderful wife Sue, for her invaluable help in editing and proof reading this book.

Sue and I would like to take the opportunity to thank everyone involved in helping Teddy on his epic journey to us.

Huge thanks to Trisha for caring for Teddy so well while we battled to make the arrangements to bring him to the UK and for what has become a lasting friendship. We are also grateful to her husband, Triantafillos, for his understanding and kindness.

To Rebecca for spotting little Teddy up in the hills of Poros and for rescuing him with Trisha. Also to Nikos and Litsa for all their excellent veterinary care for Teddy, as well as their patience and assistance with my endless administrative requests and for their continuing help with the animals in need on the island.

To Michael for being a great support to Trisha.

To Kate Daisy Grant for putting me in touch with Andrew, who in turn kindly linked me up with Greek Animal Rescue.

To Nena and Diane at Greek Animal Rescue who – despite having so many people to help as well as their own animals – spent so much time offering me invaluable advice and guidance. To Cordelia at Nine Lives Greece, Andy at Spartan Cats and Linda at CARAT for their support and advice.

To Victoria at Greek Pet Transport and Natalie at Animal Couriers for their time and advice.

To Mark and Kat for their help in solving a puzzle.

To Karen for her contribution about Nine Lives Greece in the Athens chapter.

To Eva for her support and for her contribution to the chapter on Lesvos.

To Karen at DEFRA for her assistance.

To Karen and Daisy at the Foreign and Commonwealth Office and "BD" at the Legalisation Office for their help with obtaining the dreaded Apostille.

To Sue and Merna for witnessing and certifying the adoption papers so we could get the Apostille.

To Gregory at Memory of Greece and Richard at RePrint for their help in producing copies of the documents.

To Marinos for helping with the transfer of the documents to and from Piraeus.

To the Public Notary in Brighton for her advice.

To the Greek Embassy (UK) for at least considering my request.

To the three Greek Ministry Vets who worked so hard to process the Health Certificates (practically shutting down their office department for the morning in order to achieve it).

To the Head of Vets in Greece for her help in reaching the correct department.

To Chris and her Animal Hotel for looking after Teddy and Vincent while the Freedom Bus had her air con fixed.

To Ali and Helen at SkyPets International for their help with the UK Customs declaration and VAT.

To Martin for being so organised in his responses for Vincent's paperwork and for being a new chum.

To Robert and his wife Brenda for driving the cats all the way from Poros, right around the Saronic Gulf to their drop-off point on the Greek mainland – and then having to drive all the way back again to get home.

To "Andrea" for her singularly courageous and level-headed approach to what was probably one of the most stressful mornings of her life: we owe her a great deal. She was a hero that day.

To the star that is Rachel at Thompson Pet Transport who has to be one of the kindest, patient, organised, helpful people I've ever worked with.

And, finally, to Lynda, Julie and Frank who drive Stella Blue – the "Freedom Bus" – all the way from Athens, halfway round Greece, through Italy, Switzerland and France, to the UK. They look after their passengers with all the love, care and empathy in the world, negotiating bureaucracy, diplomacy and Covid along the way, as well as all the uncertainties that circumstances bring about with such optimism and determination. They're the best! facebook.com/groups/thompsonpettravel

So many people for one little ginger cat, thank you, thank you all.

The Charities

There are so many animal charities in Greece. If you have a favourite or one to whom you regularly donate, please continue to do so. I have chosen to donate the proceeds from the sale of this book equally to the following charities who were instrumental in helping me to overcome the obstacles that faced Teddy from the point he was first rescued to his eventual transport home, and one charity local to us in Brighton.

Greek Animal Rescue
Working to alleviate the suffering of animals in Greece since 1989

Greek Animal Rescue

Founded by the late Vesna Jones following a trip to Greece in 1987 when she was moved by the neglect and plight of so many animals. The charity is run by unpaid volunteers, dedicated to helping those animals in need, relying entirely on donations. They promote, co-ordinate and fund sterilising campaigns, assist local organisations and individuals involved in animal welfare in their community, and lobby the Greek government for better, properly implemented animal welfare legislation.
greekanimalrescue.com

GREEK CAT WELFARE SOCIETY (UK)

Greek Cat Welfare Society UK

Have been promoting the care and welfare of cats in Greece since 1992. They are currently supporting over 30 local groups with grants, equipment, supplies and vets/nurses, in areas including Athens, Crete, Rhodes, Samos, Skyros and Thessaloniki. Their TNR (Trap, Neuter, Release) work is carried out by volunteer vets and nurses, and they also give material/financial support to local volunteer groups... Reducing the number of strays benefits them directly, as well as reducing the negative perceptions of some of the local human population. They continue to support those neutered cats with both feeding and healthcare programmes.
greekcats.org.uk

nine lives greece οι εφταψυχες **Nine Lives Greece – Οι Εφτάψυχες**

Nine Lives Greece – Οι Εφτάψυχες – started working in 2006 and became a recognized Greek charity in 2008, improving conditions for existing and future felines in the city of Athens and beyond. Their volunteers assist in feeding some 500 cats a day, as well as fundraising, TNR, anti-parasite treatments, and enabling access to veterinary care and rehoming.
ninelivesgreece.com

CARAT Caring for the animals trust **CARAT: Caring for the animals trust**

CARAT support around 17 small animal welfare societies by funding sterilisation of strays and pets, rescuing abandoned donkeys, supplying equipment and medication, financing rehoming, helping with building costs of stables, kennel blocks and clinics and producing educational leaflets in Greek.
caringfortheanimalstrust.co.uk

CITY CAT SHELTER **City Cat Shelter: Brighton**

City Cat Shelter homes about 250 unwanted cats in per year Brighton: they are entirely self-funded and run by donations and volunteers. They also offer community neutering, microchipping and advice on cat health.
citycatshelter.com

Appendix
The Adoption Process from Greece to the UK

This appendix to the book contains information that might be helpful for anyone thinking of adopting from Greece using an overland transport method. Things may change with time and the following information is as I understood it in July 2021. If you are adopting through a Greek animal rescue organisation they will almost certainly be able to guide you through the process. If you are trying to do it independently, then I would recommend getting help from Thompson Pet Transport as their assistance and advice on the bureaucratic complexities was invaluable to me.

So, you've fallen in love with a stray cat (or dog) and you want to bring it from Greece to the UK, what do you need to do? The following is a list of the things I had to have in place:

Pet Passport
Adoption Papers
Authorisation of a Representative (Declaration of Responsibility)
Pet Registration
ID
Apostille
IPAFFS registration
Health Certificate
Ministry Vet
Transport Method
UK Customs Agent

Pet Passport

Prior to Brexit, all animals used to have a Pet Passport and as long as the Greek vet looking after the animal at their end is still able to provide one I would recommend getting it. Even if some websites/official advice suggests it is not necessary if you have a valid Health Certificate.

I'm pretty sure the Ministry Vet would want to see that form of evidence, even if Border Control did not.

The Pet Passport has a unique booklet number assigned to your pet and includes:

- Details of Ownership (Name, address, telephone number)
- Description of the animal
- Transponder code, position and date of application (microchip)
- The details of the vet issuing the passport
- Rabies Vaccination details (batch number and dates)
- Other vaccinations (e.g. Tricat Trio, FeLV)
- Anti-echinococcus treatment details
- "Other Parasite" treatment (ie. Fleas/ticks etc)
- Clinical Examination (declared fit for transport just before the journey)

Adoption Papers

This became complicated.

A/ If the animal is a gift (e.g. a Greek friend's kitten) then you need to draw up your own adoption papers. This is what I did and I've included a redacted example of what I included. However, because I produced them in English from my end, they then became subject to needing an 'Apostille' (authentication issued to the document for use in countries that participate in the Hague Convention of 1961). Now, I'm not 100% sure, but I think that had the adoption papers been written by the person who was gifting the cat to me AND were written in Greek, then as they originated in Greece, an Apostille might not have been necessary. This is my own understanding of the situation, so not "official".

B/ If the animal was a stray/rescue, then the adoption papers have to be signed and dated by the Municipality local to the area where the animal was found. As far as I can tell the Municipalities don't seem to have their own adoption papers, so you would need to have a set of papers drawn up in Greek, covering all the important points. This would then require a visit to the Municipality to ask if they would sign them for you.

However, Greek law also states that pet marking and registration should be made within two months of birth, or within one month of finding, if the animal was a stray. So, if the animal was a stray you would need to have had it marked (transponder, tattoo) and registered on the Panhellenic Database to the local Municipality. (The local Municipalities are meant to be ultimately responsible for all strays within their jurisdiction, hence these animals should be registered to them). Having recorded the stray animal as being registered with the Municipality, you then need to register it to either the rescuer/temporary guardian or the new owner – you should seek advice on which – so that information matches with the Pet Passport and other documents (the vet should be able to help you with that).

Some of the information relating to Greek Law came from this web page. It's pretty wordy, but does set out the law as it stands ... or how it's meant to be observed, at any rate:

LAW NUMBER. 4039/2012 (Government Gazette A 15) For home pets and stray pets and to protect animals from exploitation or use for profit.

https://digihome.eu/law-number-40392012-government-gazette-a-15-for-home-pets-and-stray-pets-and-to-protect-animals-from-exploitation-or-use-for-profit/

I've included the adoption papers I drew up for Teddy (minus personal details) so you can see how this was done. I also included the Authorisation for a representative in the adoption papers so I could get an Apostille that covered both, in case there was an issue at the Health Certificate stage.

If this was copied and translated into Greek, with your pet's details then it would most likely cover both eventualities above. You would need to make clear that it had also been signed (and probably stamped) by the Municipality, along with their details. You may need to take further advice on this.

Animal Adoption Agreement

This document is the Adoption Agreement to facilitate the transfer of the cat named Teddy from his temporary home in Greece to his permanent home in the United Kingdom.

Included with this document is authorisation with nomou 105 Declaration of Responsibility giving (*name of representative*) my permission to act on my behalf as my representative at the offices of the Ministry Vet in Piraeus, Greece
and a translation into Greek of the authorisation.

I, David Burnham, am registered as Teddy's owner on the Certificate of Electronic Identification as issued in Greece and in the animal's Pet Passport No: GR 01 ....

Animal Adoption Agreement

Between
(the Temporary Guardian who has gifted the cat to the Owner)
and
David Burnham (the Owner)

Temporary Guardian (Name):	....
Address:	....
Tel:	....
e-mail:	....
ID Number:	....
Owner (Name):	David Burnham
Address:	....
Region:	....
Tel:	....
E-mail:	....
D.O.B.:	....
Passport No:	....
Place of Birth:	....
Name of Animal:	Teddy
Species:	Cat – Felis Catus
Breed:	Domestic Shorthair
Colour:	Ginger Tabby
Sex:	Male
Special Characteristics:	Letter "M" in fur on forehead
Sterile? (Yes / No)	YES
D.O.B.:	10/7/2020
Pet Passport:	GR 01 ....
Identification System:	Transponder
Identification Chip Number:	....
Date of Application/Implant of the transponder:	....
Location of the transponder:	Left Side of Neck
Applied/Implanted by Vet:	....
Address of Responsible Vet:	....
Vet Tel:	....
VAT No:	....

Conditions of the Animal Adoption Agreement

The Owner is obliged to take care of the animal, in accordance with the legislation and the provisions for the protection of animals. Law 4039/12 & 4235/14.

David Burnham is registered as the owner of the cat named Teddy.
This is confirmed by the Certificate of Electronic Identification as issued in Greece
and in the animal's Pet Passport No: GR 01 ....

The Temporary Guardian has given the animal to the Owner.
The Owner is entirely responsible for the animal.

Signature of Owner   Temporary Guardian

....

Date:

I have included the nomou105 Declaration of Responsibility here, plus a translation into Greek of the declaration I wrote. If you are visiting the Ministry Vet yourself, or if someone from a Greek Animal Rescue Organisation is helping you, you probably won't need to do that. But if you do need a nomou105 (but not an Apostille) then that might need separate verification by a local police office.

Authorisation of a Representative (Declaration of Responsibility)

If you need someone to visit the Ministry Vet on your behalf to obtain a Health Certificate, then you'll need a form nomou105. If it's written in English in your name with the details of the person you're appointing as your representative, then it may need further verification either by the Greek Embassy, the local police or even by Apostille. I'd suggest writing the whole thing in Greek and making the person who is the animal's guardian the person named on the form. Whichever way it works out, if you need a representative I would take advice on the best way of completing the form to avoid too much official complication (or if you've written the adoption papers in English, then include the nomou105 so if you then have to get an Apostille it verifies the whole lot).

The wording I used on the form in both English and Greek is below (and I included that page in with the adoption papers separately, so it was also covered by the Apostille).

Authorisation as appears on the attached Nomou 105 Declaration of Responsibility translated into Greek for clarity.

ΕΞΟΥΣΙΟΔΟΤΗΣΗ

Εγω ο David Burnham κατοικος Ην. Βασιλειου και με αρ. Διαβατηριου …………. Εξουσιοδοτω την κα ……………. με αρ. ΑΤ ΑΚ ………. κατοικο …………… οπως προβει σε ολες τις διαδικασιες για τη εκδοση πιστοποιητικου Υγειας για τον γατο μου με αρ. Ηλεκτρονικης σημανσης ……………………… οπως ειναι απαραιτητο για να την μεταφορα του μετην μεταφορικη εταιρεια Thompson pet transport

I David Burnham resident of United Kingdom with passport number ……………, authorise …………………… with ID no ……………… resident of ……………. to proceed with all the requirements needed for issuing Health Certificate for my cat with microchip number …………………… as it is needed for his transfer with the Thompson pet transport.

Date

Name

Signature

An example of the form is on the next page.

ΥΠΕΥΘΥΝΗ ΔΗΛΩΣΗ/SOLEMN DECLARATION
(άρθρο 8 Ν.1599/1986/article 8 L. 1599/1986)

Η ακρίβεια των στοιχείων που υποβάλλονται με αυτή τη δήλωση μπορεί να ελεγχθεί με βάση το αρχείο άλλων υπηρεσιών (άρθρο 8 παρ. 4 Ν. 1599/1986)/The accuracy of the information submitted with this application can be verified based on the records of other authorities (article 8, par. 4, L. 1599/1986)

ΠΡΟΣ/To(1):							
Ο – Η Όνομα/ Name:			Επώνυμο/Surname:				
Όνομα και Επώνυμο Πατέρα/Father's Name and Surname:							
Όνομα και Επώνυμο Μητέρας/Mother's Name and Surname:							
Ημερομηνία γέννησης/Date of birth(2):							
Τόπος Γέννησης/Place of Birth:							
Αριθμός Δελτίου Ταυτότητας/ID Number:			Τηλ/Tel:				
Τόπος Κατοικίας/ Place of Residence:		Οδός/ Street:		Αριθ/ No:		ΤΚ/ZIP:	
Αρ. Τηλεομοιοτύπου (Fax):			Δ/νση Ηλεκτρ. Ταχυδρομείου (Email):				

[EL] Με ατομική μου ευθύνη και γνωρίζοντας τις κυρώσεις (3), που προβλέπονται από τις διατάξεις της παρ. 6 του άρθρου 22 του Ν. 1599/1986, δηλώνω ότι:

[EN] In my personal responsibility and knowing the sanctions set in the provisions of paragraph 6 of Article 22 of Law 1599/1986, I declare that:

(4)

Ημερομηνία/Date: ....20.....

Ο – Η Δηλ./Signer

(Υπογραφή/Signature)

(1) Αναγράφεται από τον ενδιαφερόμενο πολίτη ή Αρχή ή η Υπηρεσία του δημόσιου τομέα, που απευθύνεται η αίτηση/ Filled in by the applicant of the Authority or Organization of the public sector that this application is sent to.
(2) Αναγράφεται ολογράφως/Written in full.
(3) «Όποιος εν γνώσει του δηλώνει ψευδή γεγονότα ή αρνείται ή αποκρύπτει τα αληθινά με έγγραφη υπεύθυνη δήλωση του άρθρου 8 τιμωρείται με φυλάκιση τουλάχιστον τριών μηνών. Εάν ο υπαίτιος αυτών των πράξεων σκόπευε να προσπορίσει στον εαυτόν του ή σε άλλον περιουσιακό όφελος βλάπτοντας τρίτον ή σκόπευε να βλάψει άλλον, τιμωρείται με κάθειρξη μέχρι 10 ετών./Whoever knowingly states false facts or denies or conceals the true facts with a written solemn declaration of Article 8 shall be punished with imprisonment of at least three months. If the person responsible for these acts intended to obtain pecuniary advantage harming others or intended to harm others, is punishable by imprisonment of up to 10 years.
(4) Σε περίπτωση ανεπάρκειας χώρου η δήλωση συνεχίζεται στην πίσω όψη της και υπογράφεται από τον δηλούντα ή την δηλούσα./In case of insufficient space the declaration may continue at the back side and is signed by the applicant.

Pet Registration

I've talked a bit about pet registration above. The animal's vet should be able to help you to do that. Just bear in mind that if the animal was a stray, it should be registered with the local Municipality first. You might want to take advice on whether to have the animal registered in your name, or the name of the person looking after it for you in Greece prior to departure. I'm not sure how that might influence the issuing of the Health Certificate. You are, after all, going to register the animal in the UK once it has made the journey and is at home with you.

ID

I provided copies of my UK Passport for identity and my Driving License to link identity to address.

Both the person who was looking after Teddy and the person who represented me at the Ministry Vet provided copies of their Greek Identity cards.

Teddy's ID was his transponder number and his photograph in his pet passport.

Apostille

Hopefully you won't have to get tangled up in obtaining an Apostille to verify any of your documents, but if you do then this is how I went about it (rather than getting a public notary to do it at considerable extra cost).

This is the website to start the process: www.gov.uk/get-document-legalised

Here's where to send it:
Legalisation Office
Foreign, Commonwealth and Development Office
PO Box 7656
Milton Keynes
MK11 9NS

Remember, to get an Apostille you also need to get the documents certified by a solicitor who is legally able to carry out that service. They will need to sign, date and stamp every page stating: "I .... Hereby certify this to be a true and complete copy of the original."

It takes a while and I used the FCDO-recommended courier service to make sure it came back, but you will get a fancy embossed stamp/seal and an Apostille certificate that will satisfy the Greek authorities.

IPAFFS registration

So far, so good. Now someone will need to register as an official importer of dogs, cats and ferrets with the UK government. If the animal has been rescued by a registered Greek Animal Organisation then the chances are they may well be registered with IPAFFS already and will be able to do this bit on your behalf. If not, then you will need to register yourself.

Here's a walk-through of the online process:

IPAFFS (Import of products, animals, food and feed system)

Raising an IPAFFS notification

Since Brexit, it is now a requirement to notify the UK government if you are importing an animal into the UK from the EU.

The first stage of the on-line IPAFFS completion will generate a UNN (Unique Notification Number) which must be entered into I.2.a. UNN on the Health Certificate.

This is how it works as of 1st July 2021, unless anything has been added or altered.

This is the website:
https://www.gov.uk/guidance/import-of-products-animals-food-and-feed-system

Scroll down to "START NOW"

Click: "Create sign in details"

Enter your email address

Enter confirmation code sent to your email address

Enter your full name

Create a password

Set up a recovery word in case you need it in the future

You will be sent a Government Gateway user ID to use with your password every time you sign in.

Complete your personal details

Register as an individual

First name and surname

(Complete the rest of the details)
Contact telephone number
Address
Create a security word

Check and confirm

CREATE A NEW NOTIFICATION

What are you importing?: **LIVE ANIMALS**

Country of Origin: **GREECE**

Do you know the commodity code for your animal?: **NO**
(You actually do, it's on the Health Certificate, but best to leave this blank on the IPAFFS)

Which animal are you importing?: **CATS** (or DOGS if that applies)

How many animals are you importing?: **1**

Enter any identification details you have for the animal:
Microchip/Transponder number
(only enter the microchip number, ignore passport and tattoo)
You can also enter the animal's Pet Passport Number next to this.
Make sure you've entered everything here before saving/submitting, as I found I was not able to amend it later if I had wanted to.

When are you planning to import the animal or product?:
DATE OF ENTRY INTO THE UK
You will need to enter this date otherwise you won't be able to proceed with the notification process and get the reference number you will need to be entered on the Health Certificate:

e.g. 3rd July

What is the reason for the movement of this animal?: **Rescue/Rehoming**

Provide your supporting documents:
Here, you can't upload the Health Certificate and add its number and date of issue until it's actually been done, so, **click "Save and Continue".**
You can come back to this section once you have those details.

Once the Health Certificate has been issued by the Ministry Vet, take photographs of all 4 pages of the Health Certificate showing all the details and including the Ministry Vet's stamp, signature and reference number at the top right of every page.
Enter the reference number into this IPAFFS section and upload all 4 photographs.

(I had to create a PDF of all 4 pages as the IPAFFS site only allows you to upload a single document per case.)
ALSO ENTER I.2 CERTICATE REFERENCE NUMBER AS ISSUED BY THE MINISTRY VET IN ORDER TO FINALISE THE SUBMISSION
This will finalise the submission once you click 'save and submit'.

Additional details:
Are you importing from a charity? If you are an individual, the response here is: **NO**
If it is from a charity registered in Greece in the then response is: YES
Is the place of destination the permanent address? : **YES**

Traders Addresses:

PLACE OF ORIGIN

Name: Same as Consignor on the Health Certificate (i.e. The name of the person responsible for the animal in Greece who is sending the animal to you)
Origin: The address in Greece where the animal is coming from.

Click: "Add a place of origin".
It probably won't find it on a search so click: **"Create a new place of origin"** and fill in the details.
Click save.
It should say "The place of origin has been created" so then:
Click "add to notification".

CHARITY:

Leave blank if it's not a charity that you're importing from, i.e. if it's an individual, or if the charity is not registered in Greece.
If it is a charity, then click "Add a charity of origin".
It probably won't find it on a search so click: **"Create a new charity of origin"** and fill in the details.

If the Charity is registered in Greece then use the name of the charity and their address in Greece.

So, click **“create a new charity of origin”**
Put in the charity name and relevant address in Greece.
Click save.
Click “add to notification”.

IMPORTER
This is the person adopting or receiving the animal, so enter your details
Click “Add an importer”.
Click **“Create a new importer”** and fill in your details.
Click save.
Click “add to notification”.

PLACE OF DESTINATION
It actually allows you to “SELECT” your details so if the animal is coming to live with you just click “SELECT”

Click Save and Continue

TRANSPORT DETAILS

Click “Add a transporter”
Enter “the name provided by your chosen transporter” into the Search Box Name and click SEARCH

Select the address for your transporter – all of the relevant details are very helpfully pre-entered

(There are some other handy codes relating to the transporter’s own registration here which can be useful for the Health Certificate so make a note of them e.g. Vehicle registration number)

COUNTRIES TRANSITED
Check with your transporter but I think these would be:
Select country: Greece
Select country: Italy
Click “Add another country”
Select country: France

Click “Add another country”
Select country: England
Click “Add another country”

PORT OF ENTRY
Folkstone

Click “Save and Continue”

Review and the submit the notification

Make a note of the reference number (it should be sent by email – I didn’t get one, so it’s worth making a note just in case) This is the UNN:
IMP.GB.2021.0000001-V1
IMP.GB.2021.0000001........... (this is the actual UNN, I think the V1 bit just means Version One prior to finalisation)

This is given to the Ministry Vet when they complete the Health Certificate and it gets entered here:
I.2.a. UNN (Unique Notification Number)
Example: IMP.GB.2021.0000001
The UNN is generated by the Import of products, animals, food and feed system (IPAFFS) when an import notification is created – you must give this number to the MV to add to the Health Certificate.

Make a note of these details as you go along with registration etc:

Government Gateway user ID: ....

Password : ....

Recovery Word: ....

Security Word so they can verify you: ....

Your Contact Support ID: ....

You can go back into IPAFFS when you've got your Health Certificate and Certificate Reference Number and upload it. I found it would only take one upload so I made a single document from the 8 pages I received from the Ministry Vet and uploaded it as one.

Health Certificate

Since Brexit you now have to have a veterinary certificate for the importation of dogs, cats and ferrets: GBHC157E.

It took a great deal of research to establish what information should be entered and to find individual codes for certain sections, but I have set up a guide that should make it easier to complete.

This is a signed, stamped, authorized Health Certificate that you must get from the Ministry Vet responsible for the region in which the animal is currently living.

Without that the animal cannot legally enter the UK or cross Border Control Points en route.

Without the Health Certificate being allocated a I.2. Certificate Reference Number by the Ministry Vet, you will not be able to finalise the IPAFFS notification to the UK government.

It is only valid for entry into the UK for 10 days from the date of issue. Yep, just 10 days! So, timing for the Ministry Vet visit is critical – and even more so with dogs. For dogs it must be issued within 120 hours (5 days) of arrival in the UK, as it includes treatment against *Echinococcus multilocularis* which must be administered by a veterinarian within a period of not more than 120 hours and not less than 24 hours before the time of the scheduled entry of the dog into Great Britain.

These are the things to take with you and have available when visiting the Ministry Vet (they may not all be required, but have them in case):

- A Health Certificate for the animal(s).
- Completed Pet Passport.
- Evidence of Identity and address of owner (Consignee) and guardian (Consignor) – Passport/Driving Licence photo, Greek ID cards.
- Microchip/Transponder Registration details and evidence (certificate).

- You might need a nomou 105: Greek form to complete if someone is acting on behalf of you at the Ministry Vet's office – probably completed in Greek to represent the Greek person who is sending the cat from Greece.
- Adoption Papers: depends on several factors and should be written in Greek.
- The UNN – this is the IPAFFS number you get when you raise the IPAFFS notification: already entered on the Health Certificate top right.
- This guide with its relevant information.

You may need:

An EORI number as issued by the Customs Agent acting on your behalf, but that should only be if the animal is coming from a charity or a business, not if it is coming from an individual.

As of 1st July 2021

This is how it works currently, unless anything is added or altered.

The Health Certificate can be prefilled with the information shown in the example.

Health Certificate completion information: step-by-step guide

(Page 1)

I.1 Consignor

Name: ....

Address: ....

....

Country: ....

Tel: ....

(The name and address in Greece of the natural or legal person dispatching the consignment)

I.2 Certificate reference number: **THIS IS ADDED BY THE MINISTRY VET**

This must then be added by the importer (new owner) to the IPAFFS!

(The unique mandatory code assigned by the competent authority of the third country using its own classification. **THIS IS ADDED BY THE MINISTRY VET/OV AND THE IMPORTER MUST ADD IT TO IPAFFS TO FINALISE THE NOTIFICATION**)

I.2.a. UNN (Unique Notification Number) : **IMP.GB.2021.XXXXXXX**
The UNN is generated by the Import of products, animals, food and feed system (IPAFFS) when an import notification is created – you must give this number to the MV to add to the Health Certificate.

I.3 Central Competent Authority: **GR00000 Ministry of Rural Development and Food Directorate**

I.4 Local Competent Authority: The area where the Ministry Vet works from (see list of Local Competent Authorities for your code at the end of this section on the Health Certificate)
GR03900 PIREAS

I.5 Consignee
Name: **David Burnham**
Address: ....
Country: **UK / GB**
Postal Code: ....
Tel: ....
(The name and address of the natural or legal person receiving the consignment in GB.)

I.6 Leave Blank – struck through

I.7 Country of origin: **Greece** ISO code: **GR**

I.8 Leave Blank – struck through

I.9 Country of destination: **Great Britain** ISO code: **GBR**

I.9 REGION of destination: **East Sussex** ISO code: **GB-ESX**
Regional ISO codes can be found here:
https://en.wikipedia.org/wiki/ISO_3166-2:GB

I.11 Place of dispatch
This is the same as I.1 Consignor above if the animal is being dispatched from that same address by the same person.
Name: ....
Address: ....
Country: ....
What is the APPROVAL/REGISTRATION NUMBER?
(The name, address in Greece and approval number, if required by the EU retained legislation, of the holdings or establishments from which the animals or the products come from. This seemed to get entered by the Ministry Vet.)

I.12 Place of destination
This is the same as I.5 Consignee above if the animal's destination is the same as the person receiving it.
Name: **David Burnham**
Address: ....
Country: **Great Britain**
Postal Code: ....
What is the APPROVAL NUMBER?
(The name, address in GB and approval number of where the animal(s) are going. This seemed to get entered by the Ministry Vet.)

I.13 Place of Loading: **Athens**

I.14 Date of departure:
Departure date: .... (as booked with your pet transporter)
Time of departure: .... (as booked with your pet transporter)

I.15 Means of Transport
Tick the ROAD VEHICLE box: **Road vehicle** ☑
Identification: **Registration number plate ....**
Documentary references: Not necessary – leave blank
Documentary reference
Yes that one can be left blank, it's only really relevant for flight tickets etc, but you can put in the Greek type 2 license number which your pet transporter can give you. I used that and their IPAFFS identity references: ....

I.16 Entry BCP: **GBFOLI Folkestone**

I.17 Leave Blank – struck through

I.18 Description of Commodity:

Species: **cat – Felis catus (or dog – Canis Familiaris)**

Breed: **Domestic Shorthair**

Sex: **Male**

Colour: **Ginger Tabby**

PET CAT FELIS CATUS DOMESTIC SHORTHAIR GINGER TABBY MALE

I.19 Commodity Code
(Harmonised Systems Code HS): **010619**

I.20 Quantity: **1 (One)**
(Number of animals)

I.21 Leave Blank – struck through

I.22 Number of Packages: **1 (One)**
(The number of boxes, cages or stalls, in which they're being transported (one per animal))

I.23 Seal/Container No.: **-**
The box can be filled with a '-' (dash)

I.24 Leave Blank – struck through

I.25 Commodity certified for
Tick the PETS box: **Pets** ☑

I.26 Leave Blank – struck through

I.27 For import or admission into Great Britain, Channel Islands and Isle of Man
Tick the box: ☑

I.28 Identification of the commodities

Species (Scientific Name): **cat – Felis catus (or dog – Canis Familiaris)**
Identification System: **Transponder**
Identification Number (chip number): **..............................**
Date of birth: **10/07/2020**

(Transponder code details are on Page 7 of the Pet Passport)

****

(Page 2)

II. Health Information

II.a. Certificate reference no
Top right page 2 Same as box 1.2 above
THIS IS ADDED BY THE MINISTRY VET

II.b UNN Top right page 3
Same as box 1.2.a above **IMP.GB.2021.XXXXXXX**

I the undersigned Veterinarian of......**GREECE**........ (insert name of third country)

The Ministry Vet should then set about completing this section of the Health Certificate by using the information provided by the Pet Passport. If you have pre-filled all sections then all they have to do is to verify the information from the Pet Passport and sign and stamp – and Issue the **Certificate Reference Number.**

Vaccination details at bottom of page 2

1 Transponder code: Transponder code details are on Page 7 of the Pet Passport
2 Date of Implant: Transponder code details are on Page 7 of the Pet Passport
3 Date of Vaccination: Page 9 of the Pet Passport, 1 = Rabies Vaccination Date
4 Name and manufacturer of vaccine: Page 9 of the Pet Passport, Batch label name (Probably NobiVac® Rabies)

5 Batch Number: Page 9 of the Pet Passport, Batch label number
6 Valid From: Page 9 of the Pet Passport, 2 = Rabies Vaccination valid from date
7 To: Page 9 of the Pet Passport, 3 = Rabies Vaccination valid until date
8 Date of blood sampling not required for cats and I assume, not for dogs either

****

(Page 3)

II. Health Information

II.a. Certificate reference no
Top right page 3 Same as box 1.2 above
THIS IS ADDED BY THE MINISTRY VET

II.b UNN Top right page 3
Same as box 1.2.a above **IMP.GB.2021.XXXXXXX**

Page 3 relates to dogs

If you are getting a Health Certificate for a dog your Private Vet will need to enter the details

- of the transponder number to identify the dog
- the Anti-Echinococcus treatment details and date (THE DAY BEFORE TRAVEL!)
- Your Private Vet will need to sign, stamp and date this section.

****

(Page 4)

II. Health Information

II.a. Certificate reference no
Top right page 4 Same as box 1.2 above
THIS IS ADDED BY THE MINISTRY VET
II.b UNN Top right page 4
Same as box 1.2.a above **IMP.GB.2021.XXXXXXX**

The rabies titration test is not required for the UK. There are sections on the health certificate which refer to this and refer to the animal being "destined for a body. Institute, or centre..." both sections on page 2 can be crossed out, you will notice it says "either" "or" and on page 4 the section about rabies titration can be crossed out too – at the top it says "keep as appropriate".

However, I'd rather not tinker with these sections as the MV might not like it and HCs I have had sight of don't seem to have been crossed out in these specific sections.

Check to make sure that at the bottom of page 4 the Ministry Vet has:
Put their name in capitals
The day they are issuing it: date
Their qualification and Title
Signed it
Put their official stamp on it

EVERY PAGE MUST BE STAMPED AND SIGNED BY THE MINISTRY VET – BOTTOM RIGHT

Take the Health Certificate issued by the Ministry Vet with you. If it has been completed online ask for a printed copy. Enter the II.a. Certificate reference number (written in by the Ministry Vet) into the Document Type, Reference and Date of Issue into your IPAFFS on line in order to finalise the IPAFFS notification, as well as uploading a copy of the entire Health Certificate.

EVERY PAGE MUST BE STAMPED, SIGNED AND DATED BY THE ANIMAL'S PRIVATE VET – BOTTOM LEFT
(Private Vet, date it the day before travel for dogs, date it the day before visit to Ministry Vet for cats. Remember, the Health Certificate is only valid for 10 days from date of issue to arrival in UK for cats. 5 days for dogs. So book your Ministry Vet appointment accordingly.)

An example of a Blank Health Certificate is on the following pages

Model veterinary certificate for the importation of dogs, cats and ferrets GBHC157E

COUNTRY: Countries subject to transitional import arrangements (*)

Health certificate to Great Britain, Channel Islands and Isle of Man

Part I: Details of dispatched consignment

I.1. Consignor Name Address Country Tel.	I.2. Certificate reference number / I.2.a.UNN I.3. Central Competent Authority I.4. Local Competent Authority
I.5. Consignee Name Address Country Postal Code Tel.	I.6.
I.7. Country of origin / ISO code / I.8.	I.9. Country of destination / ISO code / I.10. Region of destination / Code
I.11. Place of origin Name Address / Approval number Name Address / Approval number Name Address / Approval number	I.12. Place of destination Name Address Approval number
I.13. Place of loading	I.14. Date of departure
I.15. Means of transport Aeroplane ☐ Ship ☐ Railway wagon ☐ Road vehicle ☐ Other ☐ Identification: Documentary references:	I.16. Entry BCP in Great Britain, Channel Islands or Isle of Man I.17.
I.18. Description of commodity	I.19. Commodity code (HS code) 010619
I.21. / I.20. Quantity	I.22. Number of packages
I.23. Seal/Container No.	I.24.
I.25. Commodity certified for: Others ☐ Pets ☐ Approved bodies ☐	
I.26.	I.27. For import or admission into Great Britain, Channel Islands and Isle of Man ☐

I.28. Identification of the commodities

Species (Scientific Name)	Identification system	Identification number	Date of birth [dd/mm/yyyy]

COUNTRY: Countries subject to transitional import arrangements (*) **Dogs, cats, ferrets**

Part II: Certification

II. Health information	II.a. Certificate reference no	II.b.UNN

I, the undersigned official veterinarian of .... *(insert name of third country)* certify that the animals described in Box 1.28:

II.1. come from holdings or businesses described in Box 1.11 which are registered by the competent authority and are not subject to any ban on animal health grounds, where the animals are examined regularly and which comply with the requirements ensuring the welfare of the animals held;

II.2. showed no signs of diseases and were fit to be transported for the intended journey at the time of examination by a veterinarian authorised by the competent authority within 48 hours prior to the time of dispatch;

(1) *either* [II.3. are destined for a body, institute or centre described in Box 1.12 and approved in accordance with Annex C to Council Directive 92/65/EEC, and come from a territory or third country listed in Annex 2 to Commission Implementing Regulation (EU) No 577/2013.]

(1) *or* [II.3. were at least 12 weeks old at the time of vaccination against rabies and at least 21 days have elapsed since the completion of the primary anti-rabies vaccination (2) carried out in accordance with the validity requirements set out in Annex 3 to Regulation (EU) No 576/2013 of the European Parliament and of the Council, and any subsequent revaccination was carried out within the period of validity of the preceding vaccination (3), and

(1) *either* [they come from, and in case of transit are scheduled to transit through, a territory or third country listed in Annex 2 to Commission Implementing Regulation (EU) No 577/2013 and details of the current anti-rabies vaccination are provided in columns 1 to 7 in the table below;]

(1) *or* [they come from or are scheduled to transit through, a territory or third country listed in Part 1 of Annex 2 to Commission Regulation (EU) No 206/2010 or listed without time limit in Annex 1 to Commission Implementing Regulation (EU) 2018/659, and

- details of the current anti-rabies vaccination are provided in columns 1 to 7 in the table below, and
- a rabies antibody titration test (4), carried out on a blood sample taken by the veterinarian authorised by the competent authority not less than 30 days after the preceding vaccination and at least three months prior to the date of issue of this certificate, proved an antibody titre equal to or greater than 0,5 IU/ml (5) and any subsequent revaccination was carried out within the period of validity of the preceding vaccination, and the date of sampling for testing the immune response are provided in column 8 in the table below:]

Transponder or tattoo					Validity of vaccination		
Alphanumeric code of the animal	Date of implantation and/or reading (6) [dd/mm/yyyy]	Date of vaccination [dd/mm/yyyy]	Name and manufacturer of vaccine	Batch number	From [dd/mm/yyyy]	to [dd/mm/yyyy]	Date of blood sampling [dd/mm/yyyy]
1	2	3	4	5	6	7	8

COUNTRY: Countries subject to transitional import arrangements (*) **Dogs, cats, ferrets**

II. Health information	II.a. Certificate reference no	II.b UNN

([1]) *either* [II.4. the consignment includes dogs destined for Great Britain and those dogs have been treated against *Echinococcus multilocularis*, and the details of the treatment carried out by the administering veterinarian in accordance with Article 6 of Commission Delegated Regulation (EU) 2018/772 ([7]) ([8]) are provided in the table below:

Transponder or tattoo Alphanumeric code of the dog	Anti-Echinococcus treatment		Administering veterinarian	
	Name and manufacturer of the product	Date [dd/mm/yyyy] and time of treatment [00:00]	Name in capitals, stamp and signature	

([1]) *or* [II.4. the dogs forming part of the consignment have not been treated against Echinococcus multilocularis.]

Notes

This certificate is valid for 10 days from the date of issue by the official veterinarian. In the case of transport by sea, that period of 10 days is extended by an additional period corresponding to the duration of the journey by sea.

(*) Those countries subject to the transitional import arrangements include: an EU member State; Liechtenstein; Norway and Switzerland.

References to European Union legislation within this certificate are references to direct EU legislation which has been retained in Great Britain (retained EU law as defined in the European Union (Withdrawal) Act 2018).

References to Great Britain in this certificate include Channel Islands and Isle of Man.

Part I:

Box I.11: Place of origin: name and address of the dispatch establishment. Indicate approval or registration number.

Box I.12: Place of destination: mandatory where the animals are destined for a body, institute or centre approved in accordance with Annex C to Council Directive 92/65/EEC.

Box I.16: Do not use this box until the end of the transitional staging period.

Box I.25: Commodities certified for: indicate

- 'Pets' where dogs (Canis lupus familiaris), cats (Felis silvestris catus) or ferrets (Mustela putorius furo) are moved in accordance with Article 5(4) of Regulation (EU) No 576/2013 of the European Parliament and of the Council;
- 'Approved bodies' where dogs, cats or ferrets are moved in accordance with Article 13 of Council Directive 92/65/EEC to an approved body, institute or centre as defined in Article 2(c) of that Directive;
- 'others' where dogs, cats or ferrets are moved in accordance with Article 10 of Council Directive 92/65/EEC.

Box I.28: Identification system: select transponder or tattoo.

Identification number: indicate the transponder or tattoo alphanumeric code.

COUNTRY: Countries subject to transitional import arrangements (*) **Dogs, cats, ferrets**

II. Health information	II.a. Certificate reference no	II.b UNN

Part II:

(1) Keep as appropriate.

(2) Any revaccination must be considered a primary vaccination if it was not carried out within the period of validity of a previous vaccination.

(3) A certified copy of the identification and vaccination details of the animals concerned shall be attached to the certificate.

(4) The rabies antibody titration test referred to in point 11.3:

- must be carried out on a sample collected by a veterinarian authorised by the competent authority, at least 30 days after the date of vaccination and three months before the date of import;
- must measure a level of neutralising antibody to rabies virus in serum equal to or greater than 0,5 IU/ml;
- must be performed by a laboratory approved in accordance with Article 3 of Council Decision 2000/258/EC (list of approved laboratories available at http://ec.europa.eu/food/animals/pet-movement/approved-labs_en);
- does not have to be renewed on an animal, which following that test with satisfactory results, has been revaccinated against rabies within the period of validity of a previous vaccination.

A certified copy of the official report from the approved laboratory on the result of the rabies antibody test referred to in point 11.3 shall be attached to the certificate.

(5) By certifying this result, the official veterinarian confirms that he has verified, to the best of his ability and where necessary with contacts with the laboratory indicated in the report, the authenticity of the laboratory report on the results of the antibody titration test referred to in point II.3.

(6) In conjunction with footnote (3), the marking of the animals concerned by the implantation of a transponder or by a clearly readable tattoo applied before 3 July 2011 must be verified before any entry is made in this certificate and must always precede any vaccination, or where applicable, testing carried out on those animals.

(7) The treatment against *Echinococcus multilocularis* referred to in point II.4 must:

- be administered by a veterinarian within a period of not more than 120 hours and not less than 24 hours before the time of the scheduled entry of the dogs into Great Britain.
- consist of an approved medicinal product which contains the appropriate dose of praziquantel or pharmacologically active substances, which alone or in combination, have been proven to reduce the burden of mature and immature intestinal forms of Echinococcus multilocularis in the host species concerned.

(8) The table referred to in point 11.4 must be used to document the details of a further treatment if administered after the date the certificate was signed and prior to the scheduled entry into Great Britain.

Official Veterinarian

Name (in capital letters): Qualification and title:

Date: Signature:

Stamp:

List of Local Competent Authorities

Eventually I tracked down a webpage with this information and not only does it give you the code, but it also helped me to confirm which Ministry Vet was responsible for the region which Teddy came from. As this could be very helpful to you I've included the webpage url link below:

I.4. Local Competent Authority on the Health Certificate
The Area where the Ministry Vet for your area works from – these are the codes

Eg. Athens would be written on the Health Certificate I.4.
GR00200 ATHINA

You can find them here:

https://www.legislation.gov.uk/eudn/2009/821/annex/II/division/1/adopted

You need to scroll about a third of the way down to get to Greece if you want to check your Local Unit Code. It's under:
"GR00000 GENERAL DIRECTORATE OF VETERINARY SERVICES" – LOCAL UNITS

The Ministry Vet

Before Brexit the animal's Pet Passport was sufficient for travel to another EU member country. Sometimes, particularly with reference to rehoming strays as I understand it, the Greek government would insist on having TRACES before they would permit travel. The Trade Control and Expert System (TRACES) is an online system for health certification and tracking consignments of animals or animal products coming into or out of the UK. This guidance was withdrawn from UK Department for Environment, Food & Rural Affairs on 16th October 2019.

Following Brexit on 31st January 2021 it became a legal necessity to have a Health Certificate for an animal to enter the UK, along with IPAFFS as mentioned above. I believe that some EU countries permit the Health

Certificate to be issued by the animal's own local vet, but in Greece it has to be issued by a Ministry Vet.

Each region of Greece has its own Ministry Vet: what is called the Local Competent Authority.

Timing is crucial when making an appointment with the Ministry Vet to obtain Health Certificate authorization:

Cats – such that the Health Certificate is within the 10 day period of validity when the animal arrives in the UK.

Dogs – Best obtained the day before departure, because dogs also have to have worming treatment before travelling such that they arrive in the UK within 5 days of that treatment.

In our case, the Ministry Vet also required a detailed Journey Log ("Imerológio taxidioú") from the pet transport company, so maybe make sure you also have that in advance (although only one other Ministry Vet had asked for that in the past).

Some Ministry Vets seem happy to sign and stamp the printed copy of the Health Certificate that you or your representative provides on the day of the appointment, but others insist on using the online system and some have more experience with the procedure than others. The online version is complex and it sounds like it might not entirely match up with the Health Certificate as provided by the UK government. Plus there are various entries that have to be made before they can proceed to the next section. This caused a problem for us with the Journey Log, as the countries transited are entered during the IPAFFS section, but the Greek online Health Certificate system appears to demand considerably more detail. This is why I would suggest that the transport company you engage provides you with a Journey Log for the trip that your pet will be taking.

So, it is worth bearing in mind that although very few Ministry Vets have asked for it, the transport company's Journey Log for the trip involving your pet might be required. It may only be an issue when the Ministry Vet is using the online form and the countries are already listed as part of the IPAFFS submission. However, if they were to ask for a Journey Log at the appointment and you were unable to provide it, that could prevent the issuing of the Health Certificate. I would advise you to raise this with the transport company and either have the first page of the relevant Journey Log to hand, or else prime them to be able to provide one at short notice during your Ministry Vet appointment.

Transport Method

I highly recommend Thompson Pet Travel as they were so helpful and so caring. Different companies vary with regards to their support in the process of acquiring the necessary paperwork and with overall support for specific queries. You will also need to organise the transfer from your pet's temporary home in Greece to the pick-up point selected by the transport company, and to your home at the UK end.

It is also possible to transport animals by aircraft, but relatively few airlines provide this service and it usually means that pets would have to travel in the pressurised part of the hold. Prior to Brexit, arrangements could be made for small animals to travel in a pet carrier in the passenger cabin, but that is only allowed within EU member countries. Another issue is that on arrival in the UK your pet may be transferred to the Animal Reception Centre at Heathrow. So if you were travelling with your pet, you would have to arrange to get from arrivals in the airport to the Animal Reception Centre to collect your pet. The ARC will carry out a full PET check, which would of course require the necessary paperwork to be in order. That takes about two hours and if there's a problem the animal could wind up in quarantine. You'd need to check with the airline about exactly what documentation is required and the finer details of the process. I understand that if you travel with fewer than five animals and they are registered as your pets, then you might not need a Health Certificate as long as all of the details mentioned in the Pet Passport section are completed correctly and satisfactorily. However, post-Brexit you have to pay VAT on imported pets so you would need to check that, as well as any other Customs clearance considerations.

UK Customs Agent

I used Skypets International to deal with the Customs formalities for Teddy, as well as paying the VAT. I think the VAT is based on the value of the animal, so if your dog is a pedigree pooch then the VAT would be charged at the rate of 20% of the amount paid for the animal (EU breeders used to charge their clients VAT directly by adding it to the sales invoice, but now the invoice excludes VAT, so the UK government can collect it).

If the animal is a rescue the government now demand a VAT payment for them as well and it is based on a nominal value. This is about £60 for a cat and £100 for a dog; so the VAT would be £12 for a cat and £20 for a dog, plus a small value adjustment of an additional £6.

I'm talking about adopting here, but if you travel to the EU with your pet and then return to the UK after a period of living abroad, the animal is classified as a 'personal effect' so you shouldn't have to pay VAT, but you would have to apply for Transfer of Residence Relief on form ToR01.

The Customs Agent may need to issue an EORI code, but this code is only required for a charity or a business and shouldn't be needed as an individual. (EORI means Economic Operators Registration and Identification number for moving goods.)

Summary

I hope this Appendix helps with grasping the process as I understood it in July 2021. Things may well change as time goes along, so please seek the advice and support of your chosen Pet Transport company and keep an eye on the UK government websites. You may be able to get specific advice and support from DEFRA, but because it was all quite new when I was doing it they seemed a little unsure about how to deal with the specific questions I raised.

Adoption from Greece does seem like a daunting process, but if you work through it steadily and methodically, it can be done. The effort will always be worth it to provide a cat or dog in need with a safe, loving, forever home.

All the best,

Dave

Printed in Great Britain
by Amazon

77660267R00220